This study was undertaken as part of the Development Centre's Research Programme on the theme of Financing of Development.

3

# ALSO AVAILABLE

DEVELOPMENT CENTRE STUDIES

# REBALANCING THE PUBLIC AND PRIVATE SECTORS:

OF THE O                                                    DEVELOPMENT

Pursuant to Article 1 of the Convention signed in Paris on 14th December 1960, and which came into force on 30th September 1961, the Organisation for Economic Co-operation and Development (OECD) shall promote policies designed:

- to achieve the highest sustainable economic growth and employment and a rising standard of living in Member countries, while maintaining financial stability, and thus to contribute to the development of the world economy;
- to contribute to sound economic expansion in Member as well as non-member countries in the process of economic development; and
- to contribute to the expansion of world trade on a multilateral, non-discriminatory basis in accordance with international obligations.

The original Member countries of the OECD are Austria, Belgium, Canada, Denmark, France, Germany, Greece, Iceland, Ireland, Italy, Luxembourg, the Netherlands, Norway, Portugal, Spain, Sweden, Switzerland, Turkey, the United Kingdom and the United States. The following countries became Members subsequently through accession at the dates indicated hereafter: Japan (28th April 1964), Finland (28th January 1969), Australia (7th June 1971) and New Zealand (29th May 1973). The Commission of the European Communities takes part in the work of the OECD (Article 13 of the OECD Convention). Yugoslavia takes part in some of the work of the OECD (agreement of 28th October 1961).

*The Development Centre of the Organisation for Economic Co-operation and Development was established by decision of the OECD Council on 23rd October 1962.*

*The purpose of the Centre is to bring together the knowledge and experience available in Member countries of both economic development and the formulation and execution of general economic policies; to adapt such knowledge and experience to the actual needs of countries or regions in the process of development and to put the results at the disposal of the countries by appropriate means.*

*The Centre has a special and autonomous position within the OECD which enables it to enjoy scientific independence in the execution of its task. Nevertheless, the Centre can draw upon the experience and knowledge available in the OECD in the development field.*

Publié en français sous le titre :

LE RÉÉQUILIBRAGE ENTRE SECTEURS PUBLIC ET PRIVÉ :
L'EXPÉRIENCE DES PAYS EN DÉVELOPPEMENT

*
* *

# TABLE OF CONTENTS

# List of tables, graph and diagram

# ACKNOWLEDGEMENTS

The authors would like to thank Dimitri Germidis, who has now left his supervision of the Development Centre's research on the Financing of Development and its project on rebalancing the public and private sectors in developing countries to take up important duties elsewhere, for his constant encouragement of this research.

We would also like to thank Bruno Coquet (University of Paris-IX), Keith Griffin (University of California, Riverside) and Ernest Wilson (University of Ann Arbor, Michigan), for their comments on the preliminary versions of certain chapters.

# PREFACE

The end of the 1970s was characterised by the weakening of the traditional regulation of different types of mixed economies in developing countries. The slowing down of economic growth, the aggravation of external imbalances and the tightening of financial constraints made stabilisation and economic adjustment policies inevitable throughout the 1980s. These new economic orientations cast doubt on previously accepted models.

The time has come to evaluate what some have called "the lost decade" in development. This book offers thoughts on the transition from a system based on the search for economic independence towards one seeking better integration into the world economy as a whole. The authors then provide an analysis of the consequences of this systemic evolution for the respective roles of the public and private sectors of the economy.

Indeed, the size and interdependence of the changes taking place in the area of economic and financial liberalization require reconsideration of the balance between the public and private sectors in this context of economic transition. The importance of this book is that it supplies a structure of analysis which will allow a better interpretation of current economic transformations in developing countries.

In writing a detailed study of the reinforcing of market mechanisms and above all of the "resizing" of the public sector's role, the two authors emphasise the major recasting of development strategies which has been seen during the 1980s. They conclude, moreover, that political democratisation is necessary in order for this economic transition to receive durable acceptance among the populations of developing countries.

Louis Emmerij
President of the OECD Development Centre
February 1991

# EXECUTIVE SUMMARY


## Rebalancing the public and private sectors in developing countries: importance of research in this field

The rebalancing of the public and private sectors calls for a re-examination of the theories advocating wide government intervention in economic activity. In the developed countries, the loss of influence of Keynesian ideas has been expressed by the revision of economic policies. In the developing countries, government divestiture and the increased role of the private sector call for a complete reform of development strategies. *The rebalancing process is defined as all those actions aimed at reforming the functioning of the economic system with a view to letting market mechanisms exercise control.* Accordingly, in rebalancing the public and private sectors in the developing countries, much more is at stake than a mere redistribution of roles and responsibilities in the economy. The actions aimed at reducing the public sector thus have to be placed in the context of this progress towards an open market economy.

On the basis of a sample of ten developing countries (in Africa, Ghana, Morocco and Tunisia; in Central and Latin America, Bolivia, Chile, Jamaica and Mexico; and in Asia, Bangladesh, Malaysia and the Philippines), the rebalancing of the public and private sectors has been studied from three angles: a) it has been placed in historical perspective, on the basis of the experiences of each country, for a better understanding of the circumstances leading to the creation and strengthening of the public sector in the development strategies followed from the 1950s to the 1970s; b) the problems involved in the rebalancing process, such as the complete about-turn in development strategy under strong pressure from the economic and financial crisis in the early 1980s; c) the methods of implementing the change in balance (liberalisation of the conditions of economic activity, privatisation and restructuring of public sector enterprises) and their impact on public finances, on the allocative and productive efficiency of the economy and on social structures.

The turning point of rebalancing becomes all the more important in the light of the development strategies practised since independence by the sample countries. These strategies, based on trying to achieve economic independence and detachment

11

from the world market, called for action in two spheres: first, strong direct state presence on the market, through its taking over the production of many goods previously imported, and second, indirect state involvement, through the implementation of a regulatory framework to protect the economic fabric from domestic and foreign competition. Because the different forms of import substitution were grafted onto a variety of economic and political structures, three types of mixed economy emerged: those dominated by the state, those promoted by the state and those that serve particular interests. It is essential to understand the basis and dynamics of each of these variants in order to comprehend the respective positions of the public and the private sectors at the inception of the rebalancing process.

**The drift towards government intervention**

In all the sample countries, apart from Chile, there was an appreciable trend of state intervention during the 1970s. The increase in the weight of the public sector was a significant departure from theories of public economics (production and distribution of utilities and public services, public responsibility for natural monopolies, etc.) and of development economics (control of the "commanding heights of the economy"). Indeed, the state was no longer satisfied with the roles of "life-belt" and "promoter" state and diversified its involvement substantially, especially in the industrial, commercial and financial services sectors.

The increase in the number of public enterprises, most frequently through the creation of subsidiaries by public sector parent companies and the tightening of regulatory control, was made possible by the substantial financial resources available to most of the developing countries during the 1970s. This financing — foreign for the most part — came from two sources: export earnings from primary products and international bank loans, characterised at that time by their low real cost. The explosion of state intervention was the final phase of a mixed economy dynamics promoted or dominated by the public sector. The rapid increase in public consumption and investment was evidence of rapid adjustment by the state to the financial resources at its disposal. However, the disparity between the implementation of structural public expenditure (development projects calling for investments over several fiscal periods, the growing number of public employees) and unstable financial resources (fluctuating commodity prices, foreign debt on overflexible terms) was a harbinger of the rebalancing. By undertaking a radically opposed policy as early as 1973, Chile showed, in a different way, the limits of privatisation and financial liberalisation policies in the absence of any real constraints on foreign financing.

## Orthodox principles and economic liberalism: a necessary choice

The turning-point can be dated precisely. The fall in the developing countries' terms of trade at the beginning of the 1980s, combined with the debt crisis, suddenly dried up the state's foreign sources of finance. In addition, marked recessions resulting from these external shocks reduced the volume of tax earnings. The governments managed to adapt quickly to this financial squeeze. In a fairly short time (1982-85), most of them opted for the orthodox principles advocated by the international organisations, led by the International Monetary Fund. This choice required them to implement strict economic stabilization policies. Among the main objectives of the re-establishment of major balances were a drastic reduction in budget deficits and a marked slowdown in the growth of monetary aggregates. By eliminating the sources of domestic finance, the stabilization policies tightened the financial squeeze still further.

The difficulty of stabilizing developing economies, in a context of net financial transfers towards the creditor nations, called for the lengthy application of stabilization policies. The duration of economic and financial restrictions finally defined new operating conditions, with which the developing countries must now comply in the long term. Governments were thus compelled to limit their budget expenditure considerably and to stop turning a blind eye to poor financial performance by public sector firms. The deficit of these firms was not new and had not been looked into closely, but the exigencies of financial constraint made the problem more acute.

The adoption of structural adjustment policies led to a total revamping of the development model. These policies, which are based on increasing the allocative and productive efficiency of the economy, affect all economic agents. Public enterprises, which played a leading role in the previous model, are supposed to adapt to the requirements of the new economic environment. Consequently, they must be restructured, liquidated or privatised. In a liberalised environment, the private sector, until then discouraged by excessive regulation, should become the motive force of the nation's development. The will to divest the state in favour of the private sector is therefore a genuine reversal of responsibilities in this development model, where priority is given to competitiveness (the corollary of integration into the international trading system) rather than to national independence.

The rebalancing process stems from the will of governments, under pressure from international organisations and lenders of funds, to apply market rationality systematically and to encourage efficient behaviour. Accordingly, its planning focuses on the liberalisation of conditions of economic activity and on the restructuring and privatisation of public enterprises. Particular attention has been paid to privatisation, which represents a means of both reducing the public sector and transferring initiative and responsibility directly to the private sector. The concept of "effective privatisation" is used to clarify the change in ownership status of state-owned firms. It relies on two criteria, both essential from the viewpoint of the finality of privatisation: the application of private rationality in running the enterprise concerned and the new owner's acceptance of financial liability. The first factor emphasizes control of the enterprise; the second, financial investment in the company's modernisation and development. It should be stressed that although many transfers of ownership and management have taken place, the number of effective privatisations in the developing countries has turned out to be fairly low. For example, management contracts are excluded, since the contracting parties do not incur financial liability. In the case of transfer operations and leases, a retrospective microeconomic study has to be made before one can assess whether the privatisation was effective.

**The impact of privatisation and rebalancing**

One aim of this study is to show that the rebalancing of the public and the private sectors does not amount simply to the application of one component of the process on its own. Privatisation alone is not enough to achieve the two main objectives of rebalancing: reduction in the financial burden posed by public enterprises and improvement of the allocative and productive efficiency of the economy.

a) The impact of privatisation on the national budget depends essentially on the improvement in the privatised enterprises' financial results. If there is no such improvement, the impact over several fiscal periods is nil, or even negative, in view of the undervaluation of the assets at the time of the transfer and the possible use of the income from the transfer for consumption rather than for reducing the debt burden. Further, as public enterprises that are structurally in deficit are not concerned by effective privatisation, the expected gains in financial transfers from the state to these enterprises (operational subsidies and injections of capital) are small. In the case of public sector firms operating in substantial deficit, restructuring or even liquidation seems the most appropriate procedure. In restructuring public enterprises, the state is responsible for reorganising and modernising them, while maintaining its full control over the capital and the management. Restructuring corresponds to an attempt by a public authority to apply management criteria similar to those of private management.

b) Market competition lies at the root of economic efficiency. The transfer of ownership rights results in improvements in efficiency, but these are limited by the uncertain effect of privatisations on market structures. In the operations carried out in the sample countries, we are bound to note that the transfer of ownership has not particularly encouraged the development of competition. In certain countries privatisation has even strengthened the movement towards industrial and financial concentration (see the examples of Chile from 1973 to 1982 and Mexico since 1983). From the viewpoint of the impact on economic efficiency, the most satisfactory method is to increase the role of market forces during the privatisation process, in order to avoid the exploitation of oligopolistic or monopolistic market structures for private ends. Accordingly, the transfer to the private sector must be accompanied by genuine liberalisation of the conditions relating to domestic and foreign competition. The breaking up of monopoly market structures, which does not necessarily imply deconcentration at the national level, should enable the emergence of private producers, either local or foreign, with levels of competitiveness close to those on the international market. Genuine liberalisation comprises a number of deregulatory measures, that is to say, measures that reduce the number and scope of existing regulations (prices, customs barriers, import restrictions, etc.). To achieve a sustainable increase in the role of market forces, however, it is also essential to adapt the regulatory framework to the new competitive situation and new behaviour (process of reregulation).

The impact of privatisation on social structures also seems relatively limited. Restructurings of public enterprises, with a view either to their subsequent transfer or to the modernisation of "strategic" sectors, are much more costly from the social point of view. Pricing adjustments, the reduction of excessive staffing levels and the revision of wage scales engender high social costs. Two provisos, however, must be borne in mind: i) public enterprises are not necessarily the most appropriate means of attaining fixed social objectives; therefore, privatisation and restructuring are not bound to lead to social regression (the savings in subsidies and the income from the transfer may be used to achieve the same social objectives by more efficient means: for example, by direct redistribution to certain social groups); ii) the improvements in efficiency achieved through the combined action of liberalisation, restructuring and privatisation can improve social welfare, if competition compels the producer to lower the price of the good or service offered and/or to increase the volume for sale.

## The complementary effect of the policies

In consequence, privatisation is only one of the tools available to the governments of developing countries in their progress towards rebalancing. It seems a particularly appropriate method of reducing state involvement in those sectors of activity where it grew, without any real justification, during the 1970s. Privatisation is not a panacea, however, especially if one bears in mind the weakness of its real impact on the main aims of rebalancing. The objective restraints on the conduct of privatisation (weakness of the local capital markets, lack of potential local interest in acquisition, high number of unattractive public enterprises) call for government effort in three spheres: speeding up decision making, encouraging maximum transparency of the process and promoting the various competitive conditions that allow the potential advantages of the privatisation to be achieved in practice.

The fact that the various rebalancing procedures are complementary is also revealed at the level of the "strategic" sectors. Most of the countries in our sample have designated certain sectors of activity where public ownership and government intervention are considered to be exclusive or matters of priority. The strategic sectors reflect the scale of the public sector following the rebalancing process and centre on two poles of attraction: intervention justified by the theoretical corpus of public economics and activities deemed vital to strategies for national independence. Although these sectors are protected from privatisation, they are nonetheless subject to an active restructuring and liberalisation policy. In this perspective, these measures appear to be essential complements to privatisation policies.

**Future of the rebalancing process**

A new development model, stemming from the economic and financial crisis at the start of the 1980s, has been imposed on the developing countries. Its two keystones are integration into the world economy and better management of public funds. The rebalancing process is the interplay of these new principles at the level of the division between the public and private sectors. It is complicated to implement and faces a great deal of political and social opposition. Under these circumstances, it is important to consider how skilful the developing countries will be at achieving this change in direction, in other words, to consider whether the rebalancing process is reversible.

This will depend on progress in structural reform and the maturity of the local private sector. Of the countries included in the sample, only Chile, Mexico and Malaysia — and, to a lesser degree, Morocco and Tunisia — have reached a level of reform that would be difficult to reverse. These countries are also the ones whose economic and industrial structures are in the best position to confront international competition, and where the private sector, generally under the leadership of several large groups, disposes of sufficient financial resources to provide for its own development. For the other countries, the rebalancing process is just as necessary, but it has to take into consideration their different economic fabric. Rebalancing thus seems to be an opportunity for making small and medium-sized private enterprises more dynamic, by the removal of most of the discriminatory regulations. Whatever the case, the longevity of the rebalancing process will depend primarily on the new political alliances formed in support of or in opposition to the structural reforms.

# GENERAL INTRODUCTION

The experience of the past three decades has cast discredit on theories advocating wide government intervention. The developing countries' economic and financial difficulties at the beginning of the 1980s, in fact, drew attention to flaws in the models that had prevailed from the 1950s to the 1970s. The redefinition of the relative positions of the public and private sectors breaks with the widespread tradition of an interventionist and planner state, controlling the "commanding heights" of the national economy and promoting a development strategy based on the search for economic independence. It cannot be disputed, however, that the state has a role to play in the conduct of development. Its intervention is justified both by the theoretical corpus of public economics (in particular as regards the production and distribution of public goods and services and responsibility for natural monopolies) and by the persistence of factors that militated in the past for the extension of the public sector (weight of investments and low profitability in certain sectors of activity, support for new-fledged industries).

In the developed countries, the state exceeds the bounds of the role allotted to it by classic liberal theory. Furthermore, its weight varies considerably from one country to another. A simple comparison of the extent of government intervention in France or Sweden, on the one hand, and in the United States, on the other, reveals that apart from the weight of the public sector (expressed as a percentage of value-added, gross fixed capital formation or employment), it is important to consider the overall dynamics of the economy, principally the pressure exerted by market forces, whether domestic or foreign.

Consequently, in the rebalancing of the public and private sectors in the developing countries, more is at stake than the mere redistribution of roles and responsibilities between public and private agents in the context of a mixed economy. *The rebalancing process is defined as all those actions aimed at reforming the functioning of the economic system with a view to letting market mechanisms exercise control.* It is a major turning-point for many developing countries, since government divestiture and the growth in the role of the private sector, on the one hand, and the strengthening of the role of market forces, on the other, imply a total reform of development strategies. The measures aimed at liberalising domestic and foreign

17

market forces reflect the general direction of this reform, because they reduce indirect government intervention in the conditions of economic activity and express a certain acceptance of the rules derived from integration into the world economy. Accordingly, they call strongly into question the functioning of the mixed economy models followed by the developing countries since their independence. This work tries to throw light on the changeover to the new dynamics brought about by the rebalancing process.

The displacement of the boundary between the public and private sectors, in particular by means of actions undertaken to reduce the public sector, must be placed in the context of this evolution towards an open market economy. Only when the general direction of the reforms has been defined does the reform of the public sector really become meaningful. Reconsideration of the role of public enterprises — which, as long as the old methods of functioning applied, enjoyed a privileged status — is closely linked to the application of policies complying with the new objectives of development strategy (integration into the world economy, search for greater economic efficiency). The reform of the public sector is rendered imperative by the general acceptance of the criteria of resource allocation and profit maximisation in the assessment of companies' performance. For this reason, public enterprises are prime targets of the rebalancing process. The privatisation, restructuring or even liquidation of these enterprises is aimed at adapting them to market rationality. Accordingly, the reduction and modernisation of the public sector cannot be dissociated from systemic development towards a functioning based on market mechanisms. Furthermore, the ability of the various economic agents to adjust and adapt to the new competitive conditions and to the exigencies of competitiveness will depend on an implicit change in the balance of the public and private sectors.

In order to interpret more clearly the complex rebalancing process currently under way, the analysis developed in this work has been undertaken from three points of view: a) it has been placed in historical perspective, on the basis of national experiences, for a better understanding of the circumstances leading to the creation and strengthening of the public sector in the development strategies followed from the 1950s to the 1970s; b) the problems involved in the rebalancing process, such as the total turnaround in development strategy under strong pressure from the economic and financial crisis in the early 1980s; c) the methods of implementing the change in balance (liberalisation of the conditions of economic activity, privatisation and restructuring of public enterprises) and their impact on public finances, on the allocative and productive efficiency of the economy and on social structures.

Our discussion is based on the study of ten developing countries: in Africa, Ghana, Morocco and Tunisia; in Central and Latin America, Bolivia, Chile, Jamaica and Mexico; and in Asia, Bangladesh, Malaysia and the Philippines. Apart from geographic or demographic criteria, these countries had attained different levels of development at the start of the 1980s, in other words, at the inception of the rebalancing process. These different levels are such that they can be assessed solely on the basis of gross national product (GNP) per inhabitant (see Table 1).

*Table 1*

**POPULATION, GNP PER INHABITANT AND GROWTH RATE
IN THE SAMPLE DEVELOPING COUNTRIES**

| Country | Population (millions) | GNP per inhabitant (dollars) | | | Average annual growth rate of GDP (percentage) | |
|---|---|---|---|---|---|---|
| | 1988 | 1976 | 1982 | 1988 | 1960-70 | 1970-82 |
| Ghana | 14.0 | 580 | 360 | 400 | 2.2 | -0.5 |
| Morocco | 24.0 | 540 | 870 | 830 | 4.4 | 5.0 |
| Tunisia | 7.8 | 840 | 1 390 | 1 230 | 4.2 | 7.0 |
| Bolivia | 6.9 | 390 | 570 | 570 | 5.2 | 3.7 |
| Chile | 12.8 | 1 050 | 2 210 | 1 510 | 4.4 | 1.9 |
| Jamaica | 2.4 | 1 070 | 1 330 | 1 070 | 4.4 | -1.1 |
| Mexico | 83.7 | 1 090 | 2 270 | 1 760 | 7.6 | 6.4 |
| Bangladesh | 108.9 | 110 | 140 | 170 | 3.7 | 4.1 |
| Malaysia | 16.9 | 860 | 1 860 | 1 940 | 6.5 | 7.0 |
| Philippines | 59.9 | 410 | 820 | 630 | 5.1 | 6.0 |
| France | 55.9 | 6 550 | 11 680 | 16 090 | 5.5 | 3.2 |
| United States | 246.3 | 7 890 | 13 160 | 19 840 | 4.3 | 2.7 |

*Sources:*    *Report on World Development,* World Bank, 1978, 1984, 1990.

# Plan of the work

Particular intention is paid to the formation of the public sectors as well as the method of operation and functioning of the economic system during the phase of rising government intervention. Indeed, the shaping of the structures by the economic history of each country must be borne in mind when the problem of rebalancing is posed. It therefore seems essential to start with a country-by-country analysis of the economic bases and political intentions that paralleled these countries' efforts to achieve economic independence. Apart from the many similarities in the mid-1960s, this study enables us to distinguish three different types of mixed economy among the experiences of the sample countries. The principles and dynamics of the economic systems in place at the dawn of the rebalancing process will be presented in the first chapter of this book.

The second chapter deals with the consequences of the economic and financial breakdown in 1982 on development strategy in our sample countries. The sudden tightening of financing restrictions and the crisis in the development model that had predominated until then forced governments to examine the function and place of the public sector in the economy. Their analyses led to the adoption of policies aimed at integrating national economies into the world economy and, to this end, rebalancing economic structures in favour of the private sector. This change of direction, grounded both on economic and financial liberalisation at the domestic and foreign levels and on reduction of the public sector, corresponded expressly or impliedly to a complete restructuring of the development model. Chapter 2 presents the rationality and principal modalities of this turning-point in history, the rebalancing process in the developing countries.

The whole of Chapter 3 is devoted to privatisation operations. This procedure is the most direct way of transferring initiative and responsibility from the public sector to the private. It enables the public sector to be reduced by disseminating private activity across the economy. Presented at first as a panacea by its partisans, privatisation is a complex process that is particularly relevant at a time when most of the developing countries, after a long preparatory stage, have actually started to realise their ambitious privatisation programmes. The study examines the definition of and the theoretical justifications for privatisation and the modalities of its application. A list of privatisation operations on a country-by-country basis, grouped by sector of activity and by privatisation techniques used, is presented in Annex 2.

As many privatisation operations have already been carried out in the sample countries, it is necessary to describe the impact of privatisation and, by extension, that of the rebalancing process in general. The analysis of the repercussions on public finances, on the allocative and productive efficiency of the economy and on social structures emphasizes that the main constituents of the rebalancing process are complementary. The conclusions drawn in this fourth chapter are not applicable to every country, but on the basis of the study of ten developing countries, they do enable a more complete evaluation of what one can and should expect from privatisation and the rebalancing process.

The problem of rebalancing arises in all the developing countries. It is worth considering, however, what factors will ensure that the process is irreversible. The fifth and last chapter, essentially prospective, will present the bases of the likely dynamics of the new development model in the light of its new constraints (integration in the world economy, better management of public funds and the search for new political alliances).

*Chapter 1*

# THE DAWN OF THE REBALANCING PROCESS

The question of rebalancing the public and private sectors has been under consideration in most of the developing countries since the beginning of the 1980s. It is crucial in that it calls into question the extension of the state's economic activities. For several decades — since the 1940s in the case of most Latin American countries, and since independence in the early 1960s in the case of the former French, British, Belgian and Dutch colonies — the strengthening of the role of the state, the regulation of economic activity and the ever-increasing number of state-owned enterprises seemed part of the natural order of things. It should be noted, too, that the overweighty influence accorded to the state and the administration was often a continuation of structures set up during the colonial era. The privileged role of government and the public sector in the management of national economies was, lastly, a reflection of "the current vogue", in other words, it mirrored the dominant economic philosophy in countries both South and North.

In the first section, we shall summarise briefly the main evidence in support of the central position allotted to the state and the public sector in economic development strategies. This theoretical stage, sketched in very general terms, is essential in that rebalancing too is based on a body of economic principles; it is not merely the pragmatic response to a crisis.

After this retrospective analysis, a second section will be devoted to the national variants of the mixed economy, corresponding to the application of the ideas dominant at that time in the various countries in our sample.

This leads us to the dawn of the rebalancing process and will enable a deeper understanding of the new trends in economic policy practised after 1980, which, though clearly a break with the dogma of the past, were still to be affected by the tide of history.

## Formation of the public sector: the frame of reference

The justification for a strong public sector in developing economies — in other words the need for an active government role in the economy, backed up by a powerful administration and public enterprises and a complex regulatory apparatus — was based on two main lines of argument. On the one hand, most of the developing countries gave priority to the objective of economic independence, as an extension of the struggle for political independence from former colonial or "imperialist" powers — the "central powers", to use terminology corresponding more closely to the spirit of the age. On the other hand, the achievement of this objective led these same countries "on the periphery" to exalt the role of the state as the priority instrument of that political will.

These two main determinants of the birth of the public sector mirrored a concept of development in which economic rationality was generally subordinate to political rationality. Consequently, it will be useful at the end of this section to underline the difference between the classic theory of public economics and the theory of development dominant at the dawn of the rebalancing process, concerning justification for the government's economic role and the position of the public sector.

### *The desire for economic independence*

The finishing touch to the attainment of political sovereignty by breaking off links with colonial rulers — sometimes quite suddenly — was the abolition of the colonial alliance. Under these circumstances, economic independence called for the rejection of the international division of labour as it had been instituted under the colonial empires. This had made the colonies the suppliers of primary products to the industrialised nations via a mandatory specialisation in the production and export of unprocessed resources of the soil and subsoil. The end of the peripheral economies' "extraversion" (Amin, 1970) of necessity comes through the elimination of national economic structures based on two sectors closely linked to the world economy: the primary products export sector and the "luxury goods" (consumer durables) import sector. The model of reference is the industrialised economy, which links the intermediate and capital goods sectors with the consumer goods sector on a national basis. The final objective is to "fill in the inter-industrial matrix" (de Bernis, 1968).

To achieve this aim of "self-reliant" development, it is essential to gain independence from the world market, and this implies a drastic reduction in the economic links forged in the past with the colonial powers. The indictment of the theory of international specialisation has a slightly different colour in the case of countries, such as those of Latin America, which gained political independence long ago. The theories of CEPAL (Prebisch, in Meier, 1988; Oman & Wignaraja, 1990, Chapter 5) mainly reflect the situation in these economies. The criticism of the

24

international division of labour goes much further than mere denunciation of the effects of domination inherent in the colonial alliance. It is based on the phenomenon of structural deterioration in the terms of trade between countries that export primary products and those that export manufactured goods. According to this approach, the very principles of Ricardian analysis of comparative costs are called into question. The international division of labour founded on free trade and relative factor endowments does not lead to an equilibrium situation. Contrary to the theory, the benefits of international trade are unequally divided and lead to ongoing impoverishment of the countries exporting non-processed products, even when the trade deals are negotiated between countries that attained their political sovereignty many years earlier and have totally severed the special links that bound them to a colonial power (Singer, in Meier, 1988).

Accordingly, the only solution for the peripheral countries is to produce and export manufactured products. At this level, we may note the convergence of the Latin American theories and theories of self-reliant development, which are more concerned with the situation of the newly independent countries. Industrialisation on a national basis, therefore, seems to be the cornerstone of any policy aimed at breaking economic dependence and promoting development. The analysis of unequal trade subsequently developed by A. Emmanuel (1969) excludes any optimism of this kind, however, in that the inequality confronting international trade is based not on the type of products involved but on wage differentials. In addition, when factors such as technology and the impact of direct investment by the multinationals are taken into account, these also lead to less optimistic conclusions as regards strategies for eliminating *dependencia* (Michalet, 1985, Chapter 4). As these new views were mainly developed during the 1970s, however, they postdate the formulation of the alternatives to the liberal model which characterise the period prior to the turning-point in the rebalancing process. These models were based on the exaltation of the economic role of the state and the consequent growth in the public sector.

### Exaltation of the economic role of the state

A schematic distinction can be drawn between two different approaches to development based on industrialisation. One is based on import substitution; the other favours accumulation founded on the basic sectors. Both these approaches were favoured by most of the developing countries before the neo-liberal stance of rebalancing.

The first model, mainly drawn up by the CEPAL school, was based on the experience of the major crisis period during the 1930s and World War II. The main feature of this period was the weakening of traditional relationships between the South American countries and their usual trading partners, the United States and Europe. The substantial slowdown in imports from these countries compelled a number of Latin American countries to produce locally goods that they had traditionally imported. Hence the arrival on the scene of industrialisation in embryonic form linked to lack of supply from the industrialised countries. Subsequently, the influence of Keynesian analysis played a considerable role in the elaboration of a model in which industrialisation is encouraged by domestic demand, itself fed in part by public expenditure and the play of the multiplier effect.

The second school, whose inspiration is derived from the Soviet model, has had a more recent influence. It was fairly popular with the countries that achieved political independence in the 1960s. In this approach, the objective of self-reliant industrialisation has to be achieved by the introduction of free-will investment plans with progressive forward linkage — from the production of commodities through intermediate products and capital goods to the production of consumer goods (Hugon, 1989, p. 80 *et seq.*).

Despite the different theoretical inspiration, the two models have a great deal in common. In the first place, the main objective of independent development merges with the industrialisation process. In the second place, the possibility that this could result from the spontaneous play of market forces is excluded. The peripheral economies function in the context of a world economy. This reinforces their extraversion since it encourages the primary export activities. The only way of breaking this logic is by means of a long-term strategy based on a strong state, capable of being the motive force of the manufacturing sector. It is felt that the essential step towards encouraging intersectoral relationships and providing for overall economic cohesion is by instituting planning. The programme will be made more or less restrictive as the government thinks appropriate, but it will always be essential in order to avoid the anarchy characteristic of the market economy. Third, whether the countries adopt a centralised economy model or a mixed economy model, the vector of prime importance, industrialisation, will consist of public enterprises created and controlled by the state. If there is no cohesive local industrial fabric and no significant private initiative, the state-owned enterprises will be destined to occupy a quasi-monopoly position in the various branches where they are located. Accordingly, they will have to integrate vertically in both directions from their main activity, in order to produce the goods and services that are not available in the country owing to the limitations of the local industrial sector. The scope of the public sector is therefore not limited to specific types of activity according to the normative approach of the theory of public goods and services, but by the exigencies of industrialisation. Hence the tendency of the public enterprises to develop vertical forms of integration leading to huge industrial complexes. Fourth, the expropriation of foreign firms occupying "dominant positions" and exploiting national resources that generate foreign currency — oil, mining, plantations — also falls into the logic of industrialisation aimed at national economic independence. Such nationalisations strengthen the public sector and increase the state's financial resources, as the main public income is derived from export-import activities. Lastly, whatever the model of reference, protectionism is the rule of the day, to enable the newly fledged industries to flourish. List wins the day over Ricardo, and this also marks the defeat of the old order, the advocates of free trade involved in livestock production, plantations or export-import.

As a majority of the new leaders were members of the professional classes or the administration — including members of the former colonial administration — it is clear that an industrialisation policy based on strong state structures corresponded more closely to their past experience and their beliefs than did the market economy. It also filled the void left by the departure of colonials who had been active in the local industrial sector, which in any case was nearly always at the embryonic stage. In addition, the socialist or populist tendencies of the new leaders aimed to use the state and the public sector as instruments for redistributing the national income. Apart from an undeniable concern for equity, the fight against poverty was also intended to stimulate the growth of actual demand, which would sustain the progress of industrialisation directed first and foremost at the domestic market. The latter would principally consist of consumption by the urban populations employed by industry and, especially, the services and central government. The rural community — the vast majority of the population — was to bear the brunt of this development effort aimed at reproducing a speeded-up version of the Western economy model as it had developed since the end of the nineteenth century. This is one of the ambiguities of development models whose main foundation is the economic role of the state.

This brief presentation of "structuralist" theories of development is mainly of historical interest. The failures of the import-substitution strategies in Latin America and the "industrialising industry" strategies in Algeria have reduced their credibility. All the more so since the successes achieved by the newly industrialising countries in South-East Asia, which have agreed to play the game of comparative advantage and growth derived from exports, have been used systematically to demonstrate that policies based on the central role of the state and the rejection of the international division of labour are erroneous. However, in seeking to lend more weight to the contrast between two theories of development, the supporters of the Asiatic model have somewhat overlooked the influence of the state and the significant position of the public sector in the countries of that region. The resurgence of neo-liberal sentiment is indissociable from the crisis caused by the oil shocks. In contrast with the events in 1929, the Northern countries did not lose faith in their model of reference. To the contrary, the liberal experiments carried out in the United States and Great Britain under the leadership of President Reagan and Prime Minister Thatcher served as an example for economists specialising in research or advice to the developing countries. The International Monetary Fund (IMF) and the World Bank played a determining role in this effort to convert the South to strict economic rationality and the abandonment of "developmentalist" theories. In addition, recent analyses of public choice and the theory of rent-seekers have led to condemnation, on socio-political grounds, of the inefficient and socially regressive nature of policies based on protectionism and government interventionism (Buchanan, Tollison & Tullock, 1980;  Olson, 1988).

It is worth noting, however, along with M. Kahler (in Nelson, 1990), that the tide of monetary theory, especially at the International Monetary Fund and the World Bank, has managed to integrate certain features from the structural school. Thus, the creation of Extended Fund Facilities recognised the need to extend the time scale in the adjustment process. On the other hand, both the IMF and the World Bank, with their structural adjustment programmes, have widened the context of conditionality to include virtually all the economic variables. In so doing, they have helped to distribute what A. Hirschmann (1981) referred to as "monoeconomics": the refusal to recognise the specific characteristics of less developed economies in favour of an approach that unifies economic mechanisms. The recommendations advocating the extension of the market and the decline of the public sector are in keeping with this logic. Paradoxically, it is the governments that are asked to institute economic strategies intended to reduce significantly their power of intervention, linked to the abandonment of the mixed economy. The particular mechanisms used subsequently as a means of rebalancing the public and private sectors depended to a large extent on the governments' response to this recommendation.

### Development economics, public economics and the mixed economy

Apart from development theory, the analytical tools that can be used to understand the formation of national economies consisting of a public sector alongside a private sector are mainly supplied by the theory of public economics. This theory, which defines the role of the public sector as the provider of public goods and services, is a static approach that separates activities into two domains, the public and the private, on the basis of the characteristics of certain goods and services which are exclusively dependent on state initiative. Therefore the demarcation line defining the bounds of government intervention is strictly drawn from the outset of the analysis. This leads to the exclusion of two factors: neither the historical background to the formation of the public sector nor the dynamic play between the private and the public sectors is taken into consideration.

As the two approaches appear to be irreconcilable, we intend to propose a new methodological framework, borrowing both from the theoretical framework of public economics, the final objective of which is to take account of activities outside the market that are naturally dependent on the public sector, and from the economic development models, which were used to justify the extension of the public sector according to the objectives referred to above. This step, which it must be stressed is only at the exploratory stage, will be carried out in two phases. To start with, the concepts of the theory of public economics will be compared to the development strategies underlying the birth of the public sector, in order to highlight the radical differences between the two schools of thought. In the second phase, we shall propose a classification of the various mixed economy systems. This classification will be applied in the following section, where the various countries in the sample will be studied one by one.

## A. *The justification for the public sector*

The subject matter of the theory of public economics is all those activities that escape market logic and that, accordingly, fall within the ambit of the state's responsibility. There is clearly no question of setting out here all the analyses of this school of thought, first mooted by the Italian economist Mazzola (Musgrave & Peacock, 1964), moving on to the classical analyses of Lindahl and Wicksell, and culminating in Samuelson's general theory (1954). The most recent extensions of the concept come from the "public choice" school and the analysis of bureaucracy (Buchanan, 1980). We intend simply to summarise the basic concepts used to justify the existence of a public sector alongside the private sector. They will be compared to the justifications for the public sector contained in the development theories referred to above.

The theory of public economics aims to define the minimum position that the public sector should occupy in a market economy. Priority is given to two cases: the natural monopoly and the production of public goods and services.

The notion of the natural monopoly is linked to activities where economies of scale can be achieved. The reduction in costs depends on the increase in production and thus on the increase in market share. Bearing in mind the size of the market, the presence of several producers in this sector will prevent the optimum level of output from being achieved. If the monopoly is under the aegis of a private enterprise, the optimum allocation of resources will not be achieved because the monopolist will limit his output and force the consumer to pay high prices, thus making a monopoly profit. In order to avoid such distortions, the state should make the monopoly subject to regulations or transform it into a public enterprise. In any case, the prices of goods or services offered by public monopolies will be fixed by the central government and not by the market. The most common cases of natural monopoly are in the public utilities sector: water, gas, electricity, rail transport and communications.

Public goods and services have two specific characteristics. On the one hand, the supply of public goods and services responds to the twin principles of non-exclusion and non-appropriation. This means, first, that once an individual has access to a public good or service, admission to it will be open to all the other potential consumers. This means, second, that the demand for public goods and services will not reduce the available supply. Accordingly, the price of public goods and services should be nil, since their supply is perfectly elastic and their marginal cost is zero. The classic example of the public good is the lighthouse. Because the characteristics of public goods and services render them unattractive to private entrepreneurs, the state has to provide for their production and distribution. The financing of their production is borne by the public budget. Taxation is the substitute for the market price insofar as the vote on the budget in accordance with parliamentary procedures can be classed as a market mechanism. Leaving to one side the difficulties linked to the problem of non-revelation of preferences resulting from the principle of non-exclusion, the concern of public economics theoreticians is to demonstrate that analysis of the public sector can be integrated into general economic analysis (Greffe, 1972). According to this approach, there would therefore be no contradiction between the functioning of the public sector and that of the private sector. In both cases, the rules of economic calculation apply. Furthermore, budgetary neutrality ensures that the public sector does not disturb the optimal allocation of resources in the economy. But, in counterpart, the strict separation between the two sectors makes it difficult to take the effects of synergy into account. Any trespassing by one sector onto the other is then translated as a loss of economic efficiency.

Clearly, the concept of the role of the public sector in the various development theories prevalent over the last three decades is incompatible with the theory of public economics. The three main differences are as follows:

In the first place, whereas the theory of public economics focuses mainly on the search for conditions of Pareto optimality, the major concern of the development theories, as Ahmad underlines (in Jones, 1982), is the generation and division of economic surplus. If the development process is limited merely to industrialisation, priority is given to physical production. The public enterprises are called to act either as a motive force to make up for the lack of private initiative or as a catalyst for private investment. The two sectors are thus not viewed as strictly separate; to the contrary, the effects of interdependence are highlighted in a dynamic scenario in which the desire for economic efficiency is secondary.

In the second place, the creation of public monopolies is not limited to the question of the effects of economies of scale (natural monopolies), nor to the particular case of public goods and services. As has already been noted, the state decides to create public enterprises on the basis of economic and social objectives: strategic industries, import substitution, redistribution in favour of underprivileged strata of society. Certain activities in the public sector may be common to both theoretical approaches, but the justification for their inclusion is very different. In any case, the division of tasks between the two sectors is less strictly defined in the development models than in the analysis of public economics. Certain activities that now belong to the public sector may change over to the private sector tomorrow, or vice versa. The minimalist approach of public economics leaves a greater degree of leeway for the play of the rebalancing process in either direction.

Lastly, the public economics approach seeks to make the functioning of the public sector subject to the logic of the market; this concern is not found in the development theories, which are characterised to the contrary by mistrust of the consequences of market mechanisms in terms of equity and economic power. Government intervention through price regulation, the fixing of exchange rates, the determination of customs tariffs and quotas, the establishment of minimum wage rates and control of interest rates is therefore aimed at correcting what are deemed to be the harmful effects of the spontaneous operation of the markets. In an extreme case, planning and regulations will be simply substituted for market mechanisms.

Whereas the theory of public economics is dominated by a minimalist vision of the public sector, the development concepts tend to give priority to government intervention, on the one hand, through direct regulation of economic activities, and, on the other, by the extension of the public sector with the increase in the number of public enterprises. The application of these general principles is not uniform, however; it varies from one country to another, and in the same country from one era to another depending on changes in government policy, which in turn result from political processes that cannot really be classed as a form of market procedure. Indeed, political regimes in office do not always obey the principles of parliamentary democracy. In order to make a clearer comparison between the various national experiences, it is therefore essential to classify the different types of mixed economy.

## B. Types of mixed economy system

On the basis of the theoretical approaches mentioned above and the history of the countries in the sample, three different models of mixed economy can be distinguished. The characteristics of each system will be defined by its basic principle, its intervention instruments and its dynamics.

### Model A: The state-dominated mixed economy

— The basic principle is that the state should, to a large extent, be substituted for market mechanisms with a view to attaining a certain number of economic development objectives. The state is the guarantee of national economic independence; it can be seen at the heart of the industrialisation process; and it ensures national cohesion by fighting against social inequalities.

— The main intervention instruments are as follows: the public sector enterprises, whose function is more than the mere production and distribution of public goods and services, and which are assigned control of the "commanding heights" and strategic sectors of the economy; an extensive regulatory system that corrects the effects of market mechanisms; the creation of sectorally specialised financing bodies with two tasks: aiding private enterprises and co-operatives in accordance with

31

the stated priorities of the development plan and forming joint ventures with certain local and foreign private enterprises through the acquisition of equity capital.

— The dynamics of this type of mixed economy is directed at increasing the position and autonomy of the public sector, which is managed by a technocracy. The private sector occupies a residual position.

## Model B:  The state-promoted mixed economy

— The principle of this second type of mixed economy is based on the state and the public sector acting as the driving force in order to create an environment that encourages the gradual and concerted development of the private sector.

— The principal instruments are public enterprises created in sectors where initial investments are high, depreciation periods particularly long and profitability poor — for example, the infrastructure, basic industries, transport, communications.  The outward impact of the public sector is reinforced by a whole set of financial incentives aimed at encouraging local private initiative as well as foreign investors.

— The dynamics of this system should lead to growth in the private sector, which would gradually take over from the public enterprises.  In the same way, the regulatory apparatus should give way to market mechanisms once these have become efficient enough.  The enterprises that remain in the public sector will adopt private enterprise management criteria.

## Model C:  The mixed economy at the service of particular interests

— Principle:  the public sector creates situations that favour certain ethnic or socio-economic classes.

— The public enterprises and regulation discriminate in favour of the target groups by means of two main modalities:  on the one hand, access to public enterprises and to public financing is reserved or offered as a priority to privileged groups, and, on the other, the resources of public enterprises and public financial channels are mainly directed to "crony" private enterprises by means of public contracts, subsidised loans and subsidies.

— The dynamics of the system is indefinite in that there is an increasing merger of public and private interests. It may equally well lead to the strengthening of either sector, with the distinction between the two sectors becoming more and more artificial.

Three comments on method are necessary before applying this classification to the countries in the sample. In the first place, the models depicted above never exist in their "pure state" in reality. In each country, certain characteristics from one model or another exist side by side — in particular, certain dimensions from model C are found in countries that can be classed in category A or B. Nonetheless, at some point, one of the scenarios becomes dominant, making it possible to class the country with one model or another. In the second place, the classification of a country in one or another category may change over time. For example, an increase in a state's financial resources, linked, say, to an increase in foreign earnings, may result in a sliding over from B towards A. Lastly, political changes in the government of a country may be accompanied by a swing from one category to another at a frequency determined by "political cycles".

## National experiences

Apart from the general trend towards state interventionism and the extension of the public sector observed in all the countries in the sample during the 1970s, it is possible to identify appreciable differences from one country to another. In this perspective, the countries can be divided into three groups. The first consists of Mexico, Bolivia, Chile and Jamaica. Here the dominant role of the state was constantly affirmed during the 1970s and until the beginning of the 1980s, with the exception of Chile, where the change took place earlier. In certain cases, despite the revisions of traditional doctrine, the attachment to the state's role as leader of the economy goes back to well before the 1970s and is still strong, and this is likely to affect future rebalancing trends. In the second group, reference to the state and the public sector is important, but in the context of a mixed economy where the private sector is acknowledged to have a significant position. The state is expected to encourage its extension. This logic provides the rebalancing policies adopted since 1980 with a certain context of continuity. Morocco, Tunisia and Ghana fall into this category. Lastly, Malaysia and the Philippines will be dealt with apart, as the creation or expansion of the public sector responded to concerns of particular ethnic or business interests. It should be pointed out that Bangladesh is not included in this presentation owing to a slight historical step backwards — independence was only obtained in December 1971 — and the special circumstances that immediately followed independence. The massive exodus by part of the population of the former East Pakistan made a hole in the economic fabric, which the government had to patch up.

In dividing up the countries in our sample into these three types of mixed economy, we gave priority to the dominant trend during the period immediately prior to the turning-point in the rebalancing process. This may give the impression that the geographic location of the various countries is a determining factor. Although the influence of regional tradition on the classification with one particular model or another should not be neglected, the main explanation for the result obtained is the composition of our sample. Had Algeria, Guinea or Mozambique been selected, it would have been clearly shown that not all the Maghreb and sub-Saharan African countries can be classified with the mixed economy model where the state seeks to promote the private sector. Likewise, the extension of the sample to a greater number of African or Central American countries would have demonstrated that the use of the public sector to favour certain ethnic or other minorities is not the exclusive prerogative of the Asian countries.

### The state-dominated mixed economy

### A. Basic principles

The pre-eminence of the state is a major characteristic of Mexico, Bolivia, Jamaica and Chile (prior to 1973). The principles of this type of mixed economy were defined as long ago as 1917 in the case of Mexico, during the 1930s — under the effect of the Great Depression — in the case of Bolivia and Chile, and more recently in the case of Jamaica, which did not become independent until 1962.

In the case of Mexico, the state's economic role is defined in the Constitution of the Republic of 1917 (Michalet, 1989). Article 25 poses the central principle of the supreme responsibility of the state — la Rectoria — for "national development, to guarantee that it is total, that it strengthens the sovereignty of the Nation and its democratic regime". For this purpose, the Constitution stipulates in the same article: "The state shall complete the regulation and development of the activities that the national interest requires." It is clear that the principles laid down in the fundamental law of the Republic of the United States of Mexico do not reflect an exaggerated confidence in the benefits of the market economy and liberalism. This stance was to result in extremely strong constraints for the rebalancing policy adopted with effect from 1983. President de la Madrid's government was therefore obliged to introduce constitutional amendments aimed at a more restrictive definition of the fields of state intervention. The three sectors that make up the Mexican mixed economy are defined by Articles 26, 27 and 28: the private sector, the public sector and the social sector. The latter consists of trades unions, co-operatives in the area of production and distribution, and ejidos, traditional rural Indian communities comprising a village and common land with an elected municipality chaired by a cacique.

In Bolivia and Chile, the dominant role of the state and the public sector in the economy came to the fore later than in Mexico. According to A. Argueidas (1986), Bolivia is still attached to a notion of the role of the state that is marked by the Spanish tradition. State aid, state initiative and the all-powerful nature of the public sector are considered part of the natural order of things. Everything is expected of the state, according to an approach strongly tinged with paternalism. This attitude of dependence on the public authorities has been strengthened by the spread of socialist ideas, particularly since the Chaco war with Paraguay. The bases of "revolutionary nationalism" were laid down by the various military governments that succeeded one another with the support of the Socialist party, the Republican Socialist Party, the newly formed trades unions and the army veterans, the working classes and the middle classes. The proclaimed objective, "national reconstruction and a gradual transformation of the state towards a socialist stance", was directed mainly against the oligarchy of large landowners, the owners of the mines and traders specialising in export-import (Moore & Casanovas, in Anglade & Fortin, 1985).

This trend culminated with the National Revolution in 1952 and the arrival in power of V. Paz Estenssoro. Apart from the aim of obtaining further financial aid from the United States, the objectives of the new coalition government of the MRN (National Revolutionary Movement) and the COB (Central Obrera Boliviana) were to meet the expectations of its popular base by nationalising the tin mines, carrying out agrarian reform and applying the Bohan Plan. As early as 1942, an American economist, Mervin Bohan, had drawn up a first development model for the country, based on the following three points: diversification of the economy through the growth of oil production; import substitution in the agricultural sector, which implied extensive production on haciendas; and monetary stabilization. This was to be realised under the Siles Zuazo government between 1957 and 1960, under the direction of G. Eder, an American economist. This liberalisation programme was accompanied by a weakening of the COB and an increase in American aid. President Barrientos' "Restoration of the Revolution" Programme (1964-69) borrowed from the doctrine of the National Revolution only in rhetoric, in that it corresponded to a change in alliance in favour of the middle class *criollos*, a liberal economic stance marked by denationalisation of the Matilde copper mine and by an effort to attract private investment from abroad. The period 1969-71 was characterised by a return to populism with General Ovando followed by General Torres.

The election of General Banzer (1971-78) and the proclamation of the "New Order" entailed a change in stance in favour of foreign investments and priority export of oil and agricultural products. However, the speeches remained pro-state. Public investments accounted for 40 per cent of total investment but were mainly directed towards the extension of the road network, the development of imposing sports complexes and building. Financing was largely dependent on foreign sources: American aid, oil exports and borrowing from international commercial banks. It was unable to cope with the crisis at the end of the 1970s.

At the beginning of the century, in the "nitrate era", Chile was an adept of the international division of labour and free trade. According to Marshall (in Glade, 1986), the movement in favour of protectionism and state intervention started at the time of World War I. The conflict made nitrate exports more difficult, as the production of synthetic substitutes was being developed in Europe. The calling into question of the free-trade policy was strengthened further by the effects of the Depression in the 1930s. Indeed, state intervention helped to reduce the impact of the crisis on the Chilean economy: protectionist measures were adopted; the

35

currency was devalued; a special programme to stimulate construction was introduced; employment incentive measures helped, among other things, provide new jobs for former employees from the nitrate sector. With the creation of CORFO (Corporacion de Fomento de la Produccion) in 1939, a decisive new step was taken in the conception of the role of the state. Originally established to co-ordinate the economic reconstruction of the country following a major earthquake that occurred in the same year, CORFO was to extend the field of its activities and become the main tool of industrialisation. Henceforth the state would no longer limit its interventions to measures of general economic policy but would become a full-time player in the country's economic activity. Up to the end of the 1940s, state intervention had mainly taken the form of regulation of economic activity; subsequently, it took on forms hitherto unseen in the country, with the creation of a whole range of public enterprises in the following sectors: energy, oil production and refining, steel production, sugar-beet production, mining and industry. Foreign trade was placed under the control of a public institution. Between 1940 and 1960, half the total investment was financed directly or indirectly by public savings. With this new stance, Chile joined the group of countries according the state a dominant role in economic development.

As the oligarchy in power, which as in Bolivia was made up of large landowners linked to the banking, mining and commercial sectors, showed little interest in the development of industry, it was up to the state to promote, finance and create enterprises in this sector. On the basis of an arrangement between the land-owning oligarchy and the modernist, industrialist and urban faction mainly consisting of civil servants, executives, members of the professional classes and a narrow band of entrepreneurs, a division of labour was instituted. The public sector was granted responsibility for industrialisation through import substitution, provided that the existing regime in agriculture and livestock production was maintained and that the presence of foreign companies in the mines was not called into question (Fortin, in Anglade & Fortin, 1985). This arrangement was partially broken by the reformist President E. Frei (1964-70), who supported a major reform of land ownership and distribution and encouraged the progress towards trades unionism — the first farmers union was thus created in 1967. The accession to power in 1970 of S. Allende and the Popular Unity Party was to provoke open conflict, which was to lead to a dramatic outcome.

The Allende programme was essentially based on setting up a state-owned industrial sector comprising the nationalisation of 67 industrial enterprises, as well as the nationalisation of the copper mines and the banks. It also pledged to continue the reform of land ownership and to form a "social ownership sector" based on expropriation, the purchase of shares and a legal procedure dating from 1932, known as "intervention". The last enabled the state to take control of the management of any company deemed essential to the economy that was prevented from operating normally for various reasons, in particular by prolonged strikes. This procedure was mainly responsible for the Chilean economy's going off course in 1972 and, especially, during the first half of 1973. Indeed, the programme for nationalising the 67 industrial enterprises, which were to become the heart of the state sector, was only partially realised by the Allende government, notably owing to opposition from Congress. On the other hand, the state did "intervene" in a large number of small enterprises, under pressure from their employees and "strikes" by bosses. Between 1970 and 1973 the number of enterprises in the industrial sector controlled by the state rose from 45 to 600; more than half these operations took place in 1973.

During the first ten years of its independence (1962), Jamaica developed a public sector based on a social-democratic or "welfarist" ideology justified by the very low level of development of industry and the infrastructure, by the weakness of the local entrepreneurial class, by the tradition of a powerful local administration inherited from the colonial era and by an extremely high level of unemployment (nearly one-quarter of the active population on average). During this period, the government sought to strengthen the private sector by means of incentives, according to a mixed economy concept fairly similar to that of Morocco and Tunisia, which will be dealt with below. This trend was to be abandoned with the victory of the trades unionist Michael Manley and the National People's Party in 1972. The prime objective of the new team was to improve the living standards of the most underprivileged Jamaicans by raising the level of employment and wages and by ambitious health and education programmes. At the outset, the inspiration continued to be "welfarist" (Kennedy, in Glade, 1986). The only direct state intervention was the creation of Jamaica Nutrition Holding, a public enterprise in charge of importing essential foodstuffs. Things started to go off course beginning in 1974, when Manley, pushed by nationalistic public opinion, decided to launch an attack on the foreign companies in control of bauxite production. From then on, the government threw itself into a systematic policy of nationalisations and purchases of private enterprises in difficulties. The latter aspect of the expansion of the public sector bears a certain resemblance to the Mexican or Chilean experiences. It was to result in withdrawal by the foreign companies, the drying up of local private investment, a massive flight of capital and a surge in public expenditure, which was to culminate in a serious financial crisis and, finally, appeal to the IMF in 1978.

## B. State intervention

In all the countries in the sample, the state's capacity for intervention was to be grounded on planning, an increase in the number of public enterprises, the creation of public financing institutions, restrictions on foreign trade, wage and price regulations, restrictive codes of investment for foreign investments and so on. The system established in Mexico is the oldest and the most highly structured. It has had a definite influence on the other Latin American countries and therefore deserves special attention.

The context of intervention by the Mexican government is defined in the Constitution by means of a distinction between strategic sectors and priority sectors. The public sector is exclusively in charge of the former. In the strategic sectors, "the federal government shall always guarantee the ownership and control of bodies that are established therein". Among the strategic activities, Article 28 of the Constitution includes oil extraction and refining, basic petrochemicals, radioactive minerals, the production of nuclear and electric power and the railways. It should be pointed out that not all these sectors figured in the initial wording of the 1917 Constitution. Succeeding governments since that time have thus added to it, which is evidence of their attachment to this notion. Apart from the sectors where the state occupies an exclusive position, the Constitution also defines "priority development areas". The state may act alone or in co-operation with the private or social sectors. In the latter case, it will act as the driving or organisational force. In that the strategic sectors are defined expressly, the extent to which the priority development sectors are enlarged is crucial for the residual size of the private sector.

That is why, with a view to preparing the rebalancing process, President de la Madrid's government devoted a great deal of effort to defining the priority sectors. The objective of the PRONAFICE (Programa Nacional de Fomento Industrial y Comercio Exterior), presented in July 1984 in the context of the programmes decreed by the Planning Law, was to define the role of the various economic agents precisely "in order to clarify the areas of specialisation of each economic agent with a view to completing a model for co-operation and complementarity rather than competition one with the other". PRONAFICE's document contains a table specifying the relative positions of the various parties concerned — public enterprises, private enterprises, foreign firms, social sector enterprises — in the different branches of the Mexican economy. At the intersection of the columns listing the agents and the lines corresponding to the branches, it is specified whether the activity in question should be left to the exclusive initiative of public enterprises or based on public enterprises complemented by other enterprises. This document also lays down the conditions for priority state holding: high investment expenditure, long depreciation periods, use of new technologies. Included in this list are the iron and steel industry, fertilizers, tractors, transport equipment, diesel engines and non-ferrous metals. As regards the branches not included in the two preceding categories, a distinction is made between complementary activities and "non-recommendable" activities. In the first case, the private sector and the social sector have the initiative in a market logic. Only if the interests of the general public are not satisfied does the state reserve the right to intervene. To this end, it may use indirect methods such as regulation, financing or protection against foreign competition. If this type of intervention proves inadequate, the state may then envisage joint investments alongside the social sector or the private sector; in the latter case, it may decide to create a semi-public enterprise with a state majority. In the second group of activities, where the state's involvement is not recommended, the goods and services are not considered to be priorities or are supplied satisfactorily by the two other sectors of the economy. This part of the economy, where the state's role is excluded, includes 20 or so industrial branches.

The major role of the public enterprises is constantly referred to in the official documents. Following the logic of Article 26 of the Constitution, the Planning Law (1983-88), promulgated in January 1983, states that public enterprises are obliged to meet the objectives laid down for them in the Plan, which stresses their dominant position in "achieving national objectives, the reinforcement of the state's leading role [rectoria] in economic life and direct support for economic and social policy ...".

The public sector really took off during the 1930s. Before that period, priority had been given to the organisation of the financial sector, in particular the foundation of the Bank of Mexico, the Bank of Agricultural Credit and the Bank of Ejidal Credit, and to the development of the communications system with the creation of the National Railways Commission. The main feature of the 1930s was a more marked involvement in the country's industrialisation. The state set up specialist financial institutions such as Nacional Financiera, which was to play a leading role in industry. During this period the company PEMEX (Petroleos Mexicanos) was also created following the nationalisation of foreign oil companies in 1938 by President Cardenas. The Federal Electricity Commission (CFE) obtained a monopoly in the production and distribution of electric power. The railway companies were nationalised. Public institutions were set up to manage the country's foreign trade: Compania Exportadora e Importadora, Compania Productora e Importadora de Papel and so on. In brief, many state monopolies were gradually set up.

The next two decades followed the same trend: developing the industrial and agricultural sectors with the state as the driving force. Public control of the production of intermediate goods continued with the launch of public enterprises in fertilizers (Fertilizantes Mexicanos), the iron and steel industry (Altos Hornos de Mexico) and capital goods (Diesel Nacional, Constructora Nacional de Carros de Ferrocarril). During the 1960s, the public sector continued its expansion with the nationalisation of the electricity industry, the construction of the iron and steel complex Lazaro Cardenas-Las Truchas and the integration of most of the sugar enterprises. During the same decade, a public organisation for the distribution of basic consumer goods to the most underprivileged groups, CONASUPO (Compania Nacional de Subsistencias Populares), was set up. Lastly, the 1970s saw the state promoting high-technology industries with the creation of the Mexican Oil Institute, the Iron and Steel Research Institute and the Nuclear Research Institute. The state increased its presence in the capital goods sector by additional joint ventures with foreign enterprises (NKS, Clemex), as well as in secondary petrochemicals (Ahesivos, Poliesterino y Derivados). The nationalisation of the banks in August 1982, at the end of President Lopez Portillo's term of office, was the last episode in a systematic policy of expansion of the public sector, a policy that had been followed continuously for more than 70 years.

In the case of Bolivia, expansion of the public sector began with the nationalisation of Standard Oil and the creation of the State Mining Bank, at the end of the 1930s, followed by the creation at the beginning of the 1940s of the Bolivian Development Company for the promotion of industrial firms and of the Agricultural Bank. In 1952, under the impulsion of the Nationalist Revolutionary Movement, the tin mines were nationalised and COMIBOL was created; in addition, reforms of land ownership aimed at ending the "latifundist era" were launched. In 1969, another major operation was achieved with the nationalisation of another American oil company belonging to Gulf Oil, whose installations were transferred to YPFB. With this company and COMIBOL, the Bolivian government controlled the two most important enterprises in the country, not only from the point of view of turnover but also from that of foreign currency earnings. The adherence to the idea of a planned economy took the form of a series of Development Plans, following the first attempt in 1942 under the direction of M. Bohan. The Revolutionary Nationalist Movement government launched a Development Plan for 1962-71 in an attempt at integration into the grand design of President Kennedy's "Alliance for Progress". It was to be abandoned under Barrientos. Later, with the return of the populist military, a Minister for the Plan was created by General Ovando, while his successor, General Torres, proclaimed an Economic and Social Strategy for National Development (1971-91) aimed at "eliminating the structure of dependence and increasing popular involvement". In the mid-1970s, the Banzer government defined a National Plan for Economic and Social Development (1976-80), which, in addition to denouncing market mechanisms as a means of efficient allocation of resources, drew up a list of so-called strategic sectors (metallurgy and the heavy steel industry, basic petrochemicals, energy, transport) that fell under the exclusive responsibility of the state.

During the ten years following independence, the Jamaican government increased the number of its public financial institutions with a view to administering priority development programmes in the industrial sector (Jamaica Industrial Bank, Industrial Finance Corporation), managing distribution in agriculture (Agricultural Market Corporation) and extending the rail network (Jamaican Government Railway). At the end of the 1960s, a "Jamaicanisation" policy was applied to the foreign enterprises that managed certain public services (electricity, telephone, urban transport). Moreover, the government dominated by the Jamaican Labor Party developed programmes in favour of social housing, education and health. At the same time a set of laws aimed at promoting private investment in industry, tourism and export was adopted. They sought to encourage local private entrepreneurs to withdraw from commercial activities in order to develop productive activities. A further objective was to attract new foreign investment into industry. Promotion of the private sector was the order of the day.

The Manley government's radical stance took a dramatic turn in 1974 with the decision to attack the six North American bauxite-producing companies. In addition to a significant increase (600 per cent) in the tax on bauxite production, the government proclaimed its intention to acquire title to the mining companies' land and subsoil together with 51 per cent of their equity. The companies reacted by reducing production and investments. In view of the importance of bauxite in Jamaican exports, the trade deficit worsened considerably. Simultaneously, the government negotiated the transfer of the national bus company, the electricity production company and the telephone company to the public sector. It also took control of a cement works and a dairy that were accused of taking improper advantage of a monopoly situation. In the financial sector, three banks (one of them foreign) were nationalised in order to strengthen support to small enterprises and stimulate productive activities, especially in agriculture. In this sector, the government sought to create or safeguard jobs, on the one hand by purchasing land owned by foreign companies that were transformed into production co-operatives and, on the other, by coming to the aid of the sugar refineries. In the area of sea transport and international trade, a public company, the Jamaican Merchant Marine, was set up to reduce freight costs for bauxite and grain, and the State Trading Company was established to control foreign trade, starting with essential consumer goods. The results of private sector enterprises were eroded by the combined effect of wage rises, inflation, price controls and an overvalued exchange rate. In consequence, at the end of the 1970s, the continued expansion of the public sector was based mainly on rescuing private enterprises. Apart from taking over sugar refineries, a textile factory, a catering enterprise, a car-hire firm and a daily newspaper, the most important operation concerned the admission into the public sector of 14 hotels representing more than half of all the rooms in the hotel sector.

## C. The dynamics of the system

After this overview of national experiences of the formation of the public sector, the question that remains is as follows: to what extent will the dynamics of the state-dominated mixed economy determine the extent and modalities of the rebalancing process? Of the four countries in the sample that correspond with this model, only Chile offers a definitive response with the sudden halt in the growth of the public sector following the fall of Allende in September 1973. In the other cases, trends were still uncertain in the early 1980s and varied considerably from one country to another. In the case of Mexico, it seems that it would be difficult to reverse the rebalancing process, since it has been set up under the leadership of the state. In Bolivia, there was still strong resistance up to the mid-1980s. In Jamaica, the change of direction is viewed as the result of the deterioration in the country's economic situation.

In the case of Mexico, it is clearly stated in the PRONAFICE and in the other documents of the same era — such as the 1985 Report on the Execution of the Plan — that the list of priority or complementary sectors can change over time in one direction or another. The Report on the Execution of the Plan indicates that the fields of state intervention should not be fixed but, to the contrary, should be reassessed from time to time "so as to adapt the public presence dynamically to transformations in the economic structure". In fact, at the eve of the introduction of a large-scale policy aimed at rebalancing the public and private sectors, the whole scheme was progressing as if the new president had taken care to design the project in such a way that it accorded with the Mexican tradition of dividing responsibility between the state and the private sector. The state's *rectoria* does not seem to be called into question — to the contrary, it is strongly reaffirmed — in the perpetuation of economic policies followed since the Revolution. The state and the public sector are expected to strengthen economic activity and development facilities, particularly by the creation of an efficient credit and financing system; the exploitation of strategic resources, guarantors of national sovereignty; acting as a substitute for private initiative when this is absent or inadequate (especially in the sectors where the initial investments are high and can be depreciated only over a long period); acting as a life-belt for private enterprises in difficulty in order to safeguard employment and output levels; provision of the basic requirements of the most underprivileged social groups. These principles have inspired the establishment of the public sector since the 1930s. The lead given by President de la Madrid and his team since his arrival in power in 1982 implies a reduction of the public sector and restructuring of public enterprises. At the threshold of this experiment, the question that remains is whether this new policy will lead irresistibly to the abandonment of the principle of the pre-eminence of the state, or whether, in the end, it will rather correspond to a renovation of the Mexican tradition.

Until the middle of the 1980s, Bolivia remained particularly attached to its grand anti-liberal principles in the economic field. The National Plan for Rehabilitation and Development (1984-87) affirmed that the fundamental reason for the country's failure to satisfy its most basic needs was the organisation of the economy "according to extranational needs and interests". The main objective of the Plan is still "national control of the surplus achieved". The justification for the extension of the public sector and the reservations regarding a market economy are based on classic arguments: the lack of private initiative and market mechanisms, the size of the investments needed to develop the basic sectors, a more equitable redistribution of the national income. The influence of the doctrine of the National Revolution is still strong and may lead to the failure of the policy of structural redistribution of the roles and responsibilities of public and private agents in the economy.

In the case of Jamaica, the disastrous deterioration of the economy compelled the abandonment of the expansion of the public sector led by the Manley government. Public expenditure rose considerably, from 23 per cent of the gross domestic product (GDP) in 1970 to 35 per cent in 1975. The public deficit swelled enormously, reaching 24 per cent of GDP in 1976 as against 5 per cent in 1972. Domestic and foreign debt increased sharply. In 1976, the total exhaustion of foreign currency reserves compelled the government to apply to the IMF despite fierce opposition from part of the population. A stand-by credit arrangement was signed in 1977 for a two-year period, but it was suspended a few months later. A new agreement concluded in May 1978 was in its turn suspended at the end of 1979 following the government's inability to comply with its undertakings. The 1980 elections, commonly called the "IMF elections", were won by Edward Seaga, whose economic programme closely resembled the recommendations of the IMF and the World Bank. In 1981, the first signs of rebalancing appeared on the horizon with the creation of an Informal Committee for Divestiture. It was not until 1983, however, that a permanent structure was set up within the National Investment Bank of Jamaica, with the assistance of USAID.

### The state-promoted mixed economy

Three of the countries in the sample can be grouped under the rubric of the state-promoted mixed economy: Ghana, Morocco and Tunisia. Although they affirm the leading role of the state in the management of the economy with less force than do the Latin American states, they nonetheless accord it a central position in the institution of an economy in which the public and private sectors exist side by side. The major difference lies in the ongoing concern to act in concert with private enterprises, whether national or foreign, with a view to encouraging their development as a complement to the public enterprises.

### A. Basic principles

Fluctuation in the boundaries separating the public and private sectors, linked to alterations in government policy, is a denominator common to all three countries. In the case of Morocco, these variations depend on the state's financial resources, which themselves depend on the international price of the main export, phosphates. The leaders in Ghana and to a lesser extent in Tunisia are torn between the will to promote a dynamic private sector and a certain attraction to a socialist-inspired stance. At the beginning of the 1980s, however, in all three countries the scales were clearly weighted in favour of expanding the private sector.

A substantial segment of the current public sector in Morocco is an inheritance from the colonial era. The "phosphates boom" during the first half of the 1970s resulted in a surge in the public sector with an increase in the number of public enterprises. Under the Protectorate, France had set up two bodies to supervise the export of minerals: the Office Chérifien des Phosphates (OCP), created in 1920, and the Bureau de Recherches et de Participation Minières (BRPM), in 1928. At independence in March 1956, the local private sector was still embryonic in the industrial and services sectors. It was confined to agriculture — characterised by a very large number of small traditional farms — and trading. Foreign companies, mainly French, controlled the main part of the private industrial sector. The bank of issue was managed by the Banque de Paris et des Pays-Bas.

The First Plan, drawn up for the first five-year period following independence, was based on familiar principles: industrialisation by import substitution, self-sufficiency in food, protection of the local market. Owing to the virtual absence of private national economic actors in industry and the lack of a financial network capable of tapping local savings that had been hoarded or invested in marketable securities, the state itself was obliged to act as investor through the intermediary of public enterprises and in the context of a central plan. However, public action was viewed as a means of filling up a vacuum caused by history. The state was not setting itself up in place of private agents on a permanent basis, but rather establishing an economic, financial and institutional environment that promoted the development of local private initiative. This first stance was changed by the appreciable increase in public revenue due to the rise in the price of phosphates on the international market. The "phosphate bonanza" encouraged the state to stop increasing its direct intervention in the economy.

If A. Ben Salah, the Tunisian Minister for Planning, had remained in power after 1969, this country would undoubtedly have had to be classed as a state-dominated mixed economy. In fact, with the Ten-Year Proposals presented in 1962, the Tunisian economy was deliberately being moved towards socialism, in contrast with the liberal stance adopted shortly after independence. On the basis of centralised planning, with the support of a strong party, the Neo-Destour party — which in 1964 became the Destourian Socialist Party — whose driving force was a network of co-operatives and the increasing number of public enterprises, the Tunisian economy undertook a process of accelerated accumulation (Perkins, 1986; Guen, 1988). The final objective was to attain national economic independence based on an industrialisation process founded on a vast public sector. The creation of public enterprises and co-operatives was supposed to enable domestic exploitation and processing of mineral wealth and the production of manufactured goods as import substitutes. Priority was given to developing the interior of the country in order to break the predominance of the coastal region inherited from the days of the Protectorate. But the Tunisian farmers' refusal to abandon their individual properties and integrate into co-operatives, created by nationalising the ex-colonials' properties and neighbouring land, brought about the downfall of the Minister for the Plan in 1969.

With the arrival on the scene of H. Nouira, the former president of the Tunisian Central Bank, appointed as prime minister by President Bourguiba, a totally different stance was to be followed during the 1970s. In the new perspective, a mixed economy logic was to work for the development of a private sector focused on export in association with foreign investors. Tunisia proclaimed its ambition to become the "Singapore of the Mediterranean". With this aim in mind, a whole set of incentive measures was adopted to lighten administrative procedures and tax levies in favour of private enterprises in the export sector. Accordingly, in 1973 and 1976, more than 500 foreign firms set up in business in Tunisia, often in joint ventures with local enterprises. There was a particularly rapid boom in the textile sector. The public sector was limited to the basic industries: iron and steel industry, vehicle assembly plants and so forth. Local small and medium-sized enterprises developing labour-intensive production lines were offered substantial aid. The results were positive on the whole, owing to a favourable macroeconomic climate, characterised by a surge in oil revenues after 1973. This experience unfortunately ended in bloodshed with the repression of the general strike in 1978, triggered by the only union's protesting against the increasing social inequalities and rising unemployment. While it is true that the industrial boom had allowed a group of private entrepreneurs to get rich quickly, owing to the constraints of international competitiveness, it had also required the maintenance of low wages. Furthermore, the job creations had above all benefited female labour and had only slightly reduced the total unemployment rate, while numerous young people were arriving on the job market. These tensions were exacerbated from the economic point of view by the reduction in the number of Tunisian workers emigrating to Libya, following the break in relations with this country. After this crisis, the early 1980s were dominated by weakening at both the economic and the political levels. Support for the development of the private sector was maintained, in co-operation with foreign investors, including a preponderant number from the Arab-Persian Gulf region.

The case of Ghana illustrates fairly well a policy of unstable balance between the public and private sectors. Fluctuations in attitudes towards the private sector were closely linked to the political cycle, which accelerated after Dr. Nkrumah's presidential term (1960-66). The principles of a mixed economy system were laid down immediately following independence. It was up to the state to be the driving force, supported by a public sector "occupying the commanding heights of the economy". The first five-year plan, launched in 1959, was clearly in the Labour Party tradition, since it envisaged laying down "solid foundations to construct a welfare state". The tone was less soothing in 1963, when the seven-year plan was launched and when, according to T. Killick (1978), Dr. Nkrumah broke the colonial mould and drifted towards a socially inspired strategy by rejecting an open market economy in favour of a planned and centralised economy. This trend was rapidly called into question by the decisions taken in 1965, which pledged a policy in favour of foreign investment. Accordingly, it seems preferable to side with Dr. Asante's interpretation of the situation. His assessment of the policy followed under the First Republic accords pragmatism a decisive position over ideology: "State intervention is above all the expression of national pride" (Asante, in AAPAM, 1987).

What was sought in the end was the combined development of the public *and* the private sectors. It is true that the policy of expanding the public sector could be interpreted both as a policy combining nationalism and socialism and as the continuation of the policies pursued by the British, when the Gold Coast was part of the Empire. Indeed, the Ghana Cocoa Marketing Board was created in 1947, and the Industrial Development Corporation, which was to take charge of industrial development in the country, in 1951. Consequently, once again the roots of state interventionism derive from the dominant ideas of the immediate post-war years.

Between 1966 and 1972, Ghana experienced two political regimes, a military one led by the National Liberation Council, and a civilian one, led by Dr. Busia's Civilian Progress party. A feature they had in common was to give priority to stability over growth, by opening up the economy and encouraging return to a market economy. The most important changes compared to the previous period were a more favourable attitude towards foreign investment, the promotion of small and medium-sized enterprises and an original experiment in privatisation. Dr. Busia's government pursued a policy of developing the private sector. On the one hand it declared itself in favour of foreign investments and the formation of joint ventures between state-owned enterprises and private enterprises; on the other, it undertook not to create any new public enterprises that might compete with private sector firms. Lastly, it took measures to implement a decree, passed in 1968 by the previous military government, aimed at increasing the involvement of Ghanaians in the modern sector of the economy. Similarly, the Ghanaian Business Promotion Act of 1970 reserved certain sectors to Ghanaian nationals. This legislation fell within the logic of the Aliens Compliance Order of 1969, which had led to the expulsion of a significant number of foreigners from Ghana. The case of Malaysia, which will be examined later, is another variant of policies with an ethnic basis.

The policy of the military government in power from 1972 to 1979 followed the Ghanaian tradition of swinging the pendulum of priority between the private sector and the public. As a reaction to the previous regime, the principle of the state as the major agent in charge of the management of the economy was reaffirmed. The state's role as entrepreneur was strengthened by the transfer to public control of 55 per cent of the equity of foreign enterprises established in Ghana. It was also pointed out that "the state reserves the right to intervene directly in production in order to stimulate rapid economic development". At the same time, however, the military government declared its intention to stimulate "healthy competition between public and private enterprises" (Akuoko-Frimpong, 1989, p. 23). The five-year plan, in effect, recommended speeding up growth in the private sector's contribution to production and employment.

H. Limann's civil government (1979-81) seems in retrospect to have marked a transition between the preceding military governments, which had taken their inspiration from the Nkrumian theory of the dominant role of the public sector in the economy, and the subsequent government, which was to undertake a major policy of liberalisation and rebalancing in favour of the private sector. Dr. Limann's main decision was the promulgation in 1981 of a liberal investment code that opened the economy to foreign investment and offered private investors the guarantees and incentives they had hoped for. The action in favour of the private sector, both local and foreign, in the context of the Economic Reactivation Programme, launched as soon as the Provincial National Defense Council arrived in power at the beginning of 1982, appeared much more decisive, however, and was perhaps a real turning-point in the Ghanaian policy of oscillation between the public and private sectors.

## B. State intervention

The instruments of state intervention are aimed at creating a favourable climate for the development of private agents' activities. Depending on the means at its disposal, however, the state is tempted to increase the role played by public organisations and drift towards a different type of mixed economy.

In implementing the guidelines of Morocco's intervention policy referred to above, the government started, from the end of the 1950s, a programme of creating financial institutions: Banque du Maroc, Office des Changes, Banque Marocaine du Commerce Extérieur, Caisse de Dépôts et de Gestion, Banque Nationale de Développement et de Gestion, Banque Nationale de Développement Économique. Then, somewhat late in the day, it founded the Société Nationale d'Investissement (1966), followed the next year by Crédit Immobilier et Hôtelier and the Bourse de Casablanca. For industrial development, in 1957 the state set up the Bureau d'Etudes et de Participation Industrielle (BEPI). From 1959, the BEPI took a 50 per cent holding in the creation of the Société Marocaine de Raffinage (SOMAR) and a 40 per cent holding in the Société Marocaine de Construction Automobile (SOMACA). In both cases, the other members of the company were foreign. In the name of national sovereignty over the resources of the soil and the subsoil, the Office Chérifien des Phosphates was nationalised. It was to constitute an important source of foreign currency for the Moroccan Treasury.

The 1973 "Moroccanisation" law must not be interpreted as a manifestation of excessive nationalism. Rather, it follows the traditional logic of state promotion of the local private sector. More than 15 years after independence, the distribution and services sectors, especially the financial services sector, were still controlled by foreign firms. In order to increase the involvement of private national agents, the law compelled foreign companies to transfer at least 50 per cent of their equity capital to Moroccans. This transfer of ownership was to take place by two different methods: direct sale of at least half the capital to nationals, or an increase of capital equal to at least 50 per cent of the equity capital and reserved to shareholders of Moroccan nationality.  A first list of 325 enterprises to be "Moroccanised" was drawn up.  It concerned enterprises in the services sector (including banks, but excluding tourism) and in the industrial sector (fish canning, fertilizer manufacture, tanning, assembly of heavy goods vehicles and private cars).  By the middle of 1975, 277 enterprises had been "Moroccanised", and 36 others had been put into liquidation or fully taken over by locals.  These results were judged satisfactory by the government, which decided to interrupt this policy at the end of the same year.  Although the "Moroccanisation" law had undoubtedly increased the involvement of private Moroccan agents in the economy, it had resulted in the long-term deterioration of the business environment and discouraged the arrival of new foreign firms.  In addition, it encouraged an increase in the number of small-sized family companies which were relatively uncompetitive.

The boom stemming from the rise in the price of phosphates during the first half of the 1970s was to stimulate direct state intervention in the economy.  The Third Plan (1973-77) was characterised by a very ambitious public investment programme providing for a fourfold increase in investments over three years.  The phosphate bonanza was supposed to provide the financing for this change in industrial strategy, which was aimed less at import substitution than at encouraging export activities, especially in the processing industries (phosphate derivatives, iron and steel, agribusiness, textiles).  International subcontracting activities were also encouraged.  In parallel, the state undertook to support this new policy through the creation of special focuses for development aimed at decentralisation of industrial activity and through investment in the infrastructure:  bridges, irrigation, and so on.

The number of public enterprises, always viewed as the driving force of the implementation of the Plan's objectives, increased sharply, especially under the impetus of a strong movement towards creating subsidiaries.  However, the state continued to develop the private sector. With this aim in view, in 1973, the BEPI became the ODI (Office de Développement Industriel).  The new body continued with the task assigned to its predecessor, the acquisition of holdings in industrial enterprises from the viewpoint of venture capital.  In principle, the ODI was not meant to keep the assets in its portfolio on a long-term basis, but was to assign them to private interests once the enterprises had matured.  In addition, it had three tasks: promotion, assistance and introduction of investors, including foreigners.  As a financial partner in new companies, the ODI was to become both a promoter and an associate of potential investors.  It has played an important role in the development of new industrial networks in the areas of textiles and the mechanical and electrical industries.

In Tunisia, the bases of the public sector were laid down during the "Tunisification" period between 1958 and 1962.  At the time of independence, in 1956, the Tunisian economy was essentially rural, characterised by vast colonial properties oriented towards the export market existing side by side with small, archaic subsistence farms.  Faced with the virtual non-existence of a local entrepreneurial class and the departure of most of the French settlers, the Tunisian state became an entrepreneur state. The instruments of its action consisted of planning, strict pricing regulations (principle of prior consent), a set of measures laying down strict protectionism and public enterprises in all sectors of economic activity. The accession to monetary sovereignty was marked by the creation of the Tunisian Central Bank and of the dinar, and withdrawal from the franc zone in 1958. The financial sector is dominated by three public sector banks, which control more than half of the assets: the Caisse Mutuelle de Crédit Agricole, the Société Tunisienne de Banque and the Banque Nationale de l'Agriculture. A reform in land ownership put an end to the confused status of *habou* assets and land in common ownership.

The creation of public enterprises was justified by the desire to achieve a whole set of objectives aimed at developing the country (Ben Rejeb, 1983): the exploitation of the mineral and energy resources, the control of the strategic sectors as well as the supply of public utilities (water, electricity and transport), job promotion, promotion of sectors where private initiative fears to tread, the creation of capital-intensive units, the promotion of exports and reduction of imports, the achievement of better regional equilibrium, implementing or controlling national economic and social policy, and the improvement of the provision of administrative services by replacing the bureaucracy with public agencies. With objectives both so ambitious and so assorted, it is not surprising that the number of public enterprises increased rapidly, amounting to more than 600 at the beginning of the 1980s. This increase in number was accompanied by a reinforcement of their role in the economy. By way of example, during the period 1971-81, the average growth rate of the public enterprise value-added amounted to 15.7 per cent (see Chapter 2, "The public enterprises in question").

The state was directly involved in promotion of the tourist sector with the Société Hotelière et Touristique de Tunisie. From 1969 on, the state also intervened to encourage private initiative by means of a series of laws granting important tax advantages to local and foreign private investors. The Agence de Promotion des Investissements was created in response to Prime Minister Nouira's desire to encourage the emergence of an industrial private sector parallel to the public sector.

During Dr. Nkrumah's presidency, a whole range of public enterprises was created in Ghana: the Volta River Authority, Ghana Airways Corporation, the State Fishing Corporation, the State Farm Corporation, the Ghana National Trading Corporation, the State Gold Mining Corporation, as well as a large number of enterprises in the industrial sector, grouped under the aegis of the Ghana Industrial Holding Corporation (GIHOC). Breaking with the line followed during the First Republic, the military government of the National Liberation Council tried an experiment with privatisation. A list of 20 public enterprises was drawn up, 13 of which were to be transformed into joint ventures and 7 sold to the private sector. This policy did not achieve the success that had been expected. Only four enterprises were purchased by private investors in sectors of only minor importance, such as laundry, furniture manufacture, baking and tyre repairs. In addition, this policy provoked strong emotions in the population and led the government to cancel its plan to privatise the State Pharmaceutical Factory, the only public enterprise on the list for privatisation which was of an appreciable size. This failure halted any further attempt at privatisation until the early 1980s. In the meantime, the new military team in power between 1972 and 1979, in the name of making the private sector more dynamic by means of state intervention, set up a series of new public bodies: Bank of Ghana, National Investment Bank, Agricultural Development Bank, Capital Investment Board, Office of Business Promotion, Ghanaian Business Bureau of Management Development and the Productivity Institute.

## C. The dynamics of the system

The dynamics of the state-promoted mixed economy is largely dominated by two factors. On the one hand, the increase of the state's financial resources is accompanied, as a general rule, by an increase in the number of public enterprises and growth in public investment. On the other hand, political cycles and changes in the teams in power lay stress on particular variations in the debate on the balance between the private and the public sector. Over many years, however, and particularly since the end of the 1970s, recognition of the driving role played by the private agents seems to have been established. The choice of a rebalancing policy would therefore be in the context of a fluctuating continuum and would no doubt lead to the stabilization of this type of mixed economy. However, it will be taking place in very disparate national environments.

Morocco's dynamic industrial policy, based on the growth in public revenues, continued until the "planned pause" from 1978 to 1980, although the fall in phosphates prices goes back to 1976. Nonetheless, the trend towards the expansion of industrial investments was maintained by means of increased participation by the public budget and greater resort to foreign debt. The planned pause aimed to stabilize the rise in public expenditure and reduce imports while endeavouring to increase exports. In addition, under pressure from King Hassan II, it was decided to carry out a systematic examination of state interventions and the functioning of the public enterprises. In 1979, under the leadership of A. Jouahri, a minister under the direct aegis of the prime minister, a study was undertaken to "rethink the role of public enterprises as the priority instrument of the government's economic and financial policy with a view to achieving development objectives" (cited by Khouzam, 1988). The report was never published, but its main conclusions are known. They recognise the need to revitalise public enterprises by reducing the central government's control over their operations. The Jouahri report did not propose transfer of ownership to the private sector, but it did recommend privatisation of the management of a limited number of firms. Along the lines of the Nora report published in France in the mid-1960s, the following basic principle was laid down: "public enterprises shall behave and be managed like private enterprises, in other words without privileges, without being a burden on the public and without administrative controls." Following the Jouahri report, a Committee of Vigilance was set up in 1983, consisting of the Ministries of Finance, Economic Affairs and Public Works, with the aim of reforming relationships between the state and the public enterprises, the first item on its agenda being the problem of arrears. In addition, it helped to pave the way for a future privatisation programme by making a financial examination of the public portfolio.

In parallel, the question of making the private sector more dynamic came back onto the agenda. This revision of the strategy that had been followed during the oil bonanza was to be hastened forward by the sudden crisis in 1983, which was linked to a whole series of disasters: an unprecedented drought for two consecutive years, a rise in the value of the dollar and in interest rates, which made debt service more expensive, plus increased expenses resulting from military operations in the Western Sahara. From this time onwards, Morocco, like other countries in the sample, began a stabilization and liberalisation policy that was to lead to a total rethinking of the balance between the private and public sectors in favour of the former. It was a definite shift in stance, but in no way was it an indictment of the traditional policy of the Moroccan state, which had always exerted itself to develop a mixed economy in which the private sector had an important place. The question was whether the emergency caused by the economic crisis would be dealt with by private agents capable of taking over the reins from the state.

The performance of the Tunisian economy during the liberal 1970s was remarkable. Between 1971 and 1976, during the Fourth Plan, the average annual growth rate was 8.5 per cent; then 5.8 per cent during the following Plan. The savings rate rose from 19 per cent in 1971 to 25 per cent in 1981, covering 85 per cent of investment borrowing requirements. Foreign debt fell from 41 per cent of the gross national product (GNP) in 1971 to 38 per cent in 1981. However, although the oil shock played a determining role in the break with liberal dynamics, the Tunisian economy was structurally weakened by its heavy dependence on foreign revenues. The main sources of foreign currency — oil, fruit and vegetables, textiles, tourism, transfers from emigrant workers — were fragile. In this connection, the deterioration in relations with Libya and the return of 30 000 emigrant workers was one cause of the serious events in 1978. Subsequently, the European Community's circumspect attitude towards imports of textile and agricultural products threatened the expansion of Tunisian exports. Lastly, the uncertainties of the political climate in the region had a significant effect on earnings from the tourist industry. This instability of the Tunisian model combined with a surge in the fundamentalist movement (Ravenel, 1987) may hold back the choice of a rebalancing policy that remains at the mercy of violent reactions from the population like those in 1978 and 1984.

Whilst affirming that the state should continue to play a pivotal role in the economy, the Provisional National Defense Council, which was installed in power in 1982 in Ghana, proclaimed the need to reform the management of public enterprises in the direction of efficiency and profitability and declared itself ready to encourage the development of the private sector. Although the new status accorded to the private sector must be defined as "complementary to the public sector", it seems that a new determination is dawning, because the deterioration in the economy had become untenable and because of the population's lassitude. In this case, it would mean that there was a permanent trend in Ghana toward an economy where the private sector is accorded a predominant position.

## Promotion of the public sector in favour of particular interests

The extension of the role of the state and the public enterprises is generally justified by the interest of the whole population and not by that of a particular social group, although for certain distrustful observers, the movement often leads to strengthening the power of the technocracy. Malaysia and the Philippines are two special cases, in that the growth of the public sector was carried out to the advantage of part of the population — openly in the first case, on the basis of an ethnic criterion, and covertly in the second, through the merger of the public and private sectors.

### A. Basic principles

The experience in Malaysia is unique in more than one respect. In the first place, contrary to the findings in the other countries in the sample, accession to independence in 1957 was not accompanied by the adoption of an economic system where the state played a central role. A liberal-inspired policy was followed over a 12-year period. Second, the reduction of the position of the private sector from 1969 onwards was the result of an initial rebalancing process that was interethnic in character. Nonetheless, the present situation has largely wiped out Malaysia's idiosyncrasy: the new rebalancing process, this time in favour of the private sector, obeys a logic closely comparable to that predominating in the other countries that had undertaken a similar process.

The period 1957-69 was marked by a policy of non-intervention by the state and by the continuation of the *laissez-faire* policy that had prevailed in the past. The public sector was then strictly limited to the activities already in the corpus of public economics. The 20 or so existing state-owned enterprises were limited to the production and distribution of electricity and water, road and rail transport, cultural activities and, above all, the financial sector. The private sector was largely in the hands of three communities other than native Malays: the English, Chinese and Indians. Firms of English origin had maintained their control of the export-oriented sectors: in agriculture (rubber, palm oil, cocoa), mines (tin) and services (trade,

52

marine transport, banking and insurance). The Chinese (35 per cent of the population) and the Indians (12 per cent) were involved in production and service activities aimed at the domestic market. The ethnic Malays, the Bumiputras, had been in political control since independence. The Constitution guaranteed them priority access to the public sector. In addition, they benefited from preferential treatment as regards admission to education, especially at the university, where quotas were established for students of Malaysian origin. Lastly, Islam had been declared the official religion of the new state. For their part, the Chinese and Indian minorities had received constitutional guarantees as regards freedom of enterprise, freedom of religion and the granting of Malaysian citizenship. This relatively peaceful coexistence was shattered by very violent events in May 1969, during elections preceded by an agitated electoral campaign during which racial themes had predominated. The government, controlled by the Bumiputras, decided to suspend the Constitution for 18 months; Parliament was dissolved and work started on preparing a new economic stance. The Bumiputras' finding that although they held power, this had not prevented the continued marked inequality between them and the rest of the population lay at the heart of a radical revision of the existing situation. In order to remedy this, henceforth political power was to be parallelled by economic power. A rebalancing process in favour of the public sector became the necessary condition of the division of the national income in favour of the Bumiputra community.

The New Economic Policy (NEP) was officially proposed in the Second Plan for the period 1971-75. It stated:

> The Government shall assume a larger and more positive role in the economy than in the past ... The Government shall participate more directly in the creation and operation of a large range of productive enterprises ... The need for such an effort on the part of the Government is based on the desire to develop new industrial activities in selected development areas and to create a Malaysian industrial and commercial community. Explicit efforts and consultations on the part of the Government will be required to enable a significant number of Malays and other indigenous populations to improve their experience and have greater access to industrial and commercial activities. The state's role in this project will include the construction of buildings for industrial and commercial use, direct investments in industrial and commercial enterprises which will be controlled and managed by Malays and other indigenous groups and a variety of other activities relating to financial and technical assistance. (cited by Leeds, 1989)

In addition, it stated that the aim of the NEP was to eradicate poverty without racial discrimination and to restructure the economy in order to eliminate the confusion of race with a given economic function and geographic location.

In Malaysia, the turning-point in favour of a *dirigiste* economy, with a strong public sector, was taken in order to correct the inequality in the division of the national income that had developed during the *laissez-faire* era. The Bumiputra community had not gained any benefits from the liberal economy. Accordingly, the extension of the public sector was viewed as the means of correcting the imbalance between the various communities living in the country. It was a question of setting up a new type of welfare state, founded on membership of a particular race.

In the Philippines, as in most of the other countries in the sample, the growth of the public sector and the increase in the number of state-owned enterprises were particularly rapid during the second half of the 1970s, in the period under martial law (1972-81).

The state's right to create public enterprises was written into the Constitution in the name of the national interest or defence. Successive governments during the post-war years, however, had interpreted this right restrictively. The period of "national reconstruction" between 1945 and 1950 was marked by the creation of 30 or so public enterprises that belonged to the traditional sectors of "entrepreneur state" intervention: finance, major public services (water, gas, electricity), railways, agriculture and exports. This restrictive concept of direct state intervention in economic activity was to be radically called into question with the arrival in power of President Marcos in 1966. Indeed, the new team in charge set themselves the following objectives: an increase in public expenditure in favour of the agricultural sector, a policy of cheap money for industry and strengthening measures in favour of import substitution. From 1967, the budget and foreign trade deficits widened. In 1970, the IMF was called in, a stand-by credit arrangement was signed and 15 more were to follow before the Marcos reign came to an end.

With the establishment of martial law in 1972, the mixed economy system peculiar to the Philippines was set in place. It was based on economico-political patronage, which affected both private and public sectors to such an extent that the traditional distinction lost all relevance. In defining the president's allies, S. Haggard (in Nelson, 1990) spoke of "crony capitalists". Via a network of contacts based on the "Marcos clan" and the creation of new institutions, the public finances were to be bled systematically. The public sector was to expand at high speed: between 1972 and 1984, the number of public enterprises rose from 70 to 245. The president assumed the right to transfer funds from the Central Bank into his personal accounts. His wife administered, on doubtful criteria, the international aid fund against poverty through the Ministry of Human Settlements. Transfers from state to industry served to maintain a powerful minority of rent-seekers.

## B. State intervention

The New Economic Policy decided by Malaysia comprised many quantitative objectives to be achieved by the end of a twenty-year period: the proportion of the population that had grown poorer during the previous period was to fall from 49 to 17 per cent; the percentage of equity of enterprises held by the Bumiputras was to rise to 30 per cent in 1990 as against 2.4 per cent in 1970 (this implied a reduction of the share of foreign investors from 63.3 to 30 per cent); university admission quotas in favour of the Bumiputras were to be increased.

The main result of the NEP was an increase in public expenditure and in the number of public enterprises. The growth rate of public investment rose from an average of 1.9 per cent during 1965-70 to 5.9 per cent during the next five years. Consequently, total public expenditure as a percentage of GNP increased rapidly: 24 per cent for the period 1966-70, 29 per cent in 1971-75 and 31 per cent in 1976-80. At the same time, the public deficit increased, as did indebtedness. The increase in the number of public enterprises had made public sector employment as a percentage of total employment rise from 11.9 per cent in 1970 to 14.4 per cent ten years later. This growth mainly benefited the Bumiputras, in accordance with the targets the NEP had laid down for the public enterprises. In fact, state-owned enterprises had to play a number of roles simultaneously *vis-à-vis* the Bumiputras: as customers in the industrial and commercial sectors, trustees for their assets in some enterprises, partners in joint ventures, supervisors for their industrial and commercial activities where their experience was inadequate, and catalysts for setting up enterprises in regions where the private sector was generally disinclined to invest.

Under the regime of martial law in the Philippines, the extension of the public sector cascaded over the customary boundaries of natural monopolies and the supply of public goods, and extended indiscriminately to an ever-increasing number of activities such as horse-breeding, running casinos, sardine canning, tomato growing, crafts, film production, management of clinics and conference centres and a very large number of companies in the services sector whose names were sufficiently vague to enable them to be used for various more or less respectable tasks (Briones, 1986).

The increase in the number of state-owned enterprises was based on an increase in the number of subsidiaries. The main reason for this lush growth is fairly distant from the principles defined in the Philippine Constitution. The status of public enterprise allowed this type of company to avoid the regulations and controls that applied to the administration and also to benefit from a very advantageous tax regime. This situation was particularly valuable from the point of view of staff wages. A network of subsidiaries made it possible to by-pass the regulations relating to public sector salaries by means of complementary remunerations. They also enabled the receipt of subsidies or contracts of convenience and contrived privileged access to the nationalised banks, particularly the National Development Bank and the

Philippine Development Bank. These enterprises for laundering public funds operated on an increasingly large scale. The Ministry of Human Settlements, run by President Marcos' wife, with its 73 subsidiaries, is an excellent illustration, since a large part of the resources intended for the most needy groups were transferred abroad to finance Mrs. Marcos' shopping trips and secondary residences (Haggard, 1990, p. 227). An Audit Commission enquiry in 1987 showed that 39 individuals were both members of the directorates of public enterprises and at the same time on the boards of at least ten private companies. Detailed case studies were carried out in the sugar and coconut industries, for example. A presidential commission of the so-called Good Government set up by Corazon Aquino proved that 268 companies had benefited from their privileged relationships with the Marcos family. This list does not include the companies that were directly owned by the Marcoses, nor those owned by the richest "cronies" (Haggard, 1990, p. 233).

By 1973, the public monopolies controlled by cronies had been set up in the main export sectors — sugar and coconut oil — at the distribution and funding level (Compensation Fund and specialised investment banks). The pricing and quotas policy was also used to benefit particular firms. Thus, a 100 per cent tax on filter-tip cigarettes enabled a friend of President Marcos, the chairman of the Philippine Tobacco Filter Company, to obtain a national monopoly.

The 12 public sector banks controlled more than half of the total assets of the banking sector. They enjoyed special discounting terms from the Central Bank. In 1981, when the Philippine economy was affected by the rise in interest rates and the fall in commodities prices, the debts of the bankrupt companies of the president's cronies were swapped for assets by the Philippine National Bank and the Development Bank of the Philippines. As a result of such practices, 50 per cent of the former's portfolio and 90 per cent of the latter's were found to be worthless in 1984, representing a total of $5.5 billion! Furthermore, between 1981 and 1983, the state had transferred to the Construction and Development Company of the Philippines — a front company — the equivalent of one-third of the state's tax revenue for 1983. It is unnecessary to underline that these practices, more of which could be cited, had disastrous consequences for the state's public finances and foreign debt, compelling it to apply to the IMF on an almost permanent basis.

### C. The dynamics of the system

Self-perpetuation is the rule for mixed economies whose rationality is socio-political. In addition, as the distinction between the public and private sectors is subverted by ethnic or influential divisions, the problem of rebalancing arises in different terms from those that applied to the two other systems. The only thing that can lead to change is the intervention of exogenous factors. This is what occurred in both Malaysia and the Philippines, but in each case as a result of different specific circumstances.

The Malaysian economy had experienced remarkable growth. National output increased at a rate of 7.1 per cent between 1970 and 1975 and 8.6 per cent from 1975 to 1980. During the first decade of its application, the NEP was considered a success. This performance was based on two positive factors, the most important being the steadiness of world prices in the primary products exported by the country: rubber, tin, palm oil, oil. Moreover, direct foreign investments increased appreciably, rising from $306 million in 1970 to more than $2 billion in 1980. Over the same period, the indicators showed a reduction in poverty, an increase in the Bumiputras' share in the total capital of enterprises (rising to 12.4 per cent in 1980), and an increase in the number of Bumiputras in the professional class (accountants, attorneys, doctors). For example, the number of Bumiputras in this class rose from 738 in 1970 to 9 894 in 1983. Unfortunately, this situation could not continue after 1980: Malaysia was to be dealt a severe blow by the fall in commodities prices, which was to have repercussions on the public finances, already in a fragile condition, and to lead the government to revise its policy of expanding the public sector. Rebalancing was now on the agenda.

The situation in the Philippines at the beginning of the 1980s had a profound effect on the dynamics of the rebalancing process in that, to use Leviste's words (1985), one no longer knew whether the state was in control of the public enterprises or whether the public enterprises controlled the state. This was a very special situation of state embezzlement in favour of private interests. The turning-point in 1984 was to lead to a serious re-examination of such practices, as the state no longer had sufficient resources to continue subsidising the public enterprises, and the IMF and the World Bank were somewhat reluctant to sign new accords with the government. For all that, only the failure of the elections, decided without warning by President Marcos, put an end to the dynamics of his system. Indeed, this initiative, which turned out to be fatal, was taken soon after an agreement with the IMF and the World Bank in which the government had undertaken to introduce in-depth reforms of taxes and external tariffs and to dismantle the monopolies. Naturally, the implementation of this programme had immediately been postponed. Indeed, it was scarcely compatible with the preservation of a system that had, to the contrary, to be maintained in the light of the imminent decisive election.

## Conclusion

Throughout the 1970s, all the countries in the sample accorded the state and the public sector a role as the driving force in the process of industrialisation. This was perceived as the key to development. In the past, local oligarchies or foreign interests had generally neglected the manufacturing industries and given priority to agriculture and livestock production, exploitation of the soil and subsoil and international trade. In the face of the lack of capital accumulation in industrial production, the state was viewed as the last resort. Its intervention was governed by three principles: productivist, nationalist and populist.

Productivist, in that the success of public sector enterprises was judged on their quantitative performance; it was essential to produce more power, more intermediate goods, more capital goods; above all, it was essential to produce domestically manufactured goods that used to be purchased from abroad. The concerns for optimal efficiency and allocation of resources were deemed to be subsidiary by the *entrepreneur state*.

Nationalist, in that the expansion of the public sector was bound to reduce dependence on foreigners. Production for the domestic market had to replace production for the international market. The presence of foreign companies in the primary sector or in the supply of public goods and services had to be eliminated by the *expropriator state*.

Populist, because accumulation could not be accompanied by an increase in social inequality and underemployment. The *life-belt state* had to come to the help of private enterprises in difficulty that threatened to close their doors.

The analysis of the various national experiences shows that the general mixed economy model has been applied according to very varied modalities. In any one country, the relative position of the private and public sectors has been subjected to changes over time according to the political stance of the teams in power. In certain cases, state intervention has been led astray by influential advantage or led to an economic and financial crisis. Over and above the variety of national experiences, however, an overall trend can be observed at the end of the decade. As a result of an improvement in foreign earnings and easier access to international loans, or through the arrival in power of more radical governments, growth of the public sector accelerated and was swept along by an unrestrained tide. The life-belt state and, less frequently, the expropriator state supplanted the entrepreneur state. The result was the multiform expansion of a public sector whose frontiers were no longer delimited by the desire of the state to control the strategic sectors, natural monopolies and the supply of public goods and services to the population. Faced with this multidirectional extension of the state's domain, the private sector, both local and foreign, felt under threat. Social balance, which underlies the functioning of the mixed economy, was called into question by the increasing number of government interventions; this new situation provoked violent reactions in certain cases.

At the same time, nearly everywhere public expenditure grew astronomically, aggravating government dependence on foreign sources of funding. At the beginning of the 1980s, the collapse of commodities prices, pressures on interest rates, the soaring dollar and, after 1982, the withdrawal of the international banks were to trigger a crisis in public finances everywhere. The state no longer had the means to support the reckless expansion of the public sector. The principle of efficiency could no longer be ignored when the role of the state was once again put under the microscope.

The time for rebalancing had come. However, the dynamics of its installation was to be largely governed by the concepts of the mixed economy that had reigned in the past in the countries that were ready to start along the road to the "new realism" (World Bank, *Annual Report 1983*, p. 56).

*Chapter 2*

# REBALANCING:  THE TURNING-POINT

To what extent does rebalancing break with development policies based on import substitution, national industrialisation and the pre-eminence of the state and its public agents?  In attempting to answer this question, it is important to consider the underlying reasons for rebalancing as well as the type of measures adopted for bringing this process about.

The beginning of the story is relatively simple.  The mixed economy dynamics presented in the preceding chapter had culminated during the 1970s in an explosion of government intervention.  When the mixed economy models ran out of steam or even started to be affected by the slump in the first quarter of 1980, this had naturally drawn attention to the main protagonists of the system, the public enterprises.  Thus the international organisations responsible for taking stock of the economic and financial imbalances of the developing countries soon came to view the state-owned enterprises as the embodiment of the distortions and inconsistencies created by the functioning of mixed economies.

Two factors are of particular interest in appreciating the watershed that rebalancing represents.  First of all, it seems necessary to study the conditions that led to the indictment of the public enterprises' position in the developing countries.  Second, we shall detail the move towards a more general criticism of development policy by analysing stabilization and structural adjustment programmes.

## The public enterprises in question

The indictment of the position of public enterprises focuses on the following two questions:  is the criticism based on the weight of the public enterprises, which grew so rapidly during the 1970s, or is an indictment of the governments' inability to finance their operating costs and deficits?  The further problems underlying these questions are the financial losses incurred by public enterprises and also the state's financial resources.

## Position of public enterprises in national economies

In reviewing the extent of the public sector in the sample countries, we detail both quantitatively and sectorally the effects of its growth during the years prior to the start of the rebalancing process. It is essential to note the different strata observed at the end of this growth so as to understand both certain criticisms — in particular those relating to the wide spread of public involvement — and what the possible outcome of the restructuring and privatisation policies might be.

### A. A difficult calculation

For a number of reasons, evaluating the position of the public enterprises in the economies of the sample countries is a difficult task. For one thing, it was only undertaken late in the day. Moreover, the calculation depends on the level of public holding used as a standard of reference and on whether one counts the number of subsidiaries.

In most of the countries, no systematic catalogue of the state-owned enterprises has been kept. The previous chapter emphasized that the national public sectors were born not in response to any preconceived plan but, most often, as the result of economic or political expediency, decided by a variety of organisations that had not necessarily co-ordinated their actions. In several countries, an exhaustive list of the number and position of public enterprises started to be drawn up when the public sector privatisation and restructuring programmes were prepared. Indeed, the collection of detailed data about public holdings seemed to be a preliminary to drafting and implementing such programmes. Bodies assigned the task of evaluating the public portfolio were accordingly created or reactivated (see Annex 1). In Malaysia, the CICU (Central Information Collective Unit) was created to counter the lack of information about public enterprises available to the Malaysian authorities. A similar development was initiated in Ghana, Mexico and the Philippines. In a different fashion, Morocco (following the Jouahri report) and Tunisia had undertaken similar efforts from the end of the 1970s. However, the calculations were very partial and approximate.

The lack of information at the governments' disposal leads to three comments:

a) The state's ignorance of its own portfolio, as regards both the number and the performance of its public enterprises, is symptomatic of the poor control it exercises over them. The advocates of privatisation used this situation as an argument for denouncing the public sector's lax management.

b) The sheer weight of the task of collecting data — an initial stage of any privatisation and restructuring programme — helps to explain the slow implementation of the programmes.

c) In certain countries, privatisation began despite the fact that the catalogue of the public portfolio was far from exhaustive. For this reason, it is difficult to calculate the number of privatised enterprises precisely.

The difficulties of cataloguing the public enterprises stem not only from the problems of data collection but also from certain problems of definition (Saunders & Klau, 1985; Pestiau, 1987).

The boundaries of the public sector are defined by state control over the companies' equity capital. On the basis of this criterion of public ownership, it is then worth considering the minority or majority nature of state holdings. As a general rule, such holdings are owned either by ministries, through enterprises under their aegis, or by public sector banking and financial holding companies. The actual size of the state portfolio depends on whether one takes into account minority — and, in principle, temporary — public financial holdings and subsidiaries of the public enterprises.

In the case of Mexico, the main difficulty lies in what status to accord to the holdings, often minority, of development banks such as SOMEX or NAFINSA. These holdings stem either from private enterprise rescue operations, or from venture capital operations in association with local or foreign enterprises. In Morocco, of 620 public enterprises the structure of whose capital has been identified, the state has a majority holding in only 303 (Saulniers, 1990). In 167 cases it has a holding of less than 20 per cent; clearly, these enterprises, where the state's minority holding is very low, cannot be considered as wholly public. In the case of Tunisia, there would be 600 public enterprises if the public holding of reference were 10 per cent. If the holding of reference were raised to 34 per cent, the number of state-owned firms would be almost halved! In the case of Ghana, out of 235 public sector companies, it seems that the state has direct or indirect majority holdings in 181, or more than three-quarters (Adda, 1988, p. 305).

Furthermore the public sector has been developed according to different modalities in the various developing countries. That of Mexico was constructed partially on the basis of an existing private sector (rescue operations and political nationalisations). In 1983, more than half the 1 214 entities reckoned to belong to the public sector had originated in the private sector.

In the Philippines, the reinforcement of the public sector was grounded on the increase in the number of subsidiaries. Of 245 public enterprises, 179 are subsidiaries created during the period of martial law to allow certain high officials to circumvent the rules of public administration, deemed too restrictive. Saulniers (1990) points to a similar movement in Morocco. Between 1973 and 1977, 92 per cent of the new public enterprises were created by those already in existence. This procedure was chosen in order to avoid the annoying financial controls exercised by the supervisory authorities. Four public holding companies — the Caisse des Dépôts

*Table 2*

## POSITION OF THE PUBLIC ENTERPRISES IN THE NATIONAL ECONOMIES

| | Public expenditure Central Gov. % GDP Consolidated % GDP | Number of P.E. | P.E./GNP ratio | GFCF/ GFCF tot. | Jobs (thousands) | Jobs/Total % | Sources |
|---|---|---|---|---|---|---|---|
| GHANA | 12.2 (1982) | 235 including* 181 majority | 36.5%* (1983) | 28.7%** (1982) | 552 300* | 10.2* | * PAUL (1990) ** NAIR (1988) |
| MOROCCO | 39.7 (1981-82) | 688 including* 607 companies (262 maj.) | 19.7%** (1982) | 28.1% (1982) | 250 000* (1984) | 4.5*** | * OUDGHIRI (1989) ** NAIR (1988) *** Authors' estimates |
| TUNISIA | 41.3 (1984) | 600* at 10% 307* at 34% (1984) | 24%** (1984) | 40.4%*** (1982-83) | 200 000* | 12* | * PELLETRAU (1988) ** NAIR (1988) *** Authors' estimates |
| BOLIVIA | 32.1 (1984) | 74 including* 31 subsidiaries | 17.3%** (1980-82) | 68.4%* (1981-84) | 53 200** (1982) | 3.1** | * PASTORE (1991) ** BANCO CENTRAL (1984) |
| CHILE (1973) | 32.9  39* | 507 | | 36.5% (1974) | 161 200** (1974) | 5.6** | * BALASSA (1988) ** MAMALAKIS (1988) |
| CHILE (1979) | 29.3 | 40* | | 13.2% | 125 000* | 4.3* | * MAMALAKIS (1988) |
| CHILE (1982) | 31.2  36* (1982-84) | | 12.3%** (1982-84) | 24.5%** | | | * BALASSA (1988) ** MAMALAKIS (1988) |
| JAMAICA | 42.5 (1982) | 172 including* 81 subsidiaries | 21%** (1984) | 42%*** (1984) | 50 000** (1982) | 6.9 | * GFS (1984) ** NAIR (1988) *** PASTORE (1991) |

Table 2 (continued)

| | Public expenditure Central Gov. % GDP Consolidated % GDP | Number of P.E. | P.E./GNP ratio | GFCF/GFCF tot. | Jobs (thousands) | Jobs/Total % | Sources |
|---|---|---|---|---|---|---|---|
| MEXICO | 31.6  46.1* (1982) | 1 214** | 18.2%** 5.1% if Pemex excluded (1983) | 25.5%*** (1982) | 1 100 000** (1983) | 5.1** | * DRI (1986) ** MICHALET (1989) *** NAIR (1988) |
| BANGLADESH | 12.8 (1982-84) | 289* (1984-85) | 3.2%* (1984-85) | 20%* (1984-85) | 2 770 000** (1984-85) | 9.0** | * HUMPHREY (1990) ** GHAFUR (1988) |
| MALAYSIA | 42.7  53* (1982) | 943 of which** 888 subsidiaries | 34%** (1989) | 33.0%*** (1984-85) | 300 000** | 5.8** | * RAMANADHAM (1988) ** LEEDS (1989) *** BALASSA (1988) |
| PHILIPPINES | 15.3 | 245 of which* 149 subsidiaries | 3.3%* (1983) | 22.4%* (1981-83) | 156 600* (1982) | 0.9* | * MANASAN (1988) |

et de Gestion (created in 1958), the Banque Nationale de Développement Economique (1958), the Société Nationale d'Investissement (1966) and the Office de Développement Industriel (1973) — held more than 40 companies. The number of subsidiaries amounted to 343, or 50 per cent of all Moroccan public enterprises.

In the case of Tunisia, a distinction was drawn between parent enterprises, in which the state or local authority holding was more than 34 per cent, and subsidiary enterprises, more than 50 per cent of whose capital was held by the state, by the local authorities or by the parent enterprises. Of 600 public firms, parent enterprises represented slightly more than one-sixth. In Malaysia, 888 subsidiaries are held by 55 parent companies.

Despite the imprecision of the definitions and the fragmentary data, an evaluation of the weight of the public enterprises in the national economies at the inception of the rebalancing process is proposed (see Table 2). Three major conclusions can be drawn:

a) The contribution of the public enterprises to the GDP is large, although it differs from one country to another. At the bottom of the scale, Bangladeshi and Philippine public enterprises account for only 3 per cent of GDP. In Ghana and Malaysia, their share amounts to nearly 35 per cent.

b) The contribution to gross fixed capital formation (GFCF) is very significant: 20-25 per cent in Bangladesh, the Philippines and Mexico and more than 40 per cent in Malaysia and Tunisia (Bolivia is quite different; nearly 70 per cent of investments originate with public enterprises). The public enterprises are deeply involved in the sectors where initial investments are very high and the depreciation period very long. Accordingly, their role is as the driving force of capital accumulation in the developing countries. This role is derived from the theories of development economics referred to in Chapter 1.

c) Owing to their concentration in capital-intensive sectors, the public enterprises, taken as a whole, do not employ a large labour force. Depending on the country, employment in these firms represents between 1 per cent (in the Philippines) and 12 per cent (in Tunisia) of total employment. These figures lend credence to the argument that public enterprises create very few new jobs. As a general rule, the low capital cost that they enjoy — as a result of distortions of relative prices — leads them to favour capital investment to the detriment of intensive use of labour.

A full evaluation of the weight of the public sector should take into account external savings generated by the activity of public enterprises downstream and upstream of the private sector. Undervalued prices of intermediate goods and services supplied by public sector firms improve the profitability of private sector firms and constitute disguised subsidies, which are not generally taken into account; they explain, however, the somewhat reserved attitude of the private sector towards privatisation programmes, especially those involving the public utilities (water, gas, electricity, transport). Furthermore, certain entrepreneurs probably fear the disappearance of lucrative public contracts (overbilling of supply or services contracts). These direct and indirect supports seem more widespread in the case of entrepreneurs working mainly for the local market, who are not very competitive, than for those already exposed to international competition.

## B. Sectoral distribution of public enterprises

The disparity of the data and their limited reliability make comparison among the sample countries particularly complex. The data in Table 3 must therefore be viewed with caution. When information so permits, the sectoral division of the enterprises is presented from two complementary angles: first, a breakdown of the public enterprises by sector (or, failing this, of the fraction of the public sector GDP per sector of activity); second, the relative share of the public and private sectors, assessed on the basis of either comparative value-added or gross fixed capital formation. These figures make it possible to pinpoint several characteristics common to most of the national cases.

i) Although not numerous, public enterprises are particularly active in the traditional export sectors, where they frequently have a virtual monopoly position. By way of illustration, it is worth mentioning:

   a) oil in Mexico (there are only three enterprises, but they represent 98 per cent of value-added in the sector) and Tunisia;

   b) mineral resources in Ghana, Morocco, Tunisia (only four enterprises account for 99 per cent of investments in the sector), Bolivia and Jamaica;

   c) dairy farming and plantations in Ghana, Bangladesh (20 or so enterprises totally dominate forestry and sugar refineries), Malaysia and the Philippines.

These sectors were usually controlled by foreign firms during the colonial era and sometimes even after independence. Thus public enterprises in these sectors stem from nationalisation operations, which although they occurred at different periods, were always carried out in the name of strengthening national sovereignty over natural resources. The revenues from these public enterprises were still the principal source of foreign currency for the states during the 1970s. The downturn in commodities prices at the start of the 1980s substantially reduced the profits derived from the traditional export sectors and, consequently, the transfers from the public enterprises to the national budget. This reduction was one of the

Table 3

## SECTORAL DIVISION AND WEIGHT OF THE PUBLIC ENTERPRISES AT THE DAWN OF REBALANCING[a]

| | GHANA (1983) | | MOROCCO (1985) | | | TUNISIA (1981) | | BOLIVIA (1983) | | |
|---|---|---|---|---|---|---|---|---|---|---|
| | GDP public sector | Public/private | Number | % Total Population | Public/private | Number[c] | % Total Population | % GFCF public/private (1982-83) | Number | % Total Population |
| Agriculture, forestry, fishing | 29.2 | 20% | 44 | 6.4 | 90% | 11 | 4.4 | 17.3 | 16 | 22.2 |
| Mines and extraction | 2.2 | 75% | 55 | 8.0 | 25% | 4 | 1.6 | 99.1 | 2 | 2.8 |
| Manufacturing industries | 4.7 | 25% | 176 | 25.6 | | 100 | 40.1 | 55.7 | 19 | 26.4 |
| – agri-food industry | | | 89 | 13.0 | | 20 | 8.1 | 50.7 | 5 | 6.9 |
| – chemicals | | | 14 | 2.0 | | 10 | 4.0 | 88.9 | 1 | 1.4 |
| – oil refinery | | | | | | 3 | 1.2 | | 1 | 1.4 |
| – others | | | 73 | 10.6 | | 67 | 26.9 | 29.0 | 12 | 16.7 |
| Electricity, water, gas | 2.3 | 99% | 45[b] | 6.5[b] | 90% | 4 | 1.6 | 100.0 | 9 | 12.5 |
| Transport, communications | 4.4 | 40% | 110 | 16.0 | 50% | 27 | 10.9 | 80.8 | 8 | 11.1 |
| Construction | 3.7 | 50% | 14 | 2.0 | | 15 | 6.0 | | | |
| Commerce, restaurants, hotels | 1.3 | 5% | 47 | 6.8 | | 38 | 15.3 | | 1 | 1.4 |
| Finance, insurance | 10.9 | 80% | 37 | 5.4 | 70% | 15 | 6.0 | | 15 | 20.8 |
| Other services | 41.3 | 90% | 165 | 24.0 | | 35 | 14.1 | 15.7 | 2 | 2.8 |
| TOTAL | 100 | | 693 | 100 | | 249 | 100 | 40.4 | 72[d] | 100 |

Sources and notes: Ghana, Paul (1990); Morocco, Saulniers (1990), Oudghiri (1988); Tunisia, Ministry for the Plan and Finances (1981); Bolivia, Daguino-Pastore (1991).

a. Data for Chile were not available.
b. These figures extracted from Saulniers (1990) correspond to the energy sector.
c. Partial sample of enterprises in which the Tunisian state has a majority holding.
d. Figures to which the two state holding companies, Corporacion Fomento de Bolivia (21 subsidiaries) and Corporacion de la Fuerzas Armadas para el Desarollo Nacional (10 subsidiaries), should be added.

Table 3 (continued)

| | JAMAICA (1984) | | MEXICO (1983 & 1986) | | | | BANGLADESH (1986) | | | MALAYSIA (1986) | | PHILIPPINES (1984) | | | |
|---|---|---|---|---|---|---|---|---|---|---|---|---|---|---|---|
| | Number | % Total pop. | Number (1983) | % Total pop. (1983) | % GNP public sector (1986) | Public/private (1986) | Number | % Total pop. | Public/private | Number | % Total pop. | Number | % Total pop. | % GNP public sector | Public/private |
| Agriculture, forestry, fishing | 10 | 5.8 | 24 | 4.4 | 0.0 | 0.4 | 28 | 9.7 | 100[a] | 83 | 11.0 | 20 | 8.2 | 2.6 | 0.5 |
| Mines and extraction | 5 | 2.9 | 53 | 9.7 | 1.2 | 17.2 | 15 | 5.2 | | 20 | 3.0 | 8 | 3.3 | 0.9 | 2.6 |
| Manufacturing industries | 57 | 33.1 | 335 | 61.5 | | | 175 | 60.6 | 100[a] | 169 | 23.0 | 47 | 19.2 | 8.4 | 1.7 |
| – agri-food industry | 45 | 26.2 | 118 | 21.6 | | | 23 | 8.0 | 100[b] | | | | | | |
| – chemicals | | | 35 | 6.4 | | | 26 | 9.0 | | | | | | | |
| – oil refinery | 1 | 0.6 | 3 | 0.6 | 19.5 | 98.0 | 9 | 3.1 | | | | | | | |
| – others | 11 | 6.3 | 179 | 32.9 | 4.6 | 4.0 | 117 | 40.5 | | | | | | | |
| Electricity, water, gas | 3 | 1.7 | 7 | 1.3 | 4.8 | 100.0 | 5 | 1.7 | | | | 6 | 2.4 | 13.7 | 60.1 |
| Transport, communications | 17 | 9.9 | 47 | 8.6 | 7.8 | 23.8 | 14 | 4.8 | | 48 | 7.0 | 25 | 10.2 | 2.8 | 2.5 |
| Construction | 2 | 1.2 | | | | | | | | 105 | 14.0 | 4 | 1.6 | 0.1 | 0.1 |
| Commerce, restaurants, hotels | 36 | 20.9 | 44 | 8.1 | 22.9 | 18.4 | 21 | 7.3 | | 58 | 8.0 | 24 | 9.7 | 3.0 | 0.8 |
| Finance, insurance | 19 | 11.1 | a | a | 10.5 | 32.4 | 14 | 4.8 | | 46 | 6.0 | 54 | 22.0 | 67.0 | 84.1[c] |
| Other services | 23 | 13.4 | 35 | 6.4 | 28.7 | 44.9 | 17 | 5.9 | | 207 | 28.0 | 57 | 23.3 | 1.2 | 1.0 |
| TOTAL | 172 | 100 | 545 | 100 | 100 | 100 | 289 | 100 | | 736 | 100 | 245 | 100 | 100 | 100 |

Sources and notes:   Mexico, Casar & Perez (1988) and Secretaria de Hacienda (1990); Bangladesh, Humphrey (1990); Malaysia, Ministry for Public Enterprises (1989); Philippines, Manasan (1988).

a.   The data are based on a partial sample of 545 enterprises excluding in particular the nationalisations of 1982 in the financial sector.
b.   Market share of the public enterprises for forestry, fertilizers and sugar refineries.
c.   Percentage of total value-added of the financial sector only.

factors of rebalancing, since part of the profits of these enterprises had been used to cover the deficits of those in other sectors (see below, "The public enterprises on trial").

ii) The public enterprises also occupy a dominant position in the provision of public utilities, such as the production and distribution of water, gas, electricity and marine, rail and urban transport. These sectors are the "natural" field for state intervention. Public ownership of such enterprises, generally combined with a fairly uncompetitive market structure, is justified by the corpus of public economics (existence of natural monopolies, public goods and services, external effects). These sectors have been entrusted to public enterprises since independence, forming one of the oldest strata of the public sector. In certain cases, they were already under the aegis of the colonial administration. Unlike the first group, however, they are the main cause of the public sector deficit.

iii) In general, with the exception of Ghana, Malaysia and the Philippines, the industrial sector contains the greatest number of public enterprises. For example, there are 176 industrial public enterprises in Morocco and 19 in Bolivia (that is, a quarter of the total). In Tunisia, of a partial sample of 249 enterprises, 100 belong to the industrial sector. In Bangladesh and Mexico, the proportion is even greater (respectively, 175 and 335 enterprises, or more than 60 per cent of the total number). However, this involvement of public enterprises in the competitive industrial sector is difficult to analyse, since it fulfils two objectives.

On the one hand, it corresponds to the sectors that the state deems strategic. Their definition depends not on the theory of public economics but on that of development economics according to a logic of national independence examined in the previous chapter. The constitution of this group of enterprises therefore reflects a deliberate state strategy to control the "commanding heights" of the economy. They are generally situated downstream from export activities, which are also conducted by public enterprises (oil refining and basic chemicals in Mexico and Tunisia, fertilizer factories in Morocco and Tunisia and agriculture-based food industry in Ghana). They can also be found in the consumer durables sector (automobile assembly units in Morocco, Tunisia, Mexico and the Philippines), in accordance with the principle of import substitution.

On the other hand, public involvement in industry is the result of the systematic rescue of private firms in difficulties, for reasons connected less with industrial objectives than with the will to fight against unemployment. In this second perspective, the state's portfolio is very varied, not to say eccentric, since the acquisitions took place without preplanning, on the basis of interventions by the "life-belt state". The rise in the number of public enterprises during the second half of the 1970s in Jamaica, Mexico and Malaysia and during the last months of the Allende government is explained in part by this trend.

Mexico is a good example, as the reinforcement of its public sector reflects this dual movement: on one side, the deliberate creation of a state industrial core in the strategic and priority sectors, where state involvement is high as a ratio both of national output and of the public industrial sector taken as a whole; on the other side, hundreds of enterprises, often small or medium in scale and belonging to many industrial branches, most of which joined the public sector during the presidencies of de Echeverria and Lopez Portillo, between 1970 and 1982. As a result, Mexican public enterprises exceed 10 per cent of total value-added (private sector included) in only 2 branches of the 21 that make up Mexican industry: capital goods (15.2 per cent) and oil refineries and basic petrochemicals (95.8 per cent) (Michalet, 1989a). For the rest, the increase in the number of public enterprises has led them to occupy an overall marginal position in the division of sectoral value-added. A similar analysis (high concentration of industrial public sector value-added in two or three sectors, and spread of public presence throughout a great many branches) emerges from the information available relating to our sample countries. These data are presented in Table 3.

iv) The services are next in line so far as the density of public enterprises is concerned. The financial sector occupies an important position, particularly through the development banks, whose resources are mainly budgetary, and the commercial banks, most often in association with foreign banks with a minority holding. The Philippines is a perfect illustration of this situation. There are 54 public financial institutions, that is, 22 per cent of the total number of public enterprises. More significant is the fact that these financial bodies on their own represent 67 per cent of public sector GDP and 84 per cent of total value-added in this sector. The Philippine public institutions include both commercial banking activities (by controlling the five main banks in the country), the development banks (in particular the Development Bank of the Philippines) and the other financial services (export credits, sectoral loans, etc.).

In all the sample countries, the public financial and banking sector is highly developed since, during the period 1950-70, the control of sources of funding was viewed as strategic — in other words, falling within the domain of state intervention. The strengthening of the public enterprises took place in accordance with different modalities: in Morocco, through gradual development of the financial institutions during the 1960s in response to the requirements of economic activity; in Chile, through nationalisations decided by President Allende's socialist government; and in Mexico, following sudden nationalisations in 1982 by President Lopez Portillo.

71

Tourism, a branch of the services sector, is strongly but unevenly represented. As it is an important source of foreign currency for certain countries (Morocco, Tunisia, Jamaica, Mexico and the Philippines), the firms, often hotel chains or tourist complexes, are frequently controlled by public agencies. In addition, the public portfolio contains many hotels and restaurants constructed by the state or acquired from the private sector.

Lastly, the public enterprises in the commercial sector mainly comprise public offices in charge of marketing, promotion and distribution of goods, generally intended for export. These offices increased in number at the time of the drift towards state intervention during the 1970s. Over the years, they have become archetypical of the inefficiency of public enterprises, especially in the agricultural sector (low productivity, overmanning, cumbersome administration, negative impact on producers).

This sectoral analysis of the public enterprises reveals a number of strata. Public firms occupy a dominant, sometimes exclusive, position in the sectors described, either because of the goods and services produced, since government intervention accords with the theory of public economics, or through the production and distribution of consumer goods, mainly foodstuffs, that are essential to the population — activities that may be akin to goods "under state guardianship", to use Musgrave's terminology (1959) — or in view of their capacity to earn foreign currency (export products, tourism), where public enterprises have often taken the place of foreign enterprises. For the rest, the presence of public enterprises is the result of disparate interventionary measures taken by the life-belt state or of a more or less legitimate merger of the interests of government leaders and private sector managers. This class of public enterprises which grew considerably during the drift towards public intervention in the 1970s, is the most recent stratum in the public sector. These enterprises, whose existence was justified mainly on political grounds or by reason of economic expediency, were to be the first under attack from the privatisation programmes set up in the context of rebalancing.

### The public enterprises on trial

The two main criticisms of public enterprises relate to their lack of profitability and lack of efficiency, two aspects that are clearly linked. These criticisms are undeniable, as we shall observe at the outset of our examination of the performance of the public enterprises. However, the accusation loses some of its force in that, on the one hand, it cannot be applied wholesale, since not all the public enterprises incur deficits, and on the other, it is not a new phenomenon, as they did not suddenly start losing money at the beginning of the 1980s. This suggests that the changes in public deficit financing conditions played a considerable role in the indictment of the position of the public enterprises in the developing countries.

72

## A. Mediocre financial performance overall

The performance of the public enterprises must be assessed on two levels. In the first place, it is important to evaluate their financial results as precisely as possible in order to measure the weight of gross financial transfers from the state to the public enterprises and the net financial transfers in the budget deficit. Moreover, the description of the structure of financial relationships between the state and the public enterprises will enable us to identify those enterprises paying or receiving the largest sums of money from the state. In the second place, the analysis of financial performance should be completed by an analysis of the public enterprises' efficiency, particularly by comparison of output from the private and public sectors. The reduction in the governments' financial resources at the beginning of the 1980s, in fact, posed with new intensity the problem of utilisation for productive and profitable ends of funds available.

### 1. Net financial transfers and division of transfers

The evaluation of the financial performance of public enterprises in the developing countries is particularly problematical. Once again, the information is fragmentary, disparate and difficult to compare on an international basis. Comparative studies are few and fairly inconclusive (Short, 1984; Nair & Filippides, 1988). The reservations expressed regarding the reliability of the data concerning the position of public enterprises in the economy are equally relevant in the case of financial performance. It is important, however, to attempt to present the complex financial relationships between the state and the public enterprises in order to avoid premature conclusions on the criticisms directed against the latter. Therefore we propose to set out an evaluation of gross financial transfers (from the state to the public enterprises) and net financial transfers (taking into consideration transfers from public enterprises entered as income in the national budget). In effect, only net transfers enable the assessment of the public enterprises' contribution to the government's consolidated deficit[1]. Whenever the available data permit, the division of the financial transfers will lead to an identification of the main enterprises in receipt of transfers of public funds and those that make a positive contribution to the national budget. The available data are presented on a national basis since they cannot easily be compared on an international basis. In the case of Chile, Jamaica and Bangladesh, the data have proved both fragmentary and contradictory. Therefore, they have not been presented. At the end of the presentation, however, a number of general observations will be set out.

The case of Morocco is a particularly good illustration both of the weight of the public enterprises in the state budget deficit and of the strong concentration of financial transfers between a few receivers and a few contributors. The net transfer of funds from the state to the public firms has been a chronic phenomenon. Transfers reached a maximum in 1979, as a result of an ambitious investment programme, continued even though the phosphate bonanza had come to an end. Between 1983

73

and 1985, the cumulative total of transfers made up about one-quarter of the budget deficit on average. Cumulative gross transfers over this period amounted to 11.3 billion dinars, net transfers 5.7 billion dinars, resulting in a transfer from the public enterprises to the Moroccan Treasury of 5.6 billion dinars (Saulniers, 1990). The total net transfers between 1983 and 1985 would have been much greater had it not been for the Office Chérifien des Phosphates, whose total contributions to the state budget, in the form of dividends and taxes, represented approximately two-thirds of transfers from public enterprises to the state. The latter are essentially dependent on a single enterprise, but it must be noted that transfers *to* public enterprises are also concentrated on a small number of beneficiaries. The Grains Bureau and the National Railways Bureau received approximately 43 per cent of the financial flow, whereas 17 per cent was directed towards the Regional Agricultural Development Boards and 14 per cent to the gas and electricity companies (Saulniers, 1990).

The situation in Mexico has many points in common with that of Morocco. During 1977-82, the public enterprise deficit after tax amounted to slightly less than one-third of the budget deficit (similar estimates presented by Villaréal, 1988; Nair & Fillipides, 1988). However, if the state industrial sector alone is taken into consideration, between 1970 and 1984, the burden of the public enterprises on the national budget had a negative impact only during the period 1970-75. This result is due to payments from PEMEX to the state, which, over the period 1976-84, were on average two to three times higher than the losses of the public enterprises in the industrial sector (Michalet, 1989a, p. 35). While the deficit of the manufacturing industries remained relatively modest over the period 1970-84 (less than 10 per cent of the overall deficit), the losses suffered by the electricity production and distribution company and the railway company were much more significant. For example, the losses incurred by the electricity company alone for the first nine months of 1984 represented 70 per cent of the total losses of the public enterprises (Aharoni, 1986, p. 183).

In Tunisia between 1982 and 1986, the proportion of public enterprises' deficits in the national consolidated budget deficit after transfers from the state amounted to about 23 per cent on average, apart from 1983 when it totalled nearly one-third. Another factor to be borne in mind is that between 1980 and 1983 — in other words, before the start of the stabilization and rebalancing process — gross capital transfers to the public enterprises represented 15.4 per cent of the state's budget earnings and 5 per cent of the GDP (Pelletrau, 1988). These figures agree with those put forward by Nair and Philippides (1988), who obtain an average percentage of 3.9 per cent of GDP for net transfers over the period 1981-84. The deficits incurred by the railways, the phosphate mines and chemicals firms are a significant fraction of the public enterprises' drain on the government revenues.

In the Philippines, where the annual average growth rate of public enterprise expenditure was 41 per cent over the period 1975-84, the deficit of the public sector firms corresponded to 18.2 per cent of budget expenditure (Manasan, 1988). From 1981 to 1983, net transfers from the state averaged 2.8 per cent of GDP, or 45 per cent of the national deficit (Nair & Philippides, 1988). As in the preceding cases, the greater part of the deficit was generated by a few companies: the 15 leading public enterprises incurred more than 85 per cent of the deficit, led by the National Power Corporation (electricity), the Philippine Development Bank, the National Irrigation Administration and the National Development Company (Amatong, 1985).

In Ghana, budget expenditure in the form of subsidies and capital endowments to public enterprises accounted for 13 per cent of total government expenditure in 1982 (Adda, 1988, p. 307). Once again, the losses were not equally divided. In 1982 the deficit of the Cocoa Marketing Board represented 84.5 per cent of the total (98.2 per cent in 1983). The other firms with a structurally heavy deficit were the State Mining Corporation, the Ghana Water and Sewerage Corporation, the Food Production Corporation and the Ghana Railways Corporation. On the other hand, certain enterprises realised operating profits: the Electricity Corporation of Ghana, the Volta River Authority (Akuoko-Frimpong, 1990, p. 25).

In Malaysia, where the budget deficit was particularly high (16.9 per cent of GDP in 1982), the public enterprises' share amounted to 65 per cent of the public deficit between 1981 and 1984. Net transfers represented 3.3 per cent of GDP over the same period (Nair & Philippides, 1988). In addition, development expenditure amounted, on average between 1978 and 1981, to 23 per cent of the central government's consolidated deficit (Leeds, 1989, p. 55). This significant weight of the public enterprises in the government deficit should be placed in the context of their considerable importance in the Malaysian economy.

In Bolivia, between 1980 and 1984, public enterprise deficits fluctuated both in absolute terms and in comparison with the GDP or the central government deficit. In 1980, for example, public enterprises incurred one-quarter of the total deficit, at that time 9.2 per cent of the GDP. In 1982, their share fell by half, basically owing to an increase of more than 70 per cent in the budget deficit. In 1984, the share rose to 17 per cent of the deficit; the widening of the public enterprises' losses was accompanied by a more than equivalent aggravation of the state's consolidated deficit (Dagnino-Pastore, 1991).

After this presentation, two observations need to be made:

First, the public enterprises' contribution to the total government deficit is appreciable. For all the developing countries, according to Short (1984), the budget burden generated by the public enterprises during the 1970s amounted to 3.3 per cent of GDP (p. 169). It seems, however, that this financial burden is only one of the reasons for the indictment of the position of the public enterprises in the developing countries' economies. This leads to a consideration of two other factors: a) the change in the financial performance of public enterprises in the months prior to the adoption of economic stabilization programmes, b) the change in the financing conditions of public enterprise deficits, differentiating between international and domestic funding sources. These two factors, which are crucial to understanding the rebalancing process, will be analysed in the following subsection.

Second, our presentation demonstrates that some firms are in balance or in surplus, which proves that their status as members of the public sector is not necessarily fatal. Examination of a sample of public enterprises in Ghana between 1979 and 1983 reveals that half of them incurred operating losses, which means — recalling the fable of the empty glass and the full glass — that the other half must have made a profit. Between 1979 and 1984, however, the public enterprises paid a nominal interest rate of less than 1 per cent on loans granted by the public banking institutions or obtained with government backing (Adda, 1988, p. 306). In the case of Morocco, Saulniers (1990) notes that, of a group of 226 public enterprises, 159 had a positive rate of profitability, higher than 10 per cent in the case of one-third of them. In Malaysia, the return on capital invested in the public enterprises was higher than 10 per cent in 225 enterprises, or 30.6 per cent of the 736 public enterprises studied by the CICU. It is also important to note that 186 firms, one-quarter of the total, had a negative return (Ministry for Public Enterprises, 1989).

Numerous arguments are advanced to explain the mediocre financial performance of the public enterprises[2]. The state imposes constraints on the enterprises under its control, and these weigh heavily on their financial results. Under these circumstances, deterioration in results ensuing from specific constraints — for example, the supply of goods and services at low prices, which are in fact disguised subsidies — should be borne in mind when the financial performance of public sector and private sector enterprises are compared. The costs borne by the public enterprise can be classed as dividends paid to the state shareholder. Further, the state requires them to play a number of roles not directly related to their main activity. They are also involved in the fight against urban unemployment, the redistribution of income to underprivileged strata of society, regional development and the development of new activities deemed strategic. What is more, the state is not always an exemplary partner or shareholder: subsidies or capital endowments intended for the public enterprises may be featured in the budget but are not always paid or, in the best cases, their payment is considerably delayed. Capital endowments are uncertain and subject to annual budgets, which has the effect of preventing public sector firms from making long term-plans. Lastly, the state is often slow to pay its bills; thus the problem of late payments by the state is one of the main items on the agenda of public sector restructuring programmes.

## 2. Lack of efficiency based on poor allocation of resources

The public enterprises are blamed for being ill-managed and inefficient. The rare studies in this area in fact reveal that the productivity of public enterprises is generally lower than that of private enterprises. In Ghana in 1982, value-added per person in the public enterprises was one-quarter less than in the case of private firms (however, the difference was one-half in 1969-70); in the Philippines, overall factor productivity was 2.2 times higher in the private enterprises than in state firms (the differential is more marked in the case of capital than in the case of labour). In the Mexican industrial sector, on the other hand, the productivity of the public enterprises was higher than that of the private firms. However, the differential fell during the period just before the crisis, partly owing to the inability of public enterprises to lay off their personnel as rapidly and in the same proportions as their private sector counterparts.

This low productivity is the central point of the discussion of the role and position of the public enterprises in developing economies[3]. In fact, the mediocre profitability can be explained by the constraints borne by the public enterprises in the context of their activity, or one can point out the inadequacy of measuring such enterprises' performance solely on the criterion of profit. The criticism regarding efficiency is much more fundamental. It involves not only the use of input resources by the enterprises but also the mechanisms of resource allocation. The system of relative prices of factors of production is, therefore, concerned by the criticism of efficiency.

This analysis has a very different scope from that of Alchian and Demsetz (1972), which is derived from ownership rights. According to them, the principal causes of allocative and productive inefficiency are the public enterprises, which are intrinsically ill-managed owing to total lack of control by either the shareholders or the capital markets[4]. The criticism of the productivity of public entities concerns not only the public enterprises but also state intervention in the inputs market, which results in price distortions leading to the underallocation and underutilisation of resources. Accordingly, inefficiency appears to result less from the enterprises themselves than from distortions imposed on them by the state at the level of resource allocation. In this viewpoint, the overutilisation of capital in the public enterprises stems from the low cost of this particular factor of production, in comparison with private enterprises. On the other hand, the quantity (overmanning) and remuneration of the labour factor (generally higher than wages paid in the private sector) are evidence of heavy constraints exercised by the state.

The debate is not settled, since the inefficiency of public enterprises has not yet been demonstrated irrefutably. However, the advocates and critics of public enterprises and government intervention on the factors of production market, sensing the importance of the stakes, are deeply divided as to the criteria for assessing productivity and efficiency[5]. Aharoni (1986), after considering the main empirical studies on this question, concludes his chapter on the performance of public enterprises as follows:

> The empirical conclusions are much more ambiguous and offer limited support to the theory that public enterprises are less efficient than private firms. True, the financial results of public enterprises are illustrated by significant losses. However, these losses are perhaps the result of social and political imperatives that these enterprises have to respond to. In terms of efficiency, the performance of these enterprises is much less gloomy. At the level of efficient use of resources, they have been able to achieve performances comparable to private enterprises producing an identical good in the same country. (p. 215)

## B. The origins of the change in attitude towards public enterprises

The criticisms of public enterprises and government intervention converge on two points: denouncing the public enterprises' operating deficits and highlighting the meagre allocation and use of the resources made available to them. These accusations are not new, but they sounded particularly relevant when financing conditions deteriorated, that is, when the capital resources available in the economy decreased. It is important to present the inception of the stabilization policies precisely in order to determine which were the decisive elements leading to their adoption. Two factors seem to have played a leading role: the deterioration in external financing conditions and the widening of the public enterprises' deficits.

### 1. Tightening of external financing constraints

The main characteristic of most developing countries is a lack of the financial resources needed for investment programmes that would lead to more rapid economic growth. The relative scarcity of domestic capital forces them to depend on external sources of financing. This financial dependence was supposed to diminish gradually, in line with the development of national economic activities that were to have driven domestic capital accumulation. External financing sources have remained preponderant, however, as the progress towards national financial independence has proved particularly slow and difficult. The tightening of international financing constraints in the early 1980s occurred whilst most of the developing economies were still dependent on of financial flows from abroad, essentially earnings derived from exports and international bank borrowing. This external financing should be analysed in quantitative terms (volume of available resources, terms of trade) but also in the light of their potential utilisation, particularly the financing of deficits of public enterprises.

i) The fall in export earnings

The fall in export earnings is significant for at least three reasons. To begin with, it was the first to occur chronologically. From the end of the 1970s, in the case of non-oil primary products, and at the beginning of the 1980s in the case of oil, international prices fell after several consecutive years of upward movement. It was the first external shock that revealed how fragile and vulnerable the economies of the developing countries were. The sustained increase in the prices of primary products, including oil products, during the 1970s, had done little to encourage the developing countries to diversify their exports, and hence diversification remained limited. Under these circumstances, in 1980, most of the sample countries still depended on the prices of a limited number of primary products. For example, the price of copper, on which Bolivia and above all Chile depended, fell by 27 per cent during 1980 alone. Likewise, the price of jute, Bangladesh's main export, fell by 20 per cent as early as 1979 and a further 18 per cent in 1980. The price of tin, important for both Bolivia and Malaysia, dropped by 24 per cent during 1980 alone. As long ago as 1976, Morocco and, to a lesser extent, Tunisia had suffered the full impact of the collapse in phosphates prices (down 50 per cent in three quarters).

Second, this fall in export earnings derived from primary products reduced the surpluses of the public enterprises responsible for operating these traditional export channels. Now, we have emphasized that these transfers had in the past been the main method of financing the structural deficits of certain public enterprises. The loss of export earnings helped to bring the question of these deficits to the fore with new immediacy, as the governments realised that with the emergence of tight financial constraint they would no longer be able to assume all the economic responsibilities they were liable for in a mixed economy system. In this perspective of seeking the primary causes of the adoption of stabilization and rebalancing programmes, the fall in export earnings thus seems to foreshadow the structural change in the state's attitude towards financing public deficits.

Third, the fall in non-oil commodities prices beginning in 1978-79 (1976 in the case of phosphates), and in oil prices as from 1981, ended the period of improvement in terms of trade — that is, purchasing power for importing manufactured products — for the developing countries that exported primary products. The 1970s had nourished the illusion that the underlying degradation of terms of trade had passed (see graph 1). Over and above the quantitative reduction in export earnings, the deterioration in terms of trade at the beginning of the 1980s throws additional light on the tightening of financial constraint.

ii) The end of international bank borrowing

The term "international borrowing economy" refers to the system for recycling Eurocurrencies set up after the first oil shock by the international banks, based in offshore capital markets. The recession in the economies of the industrialised

# Figure 1. **Terms of trade of the sample countries**[1]
## (first semester 1975 = 100)

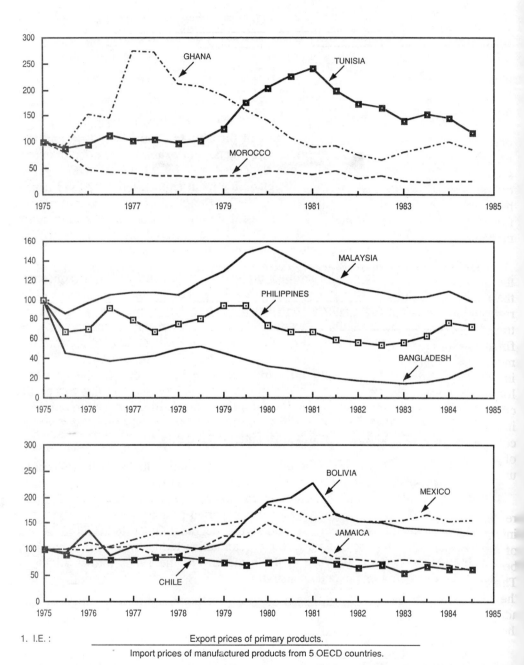

1. I.E. :     Export prices of primary products.
              Import prices of manufactured products from 5 OECD countries.

*Source :* OECD, IMF.

countries and the increase of earnings in dollars by countries with a low absorption capacity had led to overliquidity in the international banking system. The Eurobanks partially resolved their problem by lending more funds to the developing countries, which offered guarantees in the form of primary resources and/or strongly expanding industrial potential. Consequently, the international banks granted many loans on attractive financial terms: a negative real interest rate and a lack of conditionality for the borrowers. The chronic lack of local savings and the satisfactory performance from the export of traditional products led governments and public enterprises to accumulate international banking debts without worrying too much about the future burden from the loans contracted. In Malaysia, the public enterprises contracted one-third of the country's external debt (Woon, 1989, p. 246). In the Philippines, foreign loans accounted for more than half the borrowing requirements of the public sector between 1977 and 1980 (Manasan, 1988, p. 155). In Morocco, they covered on average 30 per cent of public enterprises' borrowing requirements. One should however display caution in that the public enterprises have sometimes borrowed funds on behalf of their guardian, the state, and not benefited themselves from the money lent.

The financial crisis in Mexico in August 1982 was to transform the attitude of the international banks radically. From the end of that year they drastically reduced their new commitments in the developing countries, limiting their operations to rescheduling programmes; they have only marginally revised their position since that time. The flow of international bank loans, which used to be an important source of financing for developing countries, had thus dried up. The scarcity of new loans was, moreover, accompanied by an increase in the burden of debt service owing to the rise in nominal and real interest rates and in the value of the dollar. In addition, the new loans in the mid-1980s were contracted on very different terms: strong conditionality, positive real interest rate, limited volume of new money. The end of international borrowing on extremely flexible terms, which started in 1982, has considerably reinforced financial constraint in the developing countries. In a context of net financial transfers towards the creditor countries, the problems linked to the utilisation of available capital resources have taken on a new urgency.

The deterioration of external financing conditions considerably accelerated the re-examination of public enterprise deficit. The reduction in export earnings and in international borrowing forced states to change their attitude towards the performance of public enterprises. Indeed, it would seem that their losses used to be tolerated because of the availability of abundant sources of financing on relatively easy terms. The external shocks at the beginning of the decade suddenly revealed the fragility of the functioning of the various mixed economies. When stabilization policies were adopted in an attempt to reduce the imbalances engendered by the combination of these external shocks and the collapse of the development model, domestic financing sources were reduced drastically (see below, "The choice of orthodox principles"). From then on, financial constraint was to be total, forcing states to reduce deficits that had become unsustainable.

## 2. Unsustainable public deficits

The preceding presentation aimed to demonstrate that financing the deficit is just as important as the deficit in itself. The scale of the public enterprise deficits as well as their aggravation at the start of the 1980s should not be underestimated. However, the widening of the public enterprises' operating losses seemed more a consequence than a prime cause of the crisis in the economies of the developing countries.

Not enough data are available to reach solid conclusions as to the extent of public enterprise deficits at the start of the 1980s. The general trend seems to have been one of deterioration in the financial performance of public enterprises, but not in sufficient proportions to have engendered a major crisis for the public finances.

In Tunisia, transfers of capital to the public enterprises peaked in 1977 at 5.9 per cent of GDP, as against 2.7 per cent in 1973. The transfers then stabilized at around 5 per cent of GDP between 1980 and 1983. In Mexico, despite the tripling of the losses of industrial enterprises between 1970-75 and 1976-82, their total was still low as a percentage of the overall national deficit, at about 5 per cent (Michalet, 1989a, p. 35). Similarly, the total deficit of Bolivia's public enterprises, which in 1984 stood at 4 per cent of the GDP, compared to an average of 1.6 per cent during the four previous years, remained "low" in comparison with the deficit incurred directly by the state, amounting to 19.9 per cent of GDP. For these countries it is difficult to conclude that the temporary deterioration of the public enterprises' financial results hastened the countries towards essential adjustment.

In the Philippines, the deterioration was more significant. During 1984, the percentage of transfers to public enterprises amounted to 30 per cent of budget expenditure. In addition, the fraction of the financial deficit of the public enterprises as a proportion of the total central government deficit grew by 130 per cent to 4 per cent of the GDP. This increase can be viewed as one of the factors that led to the economic stabilization programme and more generally to an awareness of the failure of the Philippine public sector. Similarly, the deficit of the Ghanaian enterprises increased ninefold at constant prices between 1979 and 1982, essentially owing to the collapse of the price of cocoa and the virtual bankruptcy of the Cocoa Marketing Board. As a percentage of sales, the deterioration was even more marked: the operating outturn of a representative sample of public enterprises rose from 4.4 per cent to 49.2 per cent in 1982 (Akuoko-Frimpong, 1989, p. 63). It is clear that this sudden deterioration in the public enterprises' accounts was a determining factor in the adoption of the stabilization policy with effect from April 1983.

The state's capacity to provide financially for the activities of the public enterprises that it itself had created in increasing numbers was thus called into question. This topic calls for an in-depth study of the birth of the public sector, and more generally the relationship between the government's financial resources and the development of the public sector. Under these circumstances, the question of rebalancing raised since the beginning of the 1980s arises in a totally different context. The tightening of financial constraints seems, in fact, to be the major factor behind the indictment of the position of the public enterprises in the economies of the developing countries. Until the period of financial constraint, public enterprise deficits had always been tolerated by the state.

The deterioration in the results of public enterprises and the tightening of borrowing conditions had three main consequences: first, a recognition that a significant part of the public sector in the developing countries was potentially insolvent; second, a consideration of the scale and composition of the public portfolio following the rapid growth in the number of public firms during the 1970s; lastly, the adoption of stabilization programmes inspired by strict economic principles that were totally at odds with the development models followed up to then.

The reduction in the state's financial resources, which was to become a rule of orthodox economic policies, and the role of the public enterprises as the scapegoats of the crisis in the mixed economies, must not in any circumstances lead to expecting the rebalancing process to solve the wrong problem. It is a matter not of calling the whole of the public sector into question but rather of revising the functioning of the public enterprises and changing the scale of the public sector. This twofold policy of restructuring and privatisation of public enterprises took place in the more general context of a revision of the foundations of the mixed economy (separation from the world market, state intervention in the conditions of economic activity, distinction between the various strata of public enterprises).

## The choice of orthodox principles

The revisions to the operating methods of mixed economies and development policies are closely linked to the choice, more or less obligatory depending on the country, of economic and financial orthodoxy. In order to highlight the logic of calling the functioning of mixed economies into question, it is worth recalling the sequence of the stabilization and structural adjustment policies. It seems, in fact, that the measures adopted to stabilize the economies had brought to light the crisis in the operation of the mixed economies early in the 1980s. This finding, however, did not take on its full significance until more comprehensive actions were undertaken with a view to permitting the gradual changeover towards an open market economy. This systemic change was to confirm the choice of orthodox principles and ratify the break with the development policies followed up to then.

*Stabilization policies — mixed economies called into question*

The stabilization policies adopted in most of the sample countries at the beginning of the 1980s are especially significant. Because they were introduced in a context of exceptional economic crisis, they are more closely akin to the starting point of a general critique of the functioning of mixed economies than to an orthodox interlude aimed at recovery from temporary imbalances.

The importance of this turning-point induced by stabilization policies can be demonstrated in two stages. The first defines the link between the modalities of the crisis affecting the sample countries and the structural weaknesses of the management of mixed economies. The second throws light on the extensions of the stabilization policies, particularly with the adoption of economic and financial liberalisation policies.

## A. The modalities of the crisis — mixed economies called into question

The deficit of the public enterprises was not the sole and determining cause of the crisis in public finances. It was the aggravation of this situation that posed with greater urgency the question of how to finance the deficit. Sometimes public enterprises have been used as scape-goats, as denunciation of their negligence can help to make the general public accept unpopular economic measures. At the same time, the trial of these enterprises also contained an indictment of the functioning of the mixed economy systems set up during the previous decades. This was on three levels:

- First, the crisis had highlighted the fragility of the state's resources. In the case of Mexico, Tunisia or Morocco, the swelling of resources stemming from the rise in oil and phosphates prices on the international market had been a providential windfall, the ephemeral nature of which was an obvious risk for the drafting of long-term investment plans. From this period, the governments became aware that their external financing arrangements were precarious and that they were still dependent on price fluctuations on the international markets, which were out of their control.

- Second, the crisis showed the limits of the logic of industrialisation based on import substitution or on industrialising industries. On the one hand, the substitution was not total. It generally succeeded in the case of local production of consumer durables, but was insufficient or non-existent as regards national production of capital goods with a more advanced technological content. To a large extent, these had to be imported. Policies based on an industrialisation process with forward linkage had no more success in getting past the stage of production of intermediate goods. Once again, the vicious circle of dependence on foreign countries appeared, and with it, the problem of access to hard currency. Moreover, local production was not competitive on the international markets as a general rule and was highly unlikely to lead to the sought-after diversification of exports. These failures revived the attacks on the inefficiency of public enterprises, due to the inflation of an excessively controlled bureaucracy that had insufficient responsibility, the more discreet proliferation of rent-seekers from the private sector prospering in the shadow of the public sector and the less common attempts to misappropriate public resources by groups pursuing their own interests.

- Lastly, the crisis was to change the theoretical references underlying economic policies[6]. Refuting the Keynesian ideas in vogue until then, those in charge of economic policies became gradually inspired by neo-liberalism, linked to the experience of Thatcherism in the United Kingdom and Reaganism in the United States. The IMF and the World Bank contributed significantly to this development by manifesting a new interest in the development of the private sector, termed "a challenge" by the Bretton Woods institutions (World Bank, 1989). The scale of the crisis and the advice of the multilateral lenders, who gradually took the place of the international banks, brought about or speeded up the awareness of the structural weakness of the development strategies followed for almost half a century by the governments of the developing countries.

The outlook for the traditional mixed economy model of reference was therefore dismal. It had not fulfilled the aspirations that had accompanied its implementation: the mechanisms of dependence linked to the traditional international division of labour had not been significantly changed; the state's financial resources had remained inadequate to the central role it had to play in the country's development. The functioning of the system was sustained by external resources procured by traditional exports, by a policy of borrowing on the international capital markets, and, at the domestic level, by money creation. These precarious methods of "balancing" the economy had made it possible to avoid asking the fundamental question of the division between wages and profits to finance accumulation. The state managed to handle the contradictory demands of the various social groups owing to foreign income and monetary illusion in an expanding economy. The sudden interruption of the facilities offered by the debt economy and the collapse of commodities prices led, in most of the countries, to significant inflationary surges, fed by the excessive swelling of budget deficits. This kind of forward flight could not continue. In all the sample countries it would lead to the adoption of stabilization policies and the abandonment of lax management of mixed economies.

The crisis that struck the countries in our sample was the complex product of external and internal factors. From one country to another the weight of the two factors varies according to the development strategies adopted in the past. Nonetheless, in every case the external shocks seem to have highlighted the structural failures of the mixed economies in question.

The deterioration of external financing conditions (export earnings from primary products, bank debt characterised by its low cost and limited conditionality) both revealed and increased the monetary "balancing" of the functioning of the mixed economies. The failures of the various mixed economy models based on import substitution were masked by the abundance of available financial resources. The turnaround, which occurred as long ago as 1976 in the case of Morocco, and only in 1981 in the case of Mexico and Tunisia, had a disastrous effect on countries that had introduced ambitious investment programmes on the basis of oil, phosphate or copper bonanzas. This change resulted in two reactions:

- Certain countries initially sought to counter the effects on growth of the deterioration in their exports by countermeasures such as increasing public expenditure. This was the case in Malaysia, in 1982-83, and in Tunisia, where the government accorded very substantial wage rises (the minimum wage was increased by 50 per cent). The main consequence of these measures was to increase the budget deficit considerably in all the countries. This was aggravated by the fall in tax revenues owing to the collapse of domestic economic activity. At the same time, the cost of servicing both external *and* domestic debt increased.

- Second, the monetary "balancing" of the mixed economies was transposed to the domestic level. Bolivia is a particularly good illustration. To palliate the collapse in export earnings from products of the Bolivian subsoil (in 1984, tin and natural gas accounted for nearly 90 per cent of total exports), the state and the public enterprises turned massively towards internal financing. Accordingly, their percentage share in total credits to the economy increased progressively, from 55 per cent in 1971-75 (with the central government taking 43.5 per cent of the total credits and the public enterprises 11.9 per cent) to more than 77 per cent in 1982-85 (respectively, 51.4 per cent and 25.7 per cent) (Dagnino-Pastore, 1991).

These two responses, which are often complementary, express the fragility of the functioning of mixed economies at both the productive and the financial levels. The rapid erosion after 1978 of the price of Ghana's main export, cocoa, had already considerably weakened the economy. Thus, in 1982 the income per inhabitant was 30 per cent less than in 1970, exports 52 per cent down, and imports reduced by 30 per cent. More than 2 million Ghanaians left the country (including many of the professional classes), and the infrastructure deteriorated substantially. Moreover, the crisis was exacerbated by the exceptional drought that struck the country in 1982-83.

In Bolivia, partly owing to the appreciable widening of the budget deficit and the monetary financing of that deficit, inflation rose to 25 000 per cent in 1985. In parallel, the fall in income per inhabitant had brought with it a reduction in tax revenues, and the investment rate fell to a historic minimum, at 5 per cent of GNP. The radical Bolivian programme of economic reforms was therefore adopted in the context of a totally weakened and drained economy.

In Jamaica, the GNP in 1980 stood at no more than three-quarters of its 1972 level. Moreover, in response to the rise in taxes on bauxite production, the foreign companies had reduced their production, aggravating the overall economic situation and widening the current balance deficit.

In Morocco, despite the recovery in phosphates prices in 1975-76, the 1973-77 Investment Plan which envisaged a tripling of public investments, was not revised downwards until the "pause" decided on in 1978. Two factors underlay this decision: a serious drought and the increase in military expenditure linked to the conflict in the Sahara. The awareness in 1978 of certain weaknesses in the Moroccan economy, sanctioned by a first agreement with the IMF, did not take the form of a general indictment of the development policy.

In the Philippines, the crisis exploded after the departure of a Chinese businessman, Dewey Dee, leaving $100 million of debts behind him. This event detonated a financial crisis, bringing into the light of day the virtually bankruptcy of the Philippine banking system, which was weakened by the numerous irrecoverable loans granted to the cronies of President Marcos. For many years, the banks had been kept afloat by systematic injections of funds from the Public Treasury and the Central Bank, which had refinanced themselves from hand to mouth by loans from international banks and by money creation. Such practices, which became generalised during the last years of the Marcos regime, considerably weakened the whole of the Philippine economy.

In the case of Chile, too, the crisis in 1981-82 took on a financial shape. The rise in the dollar and in interest rates revealed the fragility of the Chilean industrial and financial conglomerates, which had borrowed heavily from international banks to take advantage of the opportunities offered by the financial reforms of 1976. Through the Central Bank, the state came to the help of the banks by taking over their debts, establishing a favourable exchange rate for industrialists and authorising the transformation of dollar debts into pesos (Larain, 1989). The cost of this intervention between 1982 and 1985 is estimated at more than $7 billion, or 40 per cent of GDP for 1985 (Stallings, in Nelson, 1990a, p. 131). The numerous interventions by the Chilean government to prevent the bankruptcy of major private enterprises reinforced spectacularly the position of the public sector in the economy. The crisis in 1981-82 temporarily cancelled the government's privatisation and divestiture movement, which had prevailed between 1973 and 1981, as well as the economic progress (fall in unemployment, strong economic growth, diversification of exports) achieved during the same period (Yotopoulos, 1989).

According to different modalities from one country to another, the crisis took the form of a sudden and deep deterioration in the economic and financial situation, going well beyond a mere temporary recession. It is in this context of the virtual bankruptcy of the mixed economies that stabilization policies became essential.

Table 4

STABILIZATION PROGRAMMES AND MACROECONOMIC CONSTRAINTS

| | Year | Name of Programme | Stand-by Agreements (IMF) | Macroeconomic constraints |
|---|---|---|---|---|
| GHANA | April 1983 | Economic Recovery Programme (ERP) | August 1983 August 1984 October 1986 | - inflation (115% in 1981) - negative real growth rate of GDP (-7% in 1982) |
| MOROCCO | mid-1983 | | September 1983 February 1985 December 1986 | - public deficit (11.8% in 1982) - current account deficit (12.7% in 1982) |
| TUNISIA | August 1986 | Integration into the VIIth Plan | November 1986 | - current account deficit (18.3% in 1984) |
| BOLIVIA | August 1985 | New Economic Policy (NEP) "Pact for Democracy" | June 1986 | - public deficit (24% of GDP in 1984) - inflation (25 000% in 1985) |
| CHILE | end 1982 1985 | | January 1983 | - external deficit (14.5% of GDP in 1981) negative real growth of GDP (-14% in 1982) - external deficit (10.7% of GDP in 1984) |
| JAMAICA | 1977 1983 | | June 1979 April 1981 June 1984 July 1985 March 1987 | - public deficit (20% of GDP in 1977) - public deficit (19% of GDP in 1983) current account deficit (12.5% in 1982) - current account deficit (15.2% in 1985) continued growth of public borrowing |
| MEXICO | end 1982 mid-1986 | Immediate Programme for Economic Reorganisation (PIRE) then (PAC) then Economic Solidarity Pact (PSE) | January 1983 November 1986 | - public deficit (15.4% in 1982) - inflation (59% in 1982) |
| BANGLADESH | 1982 | New Industrial Policy (NIP) Revised Industrial Policy (RIP) | March 1983 December 1985 | - current account deficit (7.9% in 1981) real growth of GDP nil in 1982 |
| MALAYSIA | end 1982 | | February 1983 December 1984 October 1986 | - public deficit (16.1% in 1982) current account deficit (13.4% in 1982) - current account deficit (7.9% in 1982-83) massive flight of capital |
| PHILIPPINES | end 1983 | | | |

88

## B. The stabilization policies

The aim of the stabilization programmes was, in principle, clearly defined: reducing the strong inflationary pressures and settling the imbalances of the public finances and the external accounts by measures aimed at checking domestic demand, both private and public. The fight against inflation involved the reduction of the budget deficit, which resulted in drastic cuts in public expenditure and, consequently, a weakening of the state's customary means of intervention. The re-establishment of external balance followed the same lines: reduction of domestic absorption, heavy devaluation of the national currency, a change in commercial policies in favour of the promotion of exports and to the detriment of protectionist mechanisms. In brief, the stabilization policies were in keeping with economic and monetary orthodoxy (Haggard & Kaufman, 1988; Bienen & Waterbury, 1989).

By definition, stabilization policies, whose time scale is short-term, do not depend directly on rebalancing. In addition, until recently the experiences of stabilization in the developing countries had not generally been followed by a major revision of the logic of the functioning of mixed economies. The development of the concept of stabilization, as recommended by the IMF since the mid-1980s, has changed this situation. The framework of conditionality has been made more flexible: the IMF grants the states longer periods for implementing programmes. At the same time, co-operation between the IMF and the World Bank has increased — not without tension between the two organisations — with a view to providing better linkage between stabilization programmes and structural adjustment. Under these circumstances, the choice of economic orthodoxy during the 1980s is no longer viewed as a temporary measure but has been extended into an in-depth reform of the mixed economies, thus leading to a reconsideration of the respective position of the public and private sectors.

Table 4 shows that interventions by the IMF increased during 1982-83. Its agreements with the governments of the developing countries had to be renewed, which is evidence of the strong domestic resistance to economic and financial austerity policies. The resistance came either from the governments, owing to their reluctance to implement certain parts of the programme, or from the legitimate fears of a large sector of the population faced with a virtually certain deterioration in their living standards. It must be taken into consideration in assessing the likelihood of the success of stabilization and, beyond this, of rebalancing.

The Philippines illustrates of the governments' problems in agreeing to the conditionality of credit lines granted by the IMF. In 1982, a first stand-by agreement had been suspended, as the Philippine government had neither reduced its short-term borrowing from the international banks nor slowed the growth in the money supply. In April 1985, the IMF decided once again to suspend the second tranche of the loan then in course, after noting that the government had not kept its undertakings to reduce public expenditure. The last tranches were released on the basis of the

89

government's commitment to end agricultural subsidies, carry out tax reform and liberalise foreign trade. As soon as the IMF released the funds, however, President Marcos announced the long-awaited elections and postponed the promised reforms indefinitely, which leads one to wonder how serious his earlier undertakings really were.

In other countries in the sample, such as Morocco, Ghana, Jamaica and Mexico, the governments' attitude towards stabilization policies was totally different, because it coincided with their economic stance. The application of these policies, however, did give rise to major protest movements from within the population (in Morocco in 1981, in Tunisia in 1984, in Jamaica in 1985, etc.).

From 1978, the Moroccan government had adopted some initial stabilization measures but had produced no significant results. The 1983 agreement with the IMF and the World Bank, which was much wider and more restrictive, was therefore an extension of the earlier policy. Similarly, the two stand-by agreements signed by the Ghanaian government in 1982 were integrated into the National Recovery Programme aimed at halting the deterioration of the economy.

In Jamaica, the economic programme of the conservative candidate Seaga, the winner of the 1980 elections, was broadly inspired by monetary principles. In 1981 an agreement was signed with the IMF, followed by a second one in 1983. The results achieved up to 1985 proved extremely disappointing. The growth rate was still low, and the budget deficit, which amounted to 16 per cent of the GNP in 1981-82, had been only slightly reduced (14.2 per cent in 1985). Exports of bauxite and aluminium continued to decline following the disengagement of the foreign companies, their level in 1985 standing at 60 per cent of that achieved in 1980. Lastly, despite a 43 per cent currency devaluation in real terms, the trade balance was still in substantial deficit. The violent riots against the stabilization policy did not prevent the signature of a new programme in 1986, however.

The experience in Bolivia has a number of similarities to that in Jamaica in that the application of the stabilization measures came up against determined opposition from local political forces. It was not until August 1985, when the Paz Estensorro government passed "Supreme Decree 21060" adopting a radical "New Economic Policy" aimed at reducing the serious imbalances in the economy (hyperinflation, insolvency of the Bolivian government characterised by the suspension of servicing its external debt in 1984). This sudden and total change in stance included a number of very liberal measures in the general context of a structural adjustment programme, such as the lifting of price, foreign trade and wage restrictions. This policy, deemed by international economists to be one of the successes of abrupt stabilization policies, had positive effects as regards the fight against inflation and the rescheduling of Bolivian debt. On the other hand, wages and employment dropped, the balance of trade and public finance deficits increased. In July 1987, the publication of Supreme Decree 21660 relating to "economic reactivation", which emphasized public

90

investment (68 per cent of the total for the period 1987-89), seemed to call into question the liberalising trend. The state reaffirmed its leading role in the management of the economy; the only notable difference was a more marked stance in favour of exports.

The only country in the sample for which one can speak of a sustainable return to economic and monetary rigour is Mexico, along with Chile in the 1970s. The economic difficulties that countries had to cope with in 1982 led the new president, de la Madrid, to give priority to the fight against inflation. Three programmes were launched successively between 1982 and the end of 1987 before significant results were achieved: the PIRE (Programa Immediato de Reordinacion Economica), the PAC (Programa de Aliento y Crecimiento) and the PSE (Pacto de Solidaridad Economica). Whereas the PIRE took its inspiration from strict monetary principles, the PSE, launched in December 1987, was more heterodox in that it was principally based on a dialogue between the various social groups, aimed at agreement relating to a wage, price and public pricing freeze. This second approach proved the most effective, as the inflation of prices fell from 15 per cent in January 1988 to 1.5 per cent in July of the same year.

At the end of this rapid overview of stabilization policies, it is difficult to conclude with certainty that all the countries are now converted to the virtues of neo-liberalism. In many cases the change in direction has had to conquer fairly strong resistance, the results have remained fragile and the states finally agreed to reduce their field of intervention only because the crisis they faced had reached unbearable levels.

The choice of economic and financial orthodoxy is an important turning-point, however, in that the adoption of economic stabilization policies foreshadowed that of structural adjustment policies and policies for rebalancing the public and private sectors. This changeover from stabilization to rebalancing has at least three causes:

- In the first place, it showed that the implementation of stabilization programmes marked the end of the financing of public deficits by money creation. The monetary rigour prescribed by the IMF, supported by public and private, bilateral and multilateral lenders of funds, eliminated domestic sources of financing represented by money creation, resort to local public sector banks and government loan issues in the national currency. In view of the reduction in surpluses achieved by public enterprises in the commodities exporting sector, as well as the limits imposed on international bank borrowing (both the available financing and the cost of obtaining such loans), the states found themselves totally unable to finance the public enterprises' losses. The adoption of strict budgetary financing rules drew attention back to the main parties responsible for the public deficits, in particular to the public and parapublic enterprises. In this respect, the stabilization policies underlined the "pathological" nature of the financing conditions of the 1970s. Here too we find the two other turning-points in the changeover from stabilization to rebalancing: the application of economic policies over time and the necessary revision of the mixed economy models that had prevailed up to then.

– Second, it is worth emphasizing that the interventions by the IMF and the World Bank were overlapping more and more (Kahler, in Nelson, 1990a). This increasing blurring of the distinction between economic stabilization policies and structural adjustment policies resulted from a twofold movement. On the one hand, it consisted of the lengthening and maintenance over time of stabilization programmes, owing to both the difficulty of actually reducing economic and financial imbalances in the developing countries and the resistance of part of the population to the social costs. On the other hand, the short-term component of adjustment programmes, especially those undertaken at the sectoral level, has to be taken into account. The overlapping of the recommendations of the IMF and the World Bank, which had in fact generated a certain amount of tension between the two bodies, indicated the increasing link between the various levels of intervention. For example, sustainable stabilization of inflationary pressures or of the foreign trade balance cannot be achieved unless a liberalisation of price controls or restrictions on movements of goods and services is applied effectively. The actual relation between stabilization and adjustment is imposed by the type of structures and economic relationships involved.

– Lastly, the restricted choice of stabilization has no doubt caused or accelerated the awareness of the structural mismatches of mixed economies. From this point of view, it led to questioning the dynamics of the previous development model and, hence, the responsibilities of the main protagonists in this dynamics: the state and the public enterprises. This does not mean, however, that rebalancing can be reduced to a redrawing of the boundary between the public and private sectors: it represents a more profound change based on a new method of running the mixed economies. In the past, stabilization policies have often been simple interludes that did not call into question the logic of the previous functioning of the economy. The beginning of the 1980s was characterised by an in-depth transformation of the mixed economies based on market mechanisms and domestic and foreign competition.

Accordingly, the rebalancing process cannot be limited to an action aimed at reducing the public sector, since the mediocre performance of that sector seems not to have been the main cause of the breakdown of the mixed economy system but simply a manifestation of that breakdown. Thus rebalancing does not boil down to stabilization policies, which would amount to giving priority to exclusively short-term objectives in a situation where the very logic of the functioning of mixed economies is under indictment.

The extent to which the traditional functioning of mixed economies is reformed and the transition to a modern economy achieved depends on the programmes that liberalise market mechanisms. Their aim is a return to allocation of resources based on market criteria and is situated in the extension of the stabilization measures. There is no doubt that the keystone of this process is to open up the economy and make domestic markets subject to competition. In this context lies the whole importance of reducing the portfolio of public assets.

### The changeover to an open market economy, a new framework of reference for development policies

The economic and financial liberalisation policies, the keystones of the adjustment programmes, are aimed at directing economies towards a system of regulation based on competitive markets. By liberalising the conditions of economic activity, they seek to establish, or re-establish, a propitious environment for achieving economic decisions based on market rationality. The basic paradigm of the new rationality is the pre-eminence of competition, whether domestic or international. The generalisation of arguments in terms of efficiency and comparative advantages in the developing countries stems from acceptance of the rules of the open market economy. The freeing of prices for goods and services, deregulation of the labour market, the abandonment of "financial repression", the elimination of subsidies, the suppression of domestic rent-seekers — and, generally, of a whole set of economic and financial distortions — are the means of re-establishing coherent and adequate price indicators. The restoration of these indicators will enable better decision-making, especially in the area of productive investments. It is presumed that this behaviour will increase the efficiency of the economy and also encourage its integration into the world economy, by means of specialisation in accordance with the comparative advantages that are finally revealed.

This perception of liberalisation should be closely associated with the dominant interpretation of international organisations such as the IMF and the World Bank, in the field of development strategies. Indeed, the aim of linking stabilization and adjustment is to call the former mixed economy models strongly into question. Liberalisation is thus an essential addition to the stabilization policies, leading to growth that is both sustainable, because it is obtained through better resource allocation in the economy, and balanced, because it complies with internal and external financial constraints.

Strengthening the role of competition involves the adaptation of all enterprises in the developing countries, whether public or private. Domestic and international liberalisation in fact means that the distortions and behaviour characteristic of the old method of functioning will be, if not completely eliminated, at least attacked. This alteration of the economic and financial environment is extremely important to both the functioning of the enterprises and the general stance of development policy.

## A. Reform of the overall functioning of the economy

In order to achieve the changeover from a mixed economy — more or less dominated by the public authorities, more or less integrated into the world economy — to an open market economy, it seems essential to master the transition process politically and technically. Indeed, the scale of the reforms makes it advisable to consider, first of all, the sequence of the structural reforms and the speed at which they should be introduced. This introductory presentation will, then, enable a clearer interpretation of the real achievements by the developing countries in our sample in the context of this systemic transition.

### 1. The implementation of the transition

The conclusions derived from the experiences of the developing countries (collapse of development models based on a heavy weight of regulations and import substitution, fascination with the successes of the newly industrialising countries) and those derived from the liberal development model now in vogue[7] suggest that there is no longer any real discussion of the reasons for liberalisation. An example of this state of mind is Michaely's article (1986) on the speed and sequence of the reforms aimed at liberalising international trade; the author stresses in his introduction that "it has been demonstrated on several occasions ... that opening economies up to free trade leads to a higher income level and a higher growth rate. The fact that liberalisation policies are desirable should therefore be deemed to be established" (p. 42). Freed from the constraints of justification, the theoretical analysis concentrates on implementing liberalisation policies. Three conclusions can be drawn from all these theoretical studies, most of which focus on the Latin American region during the 1970s (mainly Argentina, Chile and Uruguay)[8].

i) Liberalisation should be undertaken after stabilization of the economy has been achieved. As Michalopoulos underlines (1987), "structural adjustment is easier if it takes place in a stable macroeconomic environment, especially with inflation under control" (p. 25). However, the appropriate moment for liberalisation remains to be determined.

ii) The sequence of liberalisation reforms is important for at least two reasons. First, the changeover from a non-liberal economy to a market economy calls for the elimination of many controls and restrictions limiting the action of competitive forces on various markets (final products, intermediate consumer goods, factors of production, capital goods). The interaction among the existing distortions creates complex situations when the time comes for them to be eliminated. Thus, over-regulation of the labour market increases the cost of the labour factor, which combined with import restrictions encourages the development of import substitution activities that are very capital-intensive. As A. Krueger emphasizes, however, "it is clear that one and the same liberalisation measure may produce different effects depending on the situations prevailing on the other markets within an economy, and that an analysis of the impact of liberalisation on a market at a given moment may lead to erroneous conclusions" (1987, p. 21). By way of example, if restrictions on inputs are lifted before restrictions on final products, the effect will be an increase in actual protection of national producers. Likewise, "the liberalisation of the inputs market at the domestic level should take place before other reforms in that, unless there is an improvement in input mobility, the potential advantages of the reforms on the products market will not be able to be achieved" (Michalopoulos, 1987, p. 27). These considerations are particularly important insofar as there are many liberalisation measures, which affect most of the markets within an economy. Next, the reversal of liberalisation policies can be costly in social terms; the sequence of the reforms and the speed of their introduction should therefore be gauged to limit the risks of reversibility (Calvo, 1987)[9].

iii) There has been much discussion of the sequence between international liberalisation of movements of goods and services and that of capital movements. In fact, one must take a third factor into account, the development of the real exchange rate, which complicates the argument considerably. Real depreciation of the exchange rate is supposed to enable a modification in the composition of production, and hence in the use of available resources, in favour of goods that can be traded on the international market. The exchange rate, which is sometimes used in economic stabilization policies as part of the fight against inflation (cf. the example of Chile from 1978 to 1981), reacts to trends in external trade, at the level both of goods and services and of capital. It therefore appears to be a mirror of overall coherence and, hence, of the credibility of the various measures undertaken by the reforming governments[10].

Two arguments are usually advanced in favour of liberalising goods and services first of all:

a) As investment decisions and the price of assets are distorted by price controls and trade restrictions, the liberalisation of capital movements will increase internal distortions (Edwards & Wijnbergen, 1986, p. 147);

b) capital movements have a much greater relative speed of adjustment compared to their underlying determinants than do movements of goods. The economic fabric responds much more slowly to the opening of the international market of goods and services. The

95

liberalisation of capital movements on the exchange rate might prove counterproductive as regards integration into the international market. However, certain authors, including Lal (1987), are in dissent.

## 2. The liberalisation measures

The increase in the number of factors likely to affect the expected results of one measure taken in isolation considerably limits the ability of these theoretical studies to make political recommendations. Depending on the macroeconomic context, the progress in stabilization and the measures aimed at liberalising the domestic markets, the same measure taken in different contexts may produce opposing results. Papageoriou, Michaely and Choski (1990), in a study of 37 liberalisation policies in 19 developing countries, reach similar conclusions. In fact, empirical studies on a significant number of experiences show that to a great extent it is the context that determines the effectiveness of one liberalisation measure or another.

Although it is difficult to discuss the sequences of liberalisation measures in the sample countries, it seems important to present the scale of liberalisation undertaken in certain countries, by means of several tables. We have already emphasized that economic and financial liberalisation calls into question the philosophy of the mixed economy model. Import substitution gives way to promotion of exports, and state intervention on the inputs market is reduced to accord more space to market forces. The tables 5-8 highlight the major efforts in liberalisation undertaken in all the sample countries. Priority is given to four areas: international trade in goods and services, internal and external capital movements, the goods and factors markets, foreign investment codes.

These tables make it clear that the implementation of these measures has a profound effect on the functioning of mixed economies. Therefore, they call for a reform of the main protagonists of the old system: the public sector enterprises. In order to adapt this sector to the new economic and financial conditions, the state pursues three main objectives: reorganising the public sector's financial situation, providing for its refocusing and modernisation with an emphasis on the strategic sectors and privatising some of the public enterprises.

## B. The reform of the functioning of the public sector

To achieve this reform of the public sector, governments first have to remedy their profound ignorance of the economic and financial results of the public and parapublic enterprises (or even their inability to enumerate the enterprises within their sphere of influence). To this end, in all the developing countries the state has submitted the main part of the public sector to an evaluation of economic and financial performance (accounting and financial audit, valuation of assets). With the political and financial support of the World Bank, the states wish to obtain these data in order to implement the first stages of privatisation, but above all to draw up an overall policy for restructuring the public sector. To organise this overall reform, two criteria of assessment were used: the strategic importance of the enterprise[11] and its economic and financial viability. By combining these two criteria used by the governments and the World Bank (see Table 9), one obtains four cases that call for a specific type of action (rehabilitation, modernisation, privatisation and liquidation) (see Shirley, 1989, p. 14). In this perspective, restructuring and privatisation immediately appear to be complementary measures to the reform of the public sector, over and above the rebalancing process. The complementary effect of the various rebalancing actions will be dealt with in Chapter 4 of this study.

The other measures for reforming the public sector, the *merger* of public enterprises or the *abolition* of those which existed only in a formal legal sense, do not necessarily affect the real economy[12]. They have been used, particularly in Mexico, because they are a way of both artificially reducing the number of public enterprises and concentrating administrative and financial control in a limited number of entities.

In restructuring public enterprises, the state, by maintaining its status as sole or principal shareholder, seeks to reinforce its effective control over their management[13]. Consequently, it assumes administrative and financial responsibility for modernising the public sector. This policy is applied to all the public enterprises, but with various end purposes:

i) In the "strategic sectors", for which state intervention is deemed exclusive or a matter of priority, the public enterprises must be adapted to the new economic and financial constraints. This adaptation, which supposes that social objectives are left to one side, takes the form of an attempt to apply market rationality in the management of the enterprise. It is necessary in order to ward off criticisms relating to the burden on the budget and the inefficiency of the state sector.

ii) Restructuring also concerns public enterprises destined for privatisation and more specifically for transfer of ownership. Two reasons can be advanced: on the one hand, it is easier to transfer ownership of a restructured public enterprise that is reorganised and earning profits; on the other hand, the state can derive higher income from the transfer operation. In Jamaica and Bangladesh, the restructuring of public enterprises is expressly considered to be a precondition of any privatisation. It nonetheless seems essential, when assessing the financial impact of privatising a restructured enterprise, to take into account the financial cost to the state of the restructuring.

Actions undertaken with a view to restructuring public enterprises, necessary as they are, are both difficult and costly, essentially from the viewpoint of the results realised.

*Table 5:* **MEASURES FOR LIBERALISATION OF FOREIGN TRADE**

**Ghana**

Customs duties are fairly uniform and not high (between 0 and 25%), but protection is provided by specific dues on imports.
1988: Simplification of these import dues, four rates are applied (5%, 10%, 25% and 35%). The system of import licences is now linked to sale of foreign currency by auction. Market exchange rate for all transactions. Liberalisation accompanied by very heavy real depreciation of the cedi between 1983 and 1987.

**Morocco**

As from 1983, gradual elimination of preliminary authorisation.
1984: Customs duty ceiling of 100%, then 60%, elimination of virtually all export certificates, liberalisation of exports of food products. In 1985, protection by means of quotas is partially replaced by tariffs.
1987: Customs duty ceiling fixed at 45%, new exports code.
1988-89: Creation of the Société marocaine de l'assurance à l'exportation.
Liberalisation accompanied, between 1983 and 1985, by a 25% real depreciation of the dirham. Between 1986 and 1987, real exchange rate stabilized, followed by a weak real appreciation over the period 1988-89.

**Tunisia**

1986: Gradual reduction of pressure on exports (elimination of import quotas and customs duties).
1987: Gradual reduction of customs duties (maximum fell from 200% to 41% and minimum from 5% to 1%).
1989: Average customs duty is now 27%, close to the target fixed by the government in 1986 (25% in 1991). Liberalisation accompanied by a real depreciation of the dinar by 15% in 1986 and by 12% in 1987. Stability in real terms since 1988.

**Bolivia**

1985: *Ex abrupto* replacement of the complex system of protection by uniform customs duty fixed at 20%. Next, gradual reduction to the rate of 10%. All products can be imported freely, apart from sugar, medecines and goods affecting state security. In order to avoid underbilling and overbilling, the government appointed two foreign enterprises to control these operations (one British and one French). Country non-member of the GATT, but a member of the Latin American Integration Association (ALADI). In 1986, very heavy real depreciation (nearly 70%) of the boliviano, low annual depreciation since 1987 (new acceleration in 1990).

*Table 5* (continued)

Chile

1974: Radical simplification of the imports regime (customs duties ranged from 0% to 750% and tariff barriers applied to more than 5 000 products). Reduction of customs duties by an average of 105% to 69%, and, in 1976, elimination of all non-tariff barriers.

1977: Withdrawal from the Andean Pact; customs duties are between 10% and 35%.

1979: Adoption of a single customs duty of 10%, adoption of a system of fixed exchange rates.

1984: Raising of customs duties to 35% following the economic crisis in 1982.

From 1985-1990: *Gradual* reduction of customs duties to 15%.

As from 1976, the exchange rate has been used for purposes of economic stabilization (revaluation to reduce inflation, "active crawling peg", tablita, then fixed exchange rates). In 1982, the system of fixed exchange rates was abandoned owing to the very high appreciation of the peso in real terms. Real depreciation was of the order of 20% per annum in 1985 and 1986. Stabilization since 1988.

Jamaica

Abolition of import quotas and reduction of customs duties to about 20 to 30% for most products. Member of CARICOM. Real depreciation of the Jamaican dollar 30% in 1984, then 10% in 1985. Slight appreciation since 1986.

Mexico

1985: Elimination of quotas for half the goods produced domestically.

1986: Membership of the GATT, whilst import licences still applied to 92% of production.

1988: Quotas relate only to 23% of products; marginal customs duty is reduced from 100% to 40% (in 1987) then to 20%, and the number of rates fell from 11 to 5; the import prices of reference (a non-tariff barrier) affect a smaller number of goods.

1989: Abolition of import licences; the average customs duty is 10.5%.

*Gradual* reduction of customs duties, quotas and export licences.

After a period of high real appreciation of the peso between 1983 and 1985, the liberalisation movement was facilitated by the weakness of the peso in 1986-87. Since 1988, there has been a tendency towards low real appreciation owing to the weakness of the dollar. Slight depreciation in 1990.

*Table 5 (end)*

**Bangladesh**

1985: First measures adopted, change from a list of free products to a list of products subject to import controls ("Control List"). Up to now, *limited progress* on reduction of quantitative restrictions and on customs duties (range of duties from 0 to 400%; 60% of textile products imported are taxed at more than 100%; distortion to the detriment of imported finished products remains in most sectors). System of very restrictive import licences. After a period of high real appreciation of the exchange rate at the beginning of the 1980s, corrected in 1985-86, a slight depreciation continued in 1987-88, supporting non-traditional exports. The 11% appreciation of the taka, in 1989, called into question the competitiveness achieved by flexible exchange-rate management.

**Malaysia**

The recommendations of the Special Action Committee on Tariffs helped to clarify and harmonise tariff protection. Reduction of customs duty was applied for agricultural products, intermediate goods and capital goods. Amendment of the law on "copyrights" (1987) to adjust it to international standards. Very rapid growth in exports of manufactured products (which now represent more than half of exports).
Slow depreciation of the ringgit since 1984, less than 10% as an annual average rate.

**Philippines**

Liberalisation undertaken as from 1979 but partially called into question in 1983-85, owing to the balance-of-payments crisis. Between 1985 and 1990, two-thirds (1 300 out of 2 000) of import restrictions were revised. The nominal rate of protection has changed but little since 1982, remaining stable in the region of 22%, but with a greater convergence of rates (reduction of marginal rates and increase of lower rates). More than 19 000 products from ASEAN benefit from a 50% reduction in customs duties. The acceleration of the liberalisation movement in 1985 was coupled by a 20% depreciation of the peso in 1986 (following a real appreciation of 10% in 1985). Stability between 1987 and 1990.

*Table 6:* FINANCIAL LIBERALISATION MEASURES

| Country | Measures |
|---|---|
| Ghana | As from 1983, restrictions on interest rate and sectoral credit allocations were eliminated in order to obtain a positive real interest rate. Gradual rise of nominal interest rates, raising the rates on bank savings deposits from 8% to 21.5% in 1989. Interest rates remain negative by about 10 points in 1989. Exchange rate unified in 1983. |
| Morocco | The main aim of the reforms was to increase financial savings. To this end, between 1983 and 1987, obligatory reserves on fixed deposits were eliminated; the maximum volumes of credits granted by the banks are now calculated on the basis of deposits; interest rates were liberalised and became positive in real terms. In addition, mandatory investments (at low interest rates) in treasury bills and securities issued by the public institutions, up to 40% of fixed deposits, were eliminated. |
| Tunisia | 1987: Elimination of need for authorisation from the Central Bank for the grant of loans by deposit-collecting banks, of the obligation (often by-passed) to lend 43% of deposits to the public sector or on long-term loans, but also increase in subsidised rates and liberalisation of interest rates. 1988: Creation of certificates of deposit (nominal divided by five in 1989). Virtually all direct controls over financial and banking activities have been eliminated. Modernisation of the Bourse des valeurs mobilières (BVM – the Securities Exchange). |
| Bolivia | 1985: Derestriction of interest rates and abolition of subsidised rates. Financial system remains restricted by the lack of national savings and uncertainty regarding the macroeconomic situation. Dollar operations facilitated for banks and residents (grant of loans, opening of accounts, etc.). Unification of exchange rates and sale by bidding under the control of the Central Bank. Despite the efforts at supervising banks, their liquidity and solvency remained poor. Reorganisation limited to date. |
| Chile | 1974-75: Derestriction of interest rates, fixing of a debt-equity ratio and liberalisation of equity purchase in banks. Unification of exchange rates following frequent devaluations. 1977: The banks are authorised to intermediate equity purchase for a monthly total of 5% of their capital and reserves. 1979-80: Reduction of prudential control over external operations. 1983: Massive intervention by the Central Bank to support the insolvent financial system. Subsequently, reinforcement of prudential control and adoption of adequate banking laws. Restriction imposed on admission to the foreign-exchange markets until 1984. |

*Table 6* (continued)

**Mexico**

As from 1988, the banks were made to compete with other financial intermediaries, determination by the banks of their interest rates, reduction of coefficients of obligatory reserves in order to increase the liquidity of the banking sector. Open market operations on state securities or public companies become the main instrument of monetary control. Since 1989, foreign investors may purchase shares at the Mexico Stock Exchange by means of "neutral" holding companies, but they may not have voting rights.

**Bangladesh**

Efforts at liberalisation dating from 1984 were called into question in 1986 by difficulties in the banking system (due to inadequate recovery of loans granted). The measures, taken in 1987, to increase the rate of recovery by the financial institutions had very limited results. The insurance sector was opened up in 1984 to private companies with appreciable success.

1987-88: Progress towards unification of the exchange rate.

1989: Measures adopted enabling the banks to fix their interest rates within limits imposed by the Central Bank; ceilings on credit were eliminated, discounting conditions facilitated, and rules relating to balance-sheet management by banks clarified. Efforts at recapitalising banks.

**Malaysia**

The reduction of the intensity of the credit-control policy, coupled with a high increase in foreign capital flows, increased the liquidity of the financial sector and increased the supply of funds for lending to the private sector by market mechanisms. The Kuala Lumpur Stock Exchange is very dynamic; financial innovation is increasing (opening of a market for bonds issued by private companies, futures markets).

1989: Vote of the law relating to financial and banking institutions, which clarifies and strengthens prudential control exercised by the Central Bank. Liberalisation of interest rates. Obligatory reserves in public securities were made more flexible. The segmentation between the money market and the capital market was reduced.

**Philippines**

The reforms undertaken to develop bank transformation mechanisms (reduction of obligatory reserves for long-term loans, restructuring of the Development Bank of the Philippines) came up against the fragmented and mono-professional structure of the Philippine banking sector.

Exchange control regulations have been gradually made more flexible since 1984, notably the transfer of foreign currency from the banking system to the Central Bank.

## Table 7: MARKET DEREGULATION MEASURES

| Country | Measures |
|---|---|
| Ghana | Price controls limited to 23 products in 1983, 17 products in 1984 and 8 products in 1985 (imported rice, sugar, baby food, cement, textiles, medicines, matches and soap). |
| Morocco | Undertaken in 1981, the liberalisation of prices of consumer goods (in 1982 and 1985, it applied to food products) and capital goods, following the reduction of public subsidies. Elimination of preliminary homologation of prices. The controls remain in force for basic products, public services and goods for which there is little competition. |
| Tunisia | 60% of agricultural and industrial prices are free of control, as against 5% in 1986. |
| Bolivia | Derestriction of prices apart from goods produced by the public sector and services recognised to be utilities. Elimination of powers of control by the Ministry of Labour and the trades unions over wage agreements, indexing of wages and minimum wages. Fixing of a very low minimum wage ($25 per month). Very heavy reduction in real wages in the public sector. |
| Chile | 1973: Elimination of all rigidities on the labour market (unions prohibited and indexation of wages now on a case-by-case basis breaking with the collective bargaining agreements). Decree 522 frees *ex abrupto* most prices of goods and services, apart from 33 regulated products (food, raw materials, etc.) and 18 supervised products. 1979: New Labour Code re-establishing certain protection for employees relating to dismissal and fixing wages. Reintroduction of indexation at 100% of noted inflation. 1982: Abandonment of indexation, deregulation of the market. Unemployment rate close to the natural rate in 1990 after five years' increase. |
| Mexico | 1985: Reduction of price controls (apart from a few products regulated by SECOFI or other public bodies, basic foodstuffs, sugar, oil and petrochemicals, in the context of the Social Pact). In 1986, 80% of the prices were freed. Gradual reduction of price differentials between the domestic and international markets (fertilizers, oil, steel). Deregulation of road transport and opening of petrochemicals to the private sector. Substantial reduction in real wages between 1988 and 1989. |

Table 8: MEASURES RELATING TO FOREIGN INVESTMENT CODES

Ghana

1985: Creation of the Ghana Investment Centre to centralise control over foreign investments; many incentives, particularly in the transfer of profits, are provided in sectors deemed priorities. Minerals Commission concentrates on the key sector of exploitation of mineral resources. Signature of an agreement with the Multilateral Investment Guarantee Agency, a subsidiary of the World Bank.

Morocco

The Investment Code, adopted in 1983, was revised in 1989, the increase in the number of tax incentives resulting in a very complex and relatively harmful system. For example, incentives relating to accelerated depreciation and subsidisation of interest rates (for the region of Casablanca) were eliminated. In June 1989, the principle of making authorisations of investments automatic two months after their filing with the authorities was instituted; at the end of this period, if no reply has been received from the authorities, this will be deemed to indicate their consent. Grounds for refusals must be given.

Tunisia

1987: Adoption of a new Investment Code in the industrial sector characterised by the elimination of prior approval, exemption from taxes (for 3 to 7 years) and from customs duty (depending on the firm's activity) and financial assistance. These incentives are bigger if the foreign enterprise is involved in export.
1988: Similar code adopted for agricultural activities.

Bolivia

Foreign investments are controlled by the Carthaginian agreement relating to joint ventures and investment periods. Investments remain concentrated in the mining sector and mainly come from the United States. At the end of 1985, signature of an agreement with the Multilateral Investment Guarantee Agency in order to stimulate foreign investments.

Chile

1977: Adoption of a very liberal investment code (Decree 600). There are no more limits on foreign holdings in Chilean enterprises, transfers of profits may be made as from the first year, and repatriation of capital at the end of three years (the conditions are more restrictive in the case of investments financed by debt conversions, Chapter 19). Income in foreign currency may be deposited on accounts abroad (the balance, after the appropriate withholding in respect of transfers of profits, must be brought back to Chile), in order to increase investors' confidence. Lastly, foreign companies have the choice between a rate of profits tax, either fixed at 49.5% for the next ten years, or at the same rate as local enterprises (35% since 1988). In 1985, certain provisions of Decree 600 were amended, in particular those relating to investment periods (extended to 20 years in the mining and industrial sectors).

Table 8 (continued)

Jamaica

Two provisions are aimed at attracting foreign investors (Industrial Incentives Act and the Export Industry Encouragement Law) by granting profits-tax reductions for nine and ten years respectively, but also import of inputs without customs duty during the same period. The effects of such measures are limited, however.

Mexico

1984-86: Foreign holding may attain 100% in the nine major sectors of the economy: capital equipment and machinery, chemicals, high technology, tourism, etc. Simplification of administrative procedures, reducing the time limits for acceptance by half and increasing the likelihood of acceptance. Important foreign investment movement towards the *maquiladoras* in the industrial sector.

1986-88: Debt-equity swaps programme for financing IDE (discount tolerated up to 30%), left on the back burner since Salinas.

Bangladesh

1987-88: Implementation of measures aimed at attracting foreign investments in the non-traditional export areas: elimination of import restrictions for export ativities (Duty Exemption/Drawback Office), guarantee on the second market variable depending on the type of exports in the context of the Export Performance Benefit (100% for non-traditional exports), financial advantages. Joint ventures with public enterprises are now possible; they are no longer obligatory with private enterprises.

Malaysia

Under the aegis of the Malaysian Industrial Development Authority, the procedures are simplified with the adoption of the "single counter". The control function is replaced by a promotion function. In 1988, foreign holdings can attain 100% of the equity capital of an enterprise exporting at least 20% of its output, or in the tourism sector. The foreign banks must create subsidiaries, then transfer more than 30% of their capital to Malay interests between now and 1994, in exchange for which they will have the possibility of developing their network and collecting funds from the public institutions.

Philippines

1987: Adoption of the Omnibus Code, a compilation of the various laws and incentives relating to IDE. However, the complex acceptance procedures remain in force, foreign holdings are limited to 40% (apart from exports and newly fledged industries) and incentives are fairly unattractive compared to the other countries in the region. Debt-assets swap programmes, launched in 1986, were victims of their own success.

Table 9

METHODS OF REFORMING THE PUBLIC SECTOR

| | Enterprise economically and financially viable | Enterprise economically and financially unviable |
|---|---|---|
| Strategic activities | Restructuring/ modernisation | Restructuring/ rehabilitation |
| Non-strategic activities | Privatisation | Liquidation |

## 1. A difficult solution to implement

The restructuring of public enterprises is based on the criticisms aimed at their method of operation. They can be grouped into four categories: a) a variety of management objectives (Ayub & Hegstad, 1983; Shirley, 1985), b) the financial cost of pursuing social objectives, c) interference by politicians in the enterprises' decision-making bodies (extravagant projects, non-economic reasoning), d) inadequate control by the shareholder (the state) over the managers of public enterprises.

The answers supplied to these problems in all the developing countries converge towards a more precise definition of management objectives: increasing autonomy in management and strengthening the state's control of economic and financial performance.

The public enterprises' new management objectives are now very clear: reduction of operating losses and, where applicable, realisation of net profits. To this end, the state grants greater autonomy of management in *employment policy* (possibility of making part of the surplus work-force redundant), *investment policy* (investment selection criteria based on economic and financial profitability) and *pricing policy* (range of price increases to achieve a satisfactory system of relative prices). As regards the pricing policy, all the sample countries have substantially increased the price of certain goods or services (rail transport, water, electricity, fertilizers, oil), in accordance with the policy of liberalising prices to reduce the number of controlled and subsidised prices. In addition, by exercising stricter control over borrowing levels, the state-shareholder hopes to obtain a satisfactory return on its investment in equity capital.

The change in the objectives and management criteria of the public enterprises, by bringing economic and financial considerations to the fore, reduces the importance of non-economic objectives. The *raison d'être* of the public enterprises, as conceived in the mixed economy models founded on the achievement of social objectives and national independence, is thus implicitly called into question. Over and above the privatisation of part of the public sector, the restructuring and modernisation of public enterprises attempt to reform completely their operating methods in order to adapt them to the new demands derived from the increasing openness to domestic and foreign competition and the continuation of financing constraint. Restructuring is therefore an essential component of rebalancing as defined in this study, in other words, concerning not only the redistribution of roles and responsibilities between the public and private sectors, but also the change in functioning of the public sector.

Two complementary types of agreement, one relating to the public sector as a whole, the other to a public enterprise individually, try to provide a more or less formal framework for restructuring the public sector.

i) The various loans granted by the World Bank — Structural Adjustment Loans (SAL), Technical Assistance Loans (TAL) and more recently Public Enterprise Loans (PEL) — carry conditions relating to the reform of public enterprises. Between 1978 and June 1988, 122 operations of this kind were approved by the World Bank (Shirley, 1989). Between June 1988 and June 1989, 24 new programmes were financed, reflecting the interest in this question (Galal, 1990). For example, Bolivia (June 1989, $35 million), Ghana, Morocco, Tunisia (July 1989, $130 million), Jamaica (May 1989, $35 million), Mexico (June 1989, $500 million) and the Philippines benefited from specific loans to facilitate the adaptation of the public sector firms' productive structures[14]. The main items in the proposed reforms follow the lines specified above, highlighting, from the first phase of the reform, the clarification of the financial relationship between the state and the public enterprises (payment of cross arrears). These reforms, both institutional and financial, define the main themes of restructuring, designed to be applicable to the entire public sector. In addition, certain restructuring programmes financed by the World Bank expressly state that the transfer of public enterprises is the final stage of the process.

ii) Certain developing countries in our sample, especially Morocco and Tunisia, have simultaneously resorted to plan contracts. "A plan contract is an agreement relating to the performance of a public enterprise, negotiated between the government as owner of the enterprises, and its directors or managers" (Nellis, 1989). One factor advanced to explain the inefficiency of the public sector is in fact the state's failure to abide by its financial and regulatory commitments[15]. Nonetheless, this approach on a case-by-case basis does not clarify the relationship between the state and the public enterprises. Plan contracts and the agreements derived from them cannot oblige the two public parties to the contract to comply strictly with their undertakings. In this connection, the relative failure of the plan contract (signed in 1982, for a two-year period) between the Moroccan government and the airline Royal Air Maroc seems in part due to the Moroccan government's failure to comply with its financial obligations under the contract (Nellis, 1989, p. 62). Thus, the absence of sanctions considerably limits the likelihood of the state's effective administrative and financial control being strengthened. Moreover, the drafting of plan contracts is particularly complex technically (estimate of the firm's economic and financial performance in a context of biased and fragmentary data) and politically (negotiation of the autonomy of the enterprise and reduction in government interference in management). Although an imperfect procedure, the plan contract permits better knowledge of the enterprise and provides an apprenticeship in market rationality for the public managers (representatives of ministries or executives of the public enterprises).

Endeavours to restructure public enterprises, like those culminating in privatisation, cannot be dissociated from the liberalisation policies adopted. These policies model an economic, financial and regulatory environment on which the operation and management of all national enterprises, both public and private, implicitly depend. Thus, the effective application of private rationality by the public managers will be facilitated, not to say imposed, by a genuine liberalisation policy (opening of certain public monopolies to competition, reduction in customs duties, pricing policy). Accordingly, it seems very difficult to separate restructuring measures from liberalisation of the conditions of economic activity, as rebalancing will then be bound to be identified as the sum of these various actions.

## 2. A costly solution

As its share in the equity of the enterprises that it rehabilitates remains unchanged, the state has to cover the borrowing requirements of investment and modernisation projects for enterprises that do not have sufficient capital accumulation to self-finance such projects. The state either directly finances the firm's investments by capital endowments or undertakes recapitalisation operations and reorganisations of balance sheets (takeover by the state of certain items on the liabilities side) in order to enable public enterprises to finance themselves directly on the capital markets, backed up by a guarantee from the sovereign state. The state, by underwriting the conduct of the rehabilitation policy, remains solely responsible for the financial results realised by the public enterprises.

The efforts undertaken by the Bangladeshi government provide a good illustration of an ambitious policy of financial reorganisation of the public industrial sector. Following the conclusions of a preliminary study on the economic and financial viability of each enterprise in this sector, a threefold action was undertaken with a view to improving their financial structure. This action took the form of injections of capital and especially of debt-equity and investment-equity swaps. Between 1981 and 1988 nearly 9 billion taka (approximately $300 million) were devoted to this financial reorganisation of the five main public industrial holding companies (BTMC, textile; BJMC, jute; BCIC, chemicals; BSEC, heavy industry; BSFIC, agriculture-based food industry). Despite these efforts, the financial performance of these enterprises remained mediocre, owing to the inadequacy of the economic restructuring undertaken in parallel.

This example, which might be found in other countries in our sample, is symptomatic of the complementary effect of the measures of economic restructuring, itself linked to the process of economic liberalisation, and of financial reorganisation. For this reason, the modernisation of the public sector is a particularly difficult task and its outcome is uncertain. Success is based essentially on the state's capacity not only to reform its traditional intervention in the management and operation of the public enterprises but also effectively to conduct programmes for adapting public enterprises to the requirements of the new economic system in the developing countries.

This presentation, deliberately brief, of the efforts undertaken to reform the public sector in many developing countries, posed the problem of restructuring the public sector and stressed the complexity of the process. Chapter 4 will return to the complementary effect of the liberalisation and privatisation measures while studying the impact of rebalancing on public finances, on economic efficiency and on social structures.

## Conclusion

The turning-point can be dated precisely. The downturn in the developing countries' terms of trade at the beginning of the 1980s, combined with the debt crisis, suddenly dried up the states' external sources of finance. Marked recessions resulting from these external shocks, moreover, reduced the volume of tax revenue. In a fairly short time (1982-85), the governments of most developing countries swung towards the orthodox philosophy advocated by the international organisations, led by the IMF.

This choice involved the application of strict economic stabilization policies, which, by eliminating the sources of domestic financing, tightened the financial constraint still further.

The difficulty of stabilizing developing economies, in a context of net financial transfers towards creditor countries, called for a prolonged application of stabilization policies. This maintenance over time of economic and financial constraints finally defined new functioning conditions, to which the developing countries henceforth had to conform on a long-term basis. The states were thus compelled to limit budget expenditure considerably and to stop tolerating poor financial performance by the public enterprises.

The widening of conditionality to virtually all the loans obtained from the Bretton Woods institutions, leading to increasing co-ordination between the IMF and the World Bank, culminated in a total reshaping of the development model. The adoption of structural adjustment policies, linked to stabilization policies, indicated that the time for adapting the economic fabric to the new operating conditions had arrived. The transition to an open market economy thus appeared as the systemic translation of the existing financial constraints. Based on an increase in the allocative and productive efficiency of the economy, the new frame of reference affected all economic agents. The public sector had to be restructured and scaled down, in a liberalised environment, and the private sector had to become the driving force of growth. The will to divest the state in favour of the private sector — the rebalancing process — is therefore a genuine inversion of responsibilities in this development model, where priority is given to competitiveness (the corollary of integration into the world economy) rather than to national independence.

# NOTES AND REFERENCES

1. According to IMF terminology, in the *Government Finance Statistics*.

2. For a detailed presentation of the explanatory factors of the performance of the public enterprises, see Chapter 8 of the *Report on World Development 1983*, World Bank; Aharoni (1986), Chapter 5; and, more recently, Nellis & Kikeri (1989).

3. It should be emphasized that the lack of profitability and inefficiency of the public enterprises had already been studied in the industrialised countries during the 1960s. In this connection, it suffices to mention the Nora report published in France in 1966, which suggested applying the principles of economic calculation to public sector firms. This report has been rediscovered by the specialists in public enterprise management at the World Bank (Nellis, 1988). The introduction of the rationalisation of budgetary choice by McNamara in the United States, followed by most of the OECD countries at more or less the same time, follows the same inspiration.

4. *Cf.* Chapter 4, "The impact on economic efficiency", for a discussion of ownership rights and X-inefficiency.

5. For the evaluation of the performance of the public enterprises, the analytical studies of Marchand *et al.* (1984), Gray (in Floyd *et al.*, 1986), Henscher (1986), Heald (1987).

6. E.g. the references of the liberal framework of reference are, in the area of liberalisation of trade, Krueger (1978 and 1981), in the area of deregulation of the capital markets, MacKinnon & Mathieson (1981).

7. Williamson (1990) speaks of Washington as the epicentre of the dominant model (see Chapter 2, "What Washington Means by Policy Reform", 1990).

8. See special number of *World Development* (1985), Connolly & Gonzalez-Vega (1987), Corbo & Melo (1987), Edwards (in Choski & Papageorgiou, 1987).

9. These questions of sequence and relative speed of the liberalisation measures are the subject of a vast body of theoretical literature. The main articles are Blejer & Sagar (1987), Codren (1987), Mussa (1987), Edwards (1989).

10. See *inter alia* in Corden (1987) the section "Developing Countries: Protection, Liberalization and Macroeconomic Policy", but also Dornbusch & Helmers (1988).

11. The reference to the strategic sectors is extremely blurred, as will be underlined in Chapter 3, "Microeconomic and empirical analysis of the privatisation operations".

12. The merger of public enterprises can however fall within a logic of achieving economies of scale or simplification of sectoral production and distribution structures. Accordingly, dismissal of surplus labour will be inevitable.

13. See Chapter 3, "The concept of privatisation: definition and justification", relating on relationships between ownership and control.

14. The figures are taken from World Bank *Annual Reports*, 1985 to 1990.

15. *Cf.* the lessons learned from the Nora Report, published in 1966, on the basis of French experience in the 1960s.

*Chapter 3*

# PRIVATISATION

Since the beginning of the 1980s, the application of policies aimed at adapting the economic structures of the developing countries to the new demands of the international environment has changed the respective roles of the public and private sectors. The reform of public sector enterprises, indeed, became an important component of the structural adjustment programmes actively supported and supervised by certain international organisations, led by the World Bank and the US Agency for International Development (USAID). Among the measures assisting in the reform of public enterprises, privatisation has been of capital importance, particularly in reducing the public sector.

Many developing countries have already undertaken ambitious privatisation programmes. Our ten sample countries have carried out more than 200 operations (for a detailed presentation, see Annex 2). The size of this movement calls for a precise analysis of what can and should be expected of privatisation operations. As a first step to this analysis, which will be set out in Chapter 4, the aim of the study will be defined, observed and detailed in the context of the countries included in our sample. The first section will therefore deal with the definition and theoretical justification of privatisation. To illustrate this normative approach to the creation of a theoretical framework, the various techniques and modalities of privatisation will be presented in the second section. Lastly, an analysis of the sectors affected by and excluded from privatisation will enable us to define its prime targets as well as the limits to its expansion.

## The concept of privatisation: definition and justification

Interest in privatisation operations grew considerably in the wake of the British experience in the early 1980s. There was a rapid increase in publications on this subject. The Reason Foundation calculated that in 1986 more than 1 000 articles dealing with privatisation or related questions were published in the main Anglo-Saxon journals. The conceptual problems, however, have only been touched on. The privatisation debate was engaged without a definition, and with no satisfactory theoretical arguments. Accordingly, it would seem useful to define the term *privatisation* as a first step to evaluating its effective impact. A second stage detailing the theoretical arguments will enable the identification of the particular channels whereby privatisation is likely to produce positive results and will compare these with empirical applications.

### Definition of privatisation

The vast body of economics literature dealing with privatisation shows a relative lack of interest in precisely defining its content[1]. As a general rule, studies have attached only a formal importance to the problems of definition and have resolved them summarily with the aid of two complementary propositions. The first, common to most of the authors, is based on the sole criterion of the ownership of the enterprise. This results in a very limited definition, which considers the transfer of ownership of part or all the capital in an enterprise as the sole factor constituting privatisation. The second proposition, which is also widespread, tends to group under the term *privatisation* all measures and policies aimed at strengthening the role of the private sector. This approach has the inconvenience of classing together a number of very disparate measures (liberalisation, restructuring and deregulation), thus making interpretation difficult.

Furthermore, the first of these definitions ignores management transfers as a method of privatisation, and the second, the specific nature of privatisation operations in the rebalancing process. The inadequacy of these presentations stems from a confused interpretation of the terms *ownership, management* and *control*. The removal of these problems of interpretation is a preliminary step to pinpointing genuine privatisation operations that can be classed as "effective privatisations" and to studying their real impact.

### A) Ownership and management

The view that transfers of shares or assets are the only method of privatisation tends to class together, on the one hand, changes in the division of the company's capital between public and private shareholders and, on the other hand, changes in its management. This one-sided interpretation of the relationships between ownership and management originates in the first works of the school of property rights (see Alchian and Demsetz (1972), on the "classic firm" where the manager and the shareholder are identical). According to this approach, privatisation of a state-owned firm's capital necessarily entails the adoption of management objectives and criteria that respond to the wishes of the private shareholders. In private firms, however there is a wide discrepancy between the objectives pursued by the owners and those pursued by its executives-managers, although in all likelihood in a diluted form. Indeed, distortions of information, allowed by an imperfect system of control and verification of the enterprise's real performance, result in the inability of the principal (the state or the shareholders) to evaluate, judge and sanction the behaviour of the agents (the managers) effectively[2].

Under these circumstances, it is no longer possible to class ownership and management together, and accordingly the relationship between the two has to be defined. Let us first of all adopt definitions similar to those proposed by J. Kay (1987): *ownership* of an asset corresponds to holding the residual financial value in that asset; *management* involves the control of those functions which are not explicitly specified in the contract subjecting the managers to the regulatory authorities and/or the public or private shareholders. On this basis, it is possible to envisage two cases at opposite ends of the spectrum in which transfer of capital and changes in the management are not linked.

In the first place, a transfer to the private sector, whether partial or integral, of a public enterprise's capital will not necessarily lead to a substantial transformation of the privatised enterprise's management methods. This situation arises from the previous behaviour of the public enterprise (adoption of private management criteria and objectives in the context of restructuring, thus limiting the innovative nature of privatised management) or from the type of regulatory environment (certain restrictions in employment, pricing and equipment, corresponding to an implied contractual specification by the public authorities)[3].

On the other hand, a complete reform in management can take place, by means of leases or management contracts, without changing the division of the capital, and accordingly without affecting the state's ownership rights. These methods of privatisation are applied in certain cases (politically difficult privatisations, uncompetitive sectors) when the state wishes to take advantage of the distinction between ownership and management.

*B) Ownership and control*

Control of an enterprise, whether public, private or privatised, falls to the shareholder who is in a position to impose the management that accords with his objectives. In the context of transfer operations, this leads to the question of how great a percentage of the capital a private investor needs to buy in order to gain effective control of the enterprise, in addition to the transfer of ownership. We shall now consider three different levels of private sector shareholding:

1) Transfer of 100 per cent of the capital

Total privatisation is relatively rare in the developing countries. Whatever the method of transfer, the assignment of capital should in theory be accompanied by a different management. The abandonment of the criteria and objectives that prevailed in the public sector (henceforth the government has no stake in the enterprise) is conditioned by the regulatory framework negotiated or imposed by the state. Restrictive regulation of pricing policies (scale of price increases in order to make a gradual transition from subsidised pricing to market pricing) or employment policy (fixed redundancy quotas) interferes with the objectives determined by the new private managers. Accordingly, the field of application of private rationality and the privatised firm's autonomy of management may be substantially reduced[4].

## 2) Transfer of a majority of the capital (more than 51 per cent)

Resulting from a partial assignment of capital, this scenario of a semi-public company dominated by private shareholders seems particularly appropriate in the developing countries in the case of politically sensitive transfers (airline or electricity companies, telecommunications, etc.). The state retains a minority share in the capital so that if, following the privatisation, the private purchasers act in a way deemed unacceptable, it will be able to oppose them. In order to assess whether transfer of control actually occurs, two precautions are essential:

With 49 per cent of the capital, the state can remain the shareholder of reference and, in the end, retain effective control over the privatised enterprise. This is particularly the case of public offerings, with the emergence of private shareownership made up of several thousands of small investors.

In many private sales of shares or assets, public or governmental interests have a partial or majority holding in the selected purchaser, in the form of a joint venture with a foreign partner or interest in the capital of the local purchaser[5]. Although such indirect public holdings are in all likelihood under the aegis of several supervisory authorities and respond to different objectives, they are added to the portion of the privatised company's capital retained by the state. In consequence, the whole of the public holding needs to be calculated in order to assess whether effective transfer of a state sector firm's capital has taken place.

## 3) Transfer of a minority holding in the capital

Consideration of this other example of partial transfer is indissociable from a study of how the enterprise's capital was divided prior to transfer. The three examples below illustrate the problems relating to transfers of control: a) The state does not own all the capital of a public enterprise; its partial divestiture (in the case of Malaysian Airlines System, 15 per cent of the capital) will then imply the transfer of control to the private sector; b) The same result is obtained, if the partial sale is interpreted as the first stage of total divestiture by the public authorities (cf. the example of the Chilean transfers); c) The minority entry, without attaining a blocking minority, of a private investor in a public firm's capital, provided the state adopts a permissive attitude, results in definite influence over the company's operation and management (see below, the privatisation of Port Kelang and the role of the Australian partner, P & 0).

Considering the state's attitude towards private behaviour becomes all the more necessary in cases where, as in Bangladesh since 1987, private sector holdings are limited to 49 per cent. Indeed, although the public authority, which still has a majority stake, seeks to limit the influence of the private partners, control of the enterprise is not transferred, and privatisation is not effective in any respect. The state's behaviour is therefore essential to success in the period subsequent to privatisation; the state encourages the private purchaser to adopt behaviour aimed at improving economic efficiency.

Many other examples highlight the will to divest the state from involvement in the everyday management of enterprises. For example, the waiver of dividend rights on state-owned equity, without giving up the voting rights or the creation of "golden shares"[6], makes the relationship between investment in the capital of an enterprise and effective transfer of control even more uncertain.

This brief presentation indicates the difficulty of proposing an average percentage that would enable one to assess whether private interests have actually taken control of privatised enterprises. However, two conclusions can be drawn:

i) For privatisation to be effective, the following criteria must be met: the adoption of management based on private rationality and financial liability for the firm's results.

ii) General analyses of privatisation, and more particularly of transfer operations, are inadequate for making a correct assessment of "effective" privatisation. Only if account is taken of the market structure and the regulatory environment accorded to each enterprise can a conceptually adequate reply be given.

C) *The concept of effective privatisation*

The criticisms set out above highlight the inadequacy of the systematic approaches to pinpointing privatisation operations. The extremely praiseworthy efforts of the World Bank (1988) and the Reason Foundation (1987-89) at providing an exhaustive list do not enable us to pick out the "effective" privatisations from among the many measures and operations strengthening the role of the private sector[7]. Measures affecting management or capital or both are grouped without differentiation, with no detailed explanation as regards the identity of the purchaser/contractor, the level of state holding or the effective control of the enterprise. The only satisfactory approach presupposes a case-by-case retrospective study of privatisation operations. Unfortunately, this approach, presented here analytically, cannot be developed owing to the limits of the information at our disposal concerning the ten sample countries. In fact, it is based on the observation over time of the two criteria that constitute effective privatisation: the adoption of behaviour denoting private rationality on the part of the purchaser or contractor, and the financial liability stemming from the operation and management of the privatised enterprise.

According to J. Kay (1987), privatisation is effective provided private agents are in charge of all the company's functions and activities, not expressly defined by the state. In this perspective, clear rules of the game need to be defined so that, on the one hand, the privatised enterprise can effectively maximise the utility of the purchaser[8] and, on the other hand, in situations where competition is restricted, the operation of these enterprises is not carried out to the detriment of the rest of the community (competitors, employees, consumers, the state). With this aim in mind, a real process of liberalisation must be undertaken, aimed at improving regulatory procedures by deregulation or reregulation.

The fundamental difference between privatisation (application of private rationality by private agents) and a certain conception of restructuring (attempt by public agents to apply private rationality) relates less to autonomy of management[9] than to the private purchaser's financial commitment. In other words, in the context of restructuring and management contracts, the state remains the backer of the public sector firms. On the other hand, "effective privatisation" is the application of private rationality by private economic agents who are responsible not only for the costs of the firm's modernisation and growth but also for any financial losses.

On the basis of this normative definition, "effective privatisation" operations, in the main leasing contracts and partial or total transfers that satisfy the two conditions set out above, will be identified and isolated from the multitude of measures that directly or indirectly strengthen the private sector. Only at this stage will it be possible to undertake a rigorous empirical study of their economic, financial and social impact. It will then be possible to dispel the uncertainty relating to the advantages and costs genuinely attributable to the privatisation operations. This is the only method that will enable us to demonstrate the deep divide between privatisation as it should be and as it is applied in the developing countries.

### What should be privatised?

Positive theories on the rationality of the transfer of ownership (partial or total assignment of a public enterprise's capital) are still relatively undeveloped. Apart from the traditional arguments put forward to explain the difference in economic and financial performance between the public and private sectors (*inter alia*, ownership rights and the logic of maximisation of profit), the theoretical propositions try to provide a conceptually satisfactory answer to the following three questions asked by L. Jones *et al.* (1988): Why transfer a public enterprise to the private sector, whom should it be transferred to, and at what price?

*A) Theories of the transfer of ownership*

The three theories presented here analyse the validity of the transfer operation in different ways. D. Bös (1986a, 1986b, 1987) seeks to explain the behaviour of the privatised enterprise (change in management objectives) by the degree of privatisation. J.J. Rosa (1988) and L. Jones *et al.* (1988) mainly study the valuation of privatised enterprises by the public authorities and the potential private purchasers.

D. Bös centres his analysis on the allocation (portion of capital transferred to the private sector) and distribution (identification of specific groups within the private sector: shareholders, employees, underprivileged groups) of the shares in a privatised enterprise.

i) The transfer operation at the level of allocation

a) Bös (1987a) adopts as a basic principle that the efficiency of a privatised enterprise depends both on its "netputs" (outputs less inputs) and on the percentage of its capital held by private agents. He then considers a point situated on the borderline of possible outputs that, by definition, eliminates X-inefficiencies. This point corresponds to a single distribution of the capital between public and private shareholders. If the privatisation results in this division of the capital between public and private owners, and consequently in full productive efficiency, it is classed as "efficient".

Privatisation does not lead solely to better use of the factors of production. It also changes the division of the gains in productive efficiency achieved by the firm. This division becomes the subject of a compromise between the public logic of maximisation of social welfare and the private logic of maximisation of profit. The body in charge of the transfer of the capital will block any additional sale of shares to the private sector once the enterprise's profitability grows at the expense of social welfare (for example, by means of a price rise in the goods produced by the privatised company). Thus, by breaking down the transfer process into its individual units, the negotiation between public and private interests results in a Pareto optimum of ownership, expressed by means of a partial transfer.

If the final objective of the transfer is maximisation of productive efficiency, however, partial transfer is an "inefficient privatisation". Whereas the sale of shares should continue as long as it increases efficiency, it is in effect stopped once the optimum welfare of the public shareholder has been achieved (1987a, p. 357). Partial transfer is then akin to an under-privatisation of capital. The reasoning becomes more complex with the introduction of differentiated net dividends (optimal, political or neutral net dividends, 1986, p. 24). The division of the capital and the achievement of "efficient privatisation" then depend on the rule of dividends' being fixed by the public authorities.

ii) The transfer operation at the level of distribution

The study of the distribution of shares and its redistributive corollary enable Bös to reach two main conclusions:

First of all, it is conceptually impossible to maintain that the division of a privatised enterprise's equity should favour small incomes rather than high incomes (1986, p. 37).

Next, the relative strength of the employees' representatives and the public or private shareholders determines how the profits derived from the privatisation of the capital will be divided[10]. If the unions are in a position of strength, they will take the whole of the private shareholders' net dividends and reduce the public shareholders' income to a minimal level below which they would refuse to privatise. The profit taken away from the public shareholders serves to increase the employees' share in the privatised company's capital or to keep surplus labour in employment. If government interests gain the upper hand, the employees' share becomes non-existent, and the public and private shareholders share the profits resulting from the privatisation (1987b, p. 362).

Bös' approach helps to explain the extent of privatisation of capital, according to the resulting impact on economic efficiency and social welfare. In addition, it answers the question of the division of the capital among the various potential purchasers (private interests, employees, underprivileged groups). The lack of an explicit presentation addressing the valuation of the privatised enterprise and its transfer price tends, nonetheless, to limit the scope of his analysis.

b) This factor is at the heart of the theory developed by J.J. Rosa. The optimum of ownership leads the rational government, which is seeking to maximise its chances of re-election by a clever policy of redistribution, to adjust the size of the public sector according to its financing conditions (1988, p. 92).

A public enterprise that has market power is just as much an instrument of the government's redistribution policy as are subsidy or regulation[11]. Both privatisation and nationalisation are justified by a different valuation of the enterprises and by a change in the opportunity cost of owning them. The state and the private investor will evaluate the profits gained from running the enterprise differently; for example, in a monopoly situation, the financial profit of a private company is only half the consumer surplus deducted by a public enterprise. Furthermore, the capital cost differs for the two agents; the private investor pays the market interest rate, while the state pays the weighted marginal cost of taxes and borrowing. "This disparity in value, compared to the condition of parity in value[12], will determine a movement towards purchase or sale, by either of the bidders, which will alter the borderline between the private and the public sector, until the two valuations coincide in the case of the marginal firm" (1988, p. 101). Subsequently, any change in the parameters for assessing the value of the firms will change the designation of a marginal firm and will thus affect the relative size of the public and private sectors. The theory of the optimum of ownership would therefore justify the nationalisation and privatisation of enterprises with market power.

c) L. Jones, P. Tandon and I. Vogelsang (1988) propose a detailed approach to the transfer operation, the final aim of which is to establish a theory that is applicable empirically.

The authors define *three values for the privatised enterprise* (two social values — one resulting from operation by the government, $V_{sg}$, and the other from operation by a private purchaser, $V_{sp}$ — and a private value for the potential purchaser, $V_{pp}$), *three transfer prices* (the minimum price acceptable to the state, the maximum price acceptable to the private investor and the actual price of the transaction), and a *parameter* $\lambda_g$ representing the value of state-held funds in relation to that of funds held by the private sector. The combination of these parameters, on the basis of a reasoning in social welfare terms, gives rise to an equation answering the three questions posed above. The transfer of a public enterprise occurs when the variation in the level of social welfare resulting from the privatisation operation is positive (dW> 0).

Accordingly, the government's decision to privatise the capital of an enterprise will depend on the two parameters that determine the impact on social welfare: the net benefit for the community, expressed by the difference between the social values of a privatised enterprise ($V_{sp}$) or under public control ($V_{sg}$), and the value for the government ($\lambda_g - 1$) of the income from the transfer (Z).

That is:  $dW = (V_{sp} - V_{sg}) + (\lambda_g - 1) Z > 0$

The transfer operation is therefore based on the private sector's capacity to provide a higher level of welfare for the community from running the enterprise, owing to greater efficiency, than the government would achieve — that is, ($V_{sp} - V_{sg}$ > 0). Moreover, Jones *et al.* take up the liberal analysis whereby the value of a dollar held by the state is higher than a dollar held by the private sector ($\lambda_g$ greater than one). The reasoning is as follows: the additional income (e.g. the income from the transfer) will enable the state to reduce taxes and withholding tax, thus reducing economic distortions and inefficiencies. The positive external effects for the community will more than compensate for the reduction in tax earnings[13].

The actual price of the transfer is situated between the minimum price acceptable to the state (it may be negative, with the state agreeing to pay for the transfer in order to increase the level of social welfare) and the maximum price at which the private purchaser decides to apply to purchase the shares, in the light of the financial value he attributes to the enterprise in question ($V_{pp}$). The high valuation of additional resources (example of the fiscal crises in the developing countries) forces the state to balance the desire for income from the transfer in the short term against the need to negotiate the highest possible transfer price with the private purchasers, within the limits of their individual evaluations.

The purchaser is chosen on the basis of the social value of the enterprise under his management ($V_{sp}$) and the purchase price offered ($V_{pp}$). Therefore the state will transfer a public enterprise not to the highest bidder but to the purchaser whose offer will give the best return in social-welfare terms. The latter is a function of the difference in social welfare resulting intrinsically from the transfer of ownership expressed by the social values ($V_{sp} - V_{sg}$), and the value for the government of the income from the transfer[14].

The approach of Jones et al. (1988) aims to compensate for market mechanisms that are absent at the time of the privatisation process. In fact, few developing countries have the combined conditions needed for such operations to be successful: inadequate assessment of the enterprises' value by the markets, small number of potential purchasers reducing the possibility for them to compete one with another. Moreover, the method has the merit of conceptualising all the questions raised by transfer of ownership of a public enterprise and of being able to integrate the more complex variants in the reasoning (in particular, various market structures). Nonetheless, this theory, which should aid decision making in the transfer of public enterprises, comes up against the problem of how to quantify the main parameters: $\lambda_g$ and the difference ($V_{sp} - V_{sg}$).

*B) Teachings about enterprises and market structures*

The three theories presented here take the view that the privatisation of the capital of public enterprises has a positive impact on economic efficiency. This finding is not formalised expressly, however, and the determinants of economic efficiency are still poorly integrated into the logic of transfer of ownership. In this perspective, particular attention should be given to market structures. The competitive or monopolistic position of the privatised enterprise is, in fact, a decisive factor in the attitude of the government and private investors towards the transfer operation.

1) J.J. Rosa's analysis concludes that enterprises with market power will be those most concerned by transfer of ownership operations (both privatisation and nationalisation)[15]. By the ownership and acquisition of companies, the government seeks to improve its redistribution policy. To this end, it generally grants its nationalised enterprises a market power that enables them to appropriate the consumer surplus by means of a discriminatory pricing policy (1988, p. 96). Market power, the extreme example of which is the monopoly, is the main ground for the difference between the government's valuation of the enterprise and the private

investor's valuation. In an entirely competitive situation, the state cannot reduce the consumer surplus, and the private entrepreneur finds that volumes of production and price levels are imposed by market forces.

Market structures should therefore be studied both before and after the transfer of ownership, in order to observe changes in behaviour and valuations. Unfortunately, Rosa's theory cannot integrate the possible changes in the market power of the companies concerned. He considers that transfer does not cast doubt upon the monopoly power granted to the nationalised company, and thus concludes that there is a relationship between the profit realised by the private investor and the surplus obtained by the state.

2) The analysis by Jones *et al.* (1988) considers both the type of purchaser involved and the market structure of the privatised company.

i) It is possible to distinguish between two types of offers: those from individual investors and those from large industrial or financial groups. The latter offer a higher price for the enterprise to be privatised, owing to the possible ensuing synergies: economies of scale, portfolio diversification, the exercise of oligopolistic or monopolistic power (purchase of a public monopoly or merger with the purchaser's activities). The effect of such synergies on economic efficiency and hence on social welfare is uncertain. It is difficult to ignore, as do Jones *et al.*, the risk of the *constitution of a private monopoly*, whose impact would be very negative in social welfare terms, by arguing that the governments' aim is to increase domestic competition (1988, p. 130). The introduction of synergies raises, without providing a satisfactory answer, the problem of balancing the maximisation of the income from the transfer against the effect on social welfare.

ii) The theory of Jones *et al.* provides a major contribution by taking into consideration market structures and their impact on transfer operations. Three scenarios are propounded: competitive balance, the possible differentiation of behaviour and the monopoly.

a) In the borderline case of competitive market equilibrium (determination of equilibrium prices and quantities), productive efficiency and social welfare are independent of effective ownership of the enterprise. Competition has the same effect on the behaviour of public and private enterprises. Accordingly, the state and private purchasers assess the value of enterprises to be privatised in the same way, which results in a similar transfer price. In this zero-sum game, the operation does not take place, owing to the costs of the deal.

b) Differentiation of public and private behaviour leads to the question of balancing productive efficiency (minimisation of costs) against allocative efficiency (use of market power to the detriment of the consumer). If the enterprise seeks greater efficiency of production without taking advantage of its position on the market, the transfer of ownership of a public enterprise will have a positive impact on social welfare. It is possible to formalise the net benefit of the transfer operation. In this context, the variation in social welfare depends on the developments in the consumer surplus, (d s(t)), and the value for the state of the pre-tax profit achieved by the private investor, (d x(t)).

That is: $d W = \Sigma r. \{d s(t) + \lambda_g . d x (t) \}$

in which r = rate of actualisation and $\lambda_g$ = premium accruing to government resources (1988, p. 69).

In a competitive situation, the privatised enterprise cannot increase its profits by reducing the consumer surplus, as the price is fixed by market forces. The profits then result either from the fall in production costs or from the increase in quantities produced. In both these examples, the privatisation of an enterprise in a competitive situation increases the welfare of the community.

c)   The transfer of ownership of a monopoly creates the opportunity for the privatised enterprise to use its market power at its discretion. The overall impact on social welfare depends on the loss of consumer good (surplus reduced by the fall in quantities produced and rise in price above its equilibrium price) and on the increase in pre-tax profit achieved by the private purchaser or the enterprise (owing to a reduction in production costs and/or behaviour aimed at maximisation of profit). This second term has a positive effect on social welfare, since it generates additional tax earnings valued by the state on the basis of its $\lambda_g$. If there is no increase in productive efficiency, and in the case of a $\lambda_g$ equal to one, the reduction in the consumer surplus is one-and-a-half times more than the increase in profit of the privatised enterprise. Under these circumstances, the privatisation operation does not take place, because it would reduce social welfare[16].

If the state values its additional resources very highly, however, as may be the case of developing countries in a fiscal crisis, the overall effect of the privatisation on social welfare becomes positive. The previous result does not presuppose that the improvements in productive efficiency are achieved. If the transfer of ownership takes place, it is to the detriment of the consumer. The intermediate case of a slight reduction in production costs no longer calls for a very high $\lambda_g$ in order to justify the privatisation operation.

Five conclusions can be drawn from this theoretical presentation:

1) The theoretical analysis developed to date is still fragmentary. No satisfactory conceptualisation of the rationality of the privatisation of the capital of public enterprises has yet been advanced.

2) The works of Rosa and of Jones *et al.* suggest that the enterprises most closely concerned by transfer operations are those with market power.

3) Under these circumstances, privatisation should be accompanied by liberalisation procedures, else the privatised firm's behaviour will reduce the welfare of society as a whole. In sum, it is a question of directing the search for financial profit towards an improvement in productive efficiency rather than towards the exploitation of market power[17].

4) The parallel implementation of a policy of liberalisation underlines the state's desire to preserve the link between privatisation and allocative and productive efficiency (shown in all the works presented). Thus combined with deregulation or reregulation measures limiting non-competitive behaviour, privatisation produces a positive impact on social welfare.

5) In the case of a competitive market structure, privatisation is validated by the difference in behaviour between public and privatised enterprises. In the case of a non-competitive market structure (oligopoly, monopoly), the public enterprise is transformed into a regulated private enterprise (*cf.* Chapter 4).

## The wide variety of privatisation procedures

The wide variety of procedures is explained by the diversity and hierarchical organisation of the objectives sought by the authorities in the context of the privatisation process. Over and above the first reasons leading to privatisation (reduction in the budget deficit and improvement in economic efficiency), the choice of procedure will reflect the opportunity of achieving certain secondary objectives as a result of the privatisation, simply by means of the technique adopted for transferring ownership or management. For example, when choosing the method of transfer of a state-owned enterprise, the authorities may give priority to the emergence of popular capitalism by means of employee or individual shareholders (public offering, staff buy-out), the setting up of economic and financial centres of interest or the development of an industrial fabric of small and medium-sized enterprises (negotiated sale of assets or shares). These underlying objectives should be borne in mind when studying the modalities of privatisation.

This section mainly presents the conclusions drawn from the empirical studies on our sample countries. It is divided into three subsections: 1) the procedures for transfer of ownership, 2) the procedures for strengthening the role of the private sector in the operation of the enterprise, 3) three examples of privatisation that stress the link between the procedure used and the objectives sought.

*Transfers of public enterprises*

There are four methods of transferring ownership: i) the public offering with resort to the stock market, ii) negotiated sale of shares or assets, iii) the staff or management buy-out and iv) the non-subscribed increase of capital. The distinction takes account not only of the type of purchasers involved but also of the practical conditions of the operation (transfer by means of a market placement, tender, sale on agreed terms, increase of capital). The use of these procedures is conditioned by the economic and financial environment prevailing in most developing countries. The non-existence or narrowness of stock markets, the difficulty of assessing the value of the assets of the companies concerned and the concentration of capital in the hands of several dominant groups are all potential checks on the satisfactory progress of transfer operations. By referring as often as possible to specific examples, the discussion below evaluates the advantages and limitations of these various mechanisms.

*A) The public offering*

This procedure, favoured in the developed countries[18], calls for conditions that are seldom completely fulfilled in the developing countries. Moreover, the complexity of the preparatory stages restricts its use to the major public enterprises.

1) The objectives of the public offering

 i) The government's first objective, in a public offering, is to show its intention to use privatisation as a means of "democratising" the shareownership of the main industrial or banking groups. This measure, which encourages direct financial participation by a wide band of the population, should help to put paid to any objections and criticisms relating to the risks of denationalisation (foreign interests taking majority holdings) or excessive concentration of capital. Accordingly, democratisation of shareownership demonstrates that privatisation is not taking place solely for the benefit of powerful national or foreign financial groups. The public offering, which seems to preserve popular interests, as it provides an opportunity to participate in the new distribution of the equity of the privatised enterprises, is therefore most often chosen in the case of politically difficult transfers (monopoly situations, enterprises with national prestige or belonging to strategic sectors). This desire to promote "popular capitalism" has been particularly prevalent in Chile since 1985. The reprivatisation of financial and banking organisations nationalised during the economic crisis from 1982-83 has been achieved mainly through public offerings[19].

126

ii) The second objective is to develop the capital and securities markets. Offering a financial investment — marketable securities — relatively unknown to the middle classes is a way of gradually converting part of monetary savings into financial savings. The increase in financial savings, and subsequent increase in demand for financial products, should increase the liquidity of the local capital markets. This would tend to provide private or public enterprises with greater ease of access to direct financing on the markets and would thus limit resort to bank borrowing.

iii) Further, the public offering allows governments to reaffirm their commitment to privatisation. The popular success of the transfers of the National Commercial Bank of Jamaica, Malaysian Airline System, Banco de Chile and Philippine National Bank were seen, often prematurely, as major turning-points in the achievement of national privatisation programmes. The political authorities interpreted these successes as legitimate grounds for continuing the privatisation programme.

iv) Lastly, popular participation in the capital of the major state-owned enterprises, which results in the splitting up of traditional ownerships, seems to be a powerful protection against possible renationalisation. Chile has particularly favoured this point of view since 1985, by encouraging an increase in the number of small individual shareholders (more than 25 000 shareholders for the transfer of Banco de Chile alone, in 1986). Under these circumstances, the privatisations carried out seem irreversible, and opposing operations that encourage "popular capitalism" becomes an extremely delicate political decision.

2) Resort to public offerings

In view of these four advantages, and despite the difficulties of implementing a public offering, 43 such operations have taken place in the sample countries (see Table 10). They have generally involved the largest public sector industrial or banking enterprises in each country, and most often a fraction of the capital or public holding in these firms. In Malaysia, 17 per cent and 30 per cent respectively of the capital in Malaysian Airline System and Malaysian International Shipping Company have been transferred. In Bangladesh, divestments that have taken place since June 1987 have permitted a maximum of only 34 per cent of the capital to be transferred by public offering. Up to the middle of 1990, public offerings in Mexico were limited to the same percentage. Only Chile and Jamaica (Banco de Chile and Banco de Santiago, Caribbean Cement) have undertaken public offerings of the entire capital or public holding.

In fact, partial public offerings fulfil three essential requirements: avoiding saturating the demand for shares from small investors, complying with certain regulatory constraints (Mexico, Bangladesh) and encouraging a gradual dilution of the state's holding in enterprises in strategic sectors. However, do these operations

127

actually result in effective privatisation of the enterprises concerned, in particular when the state retains a majority holding after the public offering (see *infra*, "The concept of privatisation:  definition and justification")[20].

3) The difficulties of implementation

Two major constraints affect developing countries wishing to start along the road towards the public offering:  the narrowness of local capital markets and the complexity of the preparatory stages.

i) Poor capacity of absorption by the local capital markets (low volume of issues, limited liquidity of the secondary market) is often advanced to explain the difficulty of implementing public offerings in the developing countries.  For these reasons, Ghana (whose government approved the modernisation of the stock market as recently as April 1989), Morocco, Tunisia and Bolivia have been unable to use the capital markets for a public offering.

In contrast, in Jamaica, despite the low volume of transactions on the Kingston Stock Exchange, two major operations have taken place: the transfers of the National Commercial Bank of Jamaica in 1986, and of Caribbean Cement in 1987.  These two public offerings alone increased stock market capitalisation by 20 per cent and accounted for 87 per cent of the funds raised directly on the markets by quoted companies[21].  Evidence of the limited absorption capacity of the Jamaican stock market was the fact that the public offering of 100 per cent of the capital in Caribbean Cement was undersubscribed, partly because it occurred less than six months after the sale of the National Commercial Bank.

Bearing in mind the limited financial resources of a large band of the population and the innovative nature of this kind of investment in most of the developing countries, the government seeks to fix the subscription price at an attractive level.  The price selected generally reflects a considerable discount compared to the potential value of the security.  In Malaysia, the discounts in the case of Malaysian Airline System and Malaysian International Shipping Corporation were substantial, with price earnings ratios much lower than the market average.  In the Philippines, the public offering of the country's largest commercial bank, the Philippine National Bank, ended with the shares substantially oversubscribed. In fact the offering had been reduced to 30 per cent of the capital, only two-thirds of this via the two securities markets in the Philippines, the Manila and Makati Stock Exchanges.  The price fixed at 170 pesos (approximately $8) gave rise to the expectation of very high capital gains.  From the time it was first quoted, the share price increased by nearly 70 per cent, in a volume of transactions four times higher than the normal level[22].

The direct involvement of insufficiently developed capital markets in the transfer process increases the uncertainty as to the success of the operation. Such involvement is inevitable, however, as the public offering ought to contribute to the modernisation of financial structures and the development of direct finance in the developing countries. To ensure the success of the public offering, the government bears a financial opportunity cost, through lower income from the transfer.

ii) The preparatory stages of a public offering are long and complex. They call for a detailed audit, an appropriate financial evaluation and a whole battery of legal provisions relating to foreign investment, limits on the size of individual nationals' holdings and the issue of new shares. The inadequacy of the financial data available about the firms concerned, the difficulty of pricing the shares satisfactorily and the complexity of the legislation are evidence of the authorities' lack of preparation.

Because most governments of developing countries cannot complete the preparatory stages efficiently, they tend to resort to foreign skills. The involvement of foreign experts — usually British, because of their experience of privatisation in general, and public offerings in particular — has become the rule in Malaysia, Jamaica and the Philippines. It is difficult to assess the amounts received by consulting firms in emoluments for their financial and legal expertise.

The financial costs of implementing public offerings are likely to be high. They ensue from the substantial undervaluation (generally more than is applied in the case of private sales of shares), the costs of preparation (valuation and legal studies) and the costs of transaction (underwriting, promotion)[23]. These expenses are the price of ensuring the success of the operation, in particular from the point of view of popular investment.

B) Private transfers of shares or assets

The sale of shares or assets to private purchasers is the transfer method most often used in the developing countries in our sample. One hundred and thirty-one such operations have taken place, that is, more than half of the total privatisations, and about three-quarters of transfers alone. Except in Ghana, Morocco, Jamaica and Malaysia, the private transfer of shares or assets has been used more than all the other privatisation techniques put together.

All the enterprises that the public authorities propose to sell are set out in official lists drawn up for potential investors. Mexico has published a list of 218 public enterprises available for privatisation. Similarly, in 1988 Ghana and the Philippines published lists of, respectively, 32 and 135 public firms "to be privatised by transfer operations". During 1989, Morocco and Malaysia took the same step. In December 1989 the Moroccan National Assembly passed a bill proposing the sale of

Table 10

## PRIVATISATION OPERATIONS: TECHNIQUES USED

| | Public offering (I) | Transfers of equity or assets (II) | Staff buy-out (III) | Unsubscribed increases of capital (IV) | Leases (V) | Management contracts (VI) | Reorganisations combined with (I,II,III,IV) | Debt-equity, debt-assets swaps (I, II) |
|---|---|---|---|---|---|---|---|---|
| GHANA | | (5) | | | | (6) | | |
| MOROCCO | | (5) | | | (2) | (7) | | |
| TUNISIA | | (20) | (1) 100% | (3) | | | (2) | |
| BOLIVIA | | (1) | | | | | (1) | |
| CHILE since 1985 | (14) | (34) | (12) including (2) 100% | (1) | | | | (6) |
| JAMAICA | (3) | (29) | (2) | | (9) | (14) | | |
| MEXICO | (13) | (18) | (4) of which (1) 100% | | | | | (1) |
| BANGLADESH since 1987 | (9) | | (9) | | | | | |
| MALAYSIA | (3) | (4) | | | (6) | (5) | (1) | |
| PHILIPPINES | (1) | (15) | | | | | | (3) |
| TOTAL (255) | (43) | (131) | (28) of which (4) 100% | (4) | (17) | (32) | (4) | (10) |
| FRANCE | (14) | (11) | (1) | (1) | | (1) | (1) | |
| UNITED KINGDOM | (14) | (19) | (12) | (1) | | (1) | (3) | |

113 enterprises. In Malaysia, the general framework of the privatisation policy, completed at the end of 1989, listed 246 public enterprises, the majority of whose capital will be able to held by the private sector[24].

## 1) Characteristics

The main difference between the two methods of transfer lies in the form of the transaction: sale of equity or assets. In the first case, the body in charge of the transfer offers a block of shares, fixing a minimum price for the operation. The transfer then takes place, either as a private sale (acquisition of a minority holding in the Chilean Telephone Company by the A. Bond Group in 1987, purchase of a majority share in the airline company Lanchile by a private consortium in 1989), or through the securities markets (market placement of virtually all the capital of several Tunisian enterprises since 1988). In the second case, the assets are sold by tender, mainly in the context of the reorganisation or fragmentation of a public enterprise. The only privatisation realised to date in Bolivia, that of ENTA, took the form of the sale of its assets (goods vehicles), following its liquidation by the public authorities. In Tunisia, the split-up of Société Hôtelière et Touristique de Tunisie resulted in sale of the assets (the hotels) to a number of different private purchasers. In Jamaica, the reorganisation of the National Hotel and Properties Group, plus an extra phase, in that the state had initially granted management contracts, ended with the actual transfer of a number of the state-owned hotels.

In comparison with public offerings, the preparatory stages of private sales are not complicated and therefore have the attraction of a procedure that is both flexible and speedily implemented. Once the list of firms available for privatisation has been drawn up, the public authorities determine a minimum transfer price for each firm, below which they will not agree to sell. On this basis, they study and compare the various competing offers. In the case of very attractive enterprises, this type of procedure entails a certain amount of bidding by the would-be purchasers. By this means, the state hopes to obtain higher income from the transfer than was envisaged when the initial price was fixed. For example, when Mexicana de Cobre, the largest copper producer in Mexico, was put up for sale, most of the major private mining companies entered several bids.

## 2) Private transfers and debt conversion

The private sale of equity or assets makes it possible to integrate debt conversion into the financial arrangements. Under this procedure, local or foreign purchasers buy claims on the secondary market, and debt instruments drawn on the target developing country, at a discount. These claims and debt instruments are denominated in hard currency. They then make an offer to the Central Bank of the country concerned to convert the debt instruments at their face value, either into the national currency or in exchange for equity or assets in companies available for privatisation. This kind of operation has seen spectacular growth in Chile, Mexico and the Philippines, which have suffered a massive outflow of capital and whose nationals have substantial reserves in hard currency deposited abroad. In these countries, the aim of introducing debt conversion mechanisms into the context of financing investments and privatisation operations is to make this capital play an active role.

In Chile, the main acquisitions of majority holdings have been financed by debt-equity swaps, as is illustrated by the transfer of COPEC (an enterprise specialising in forestry and gas) in 1986, at a value of more than $200 million. In order to finance the purchase of 40 per cent of the capital in the Chilean pension fund AFP Provida, the American bank Bankers Trust converted its own debt instruments drawn on Chile for a total of $60 million. Such financial arrangements are extremely complex and call for the involvement of a variety of intermediaries (potential investors, foreign creditor banks, the Central Bank and the body responsible for the transfer) and for many parameters to be taken into account (the discount applied and the transfer price). The failure of the transfer of the Mexican mining group CANANEA, in 1988, is evidence of the conditional and uncertain nature of such operations. In this case, the creditor bank, First Chicago, felt that the discount offered by the Mexican purchaser, Grupo Protexa, was too large and decided to withdraw from the provisional financing scheme. The British bank, Midland Bank, then offered to take the place of the defaulting bank, but the sum required, $1.3 billion, could not be raised.

The inflationary impact of debt-equity swap mechanisms has nonetheless tempered the initial enthusiasm of the public authorities. In Chile, debt conversions rose to more than $1.3 billion between the second half of 1985 and September 1989[25]. Under these circumstances, the government deemed it essential to restrict the application of debt conversions solely to privatisation operations and tourist activities. In 1988, the Philippines considerably reduced the scope for the use of debt-equity swaps as a means of financing investment and privatisation operations and subsequently favoured development of debt-assets conversions, considered less inflationary[26].

The introduction of debt conversion mechanisms helps to reinforce the discretionary nature of private sales of equity or assets. The application of unofficial discounts on debt instruments and the possible repatriation of funds transferred abroad have led the public authorities to restrict information regarding the actual amounts involved in the transactions and the identities of the purchasers. This limited transparency of the criteria for decision adopted by the transfer authorities, in comparison with a public offering, seems to be the rule for private sales, even when a transparent tender procedure is defined in advance.

3) The risks inherent in private sales

The problems encountered in the effective realisation of transfer operations are closely similar to those mentioned above in the case of public offerings: determination of the minimum transfer price, narrowness of the securities markets and selection of target firms. Nonetheless, the limited number of purchasers in the developing countries with genuine financial resources is an additional obstacle to the achievement of a satisfactory tender operation.

i) The success of such direct sale procedures, and of transfer operations in general, depends primarily on the financial position of the firms to be privatised. The tourist complexes in Tunisia, Jamaica, Mexico and the Philippines, which were intrinsically very profitable, were among the first entities transferred to private investors. Likewise, companies in the attractive sector of telecommunications in Chile and Jamaica, as well as in Mexico and Malaysia, were or will be transferred without difficulty. The risk inherent in any transfer process is as follows: the healthiest firms are likely to be transferred to the private sector with no difficulty, leaving in public ownership those firms in deficit or potentially less attractive. Such a development is likely to prohibit a significant reduction in flows of capital from the government towards public enterprises.

Moreover, the sale of a state-owned company's assets does not in any way resolve the residual responsibility for its liabilities. As a general rule, the state takes responsibility for all or part of the firm's debts when it is split up or put into liquidation. The state takes on this responsibility so that the weight of state-owned firms' liabilities neither hampers the transfer process nor handicaps possible purchasers. The coverage of the liabilities takes the form of settling cross-debts with other public sector firms, and problems relating to the reimbursement dates of loans from banking institutions, which are usually in the public sector.

ii) The valuation by potential purchasers of firms to be privatised is an essential factor in the private sale. At the level of economic and financial valuation, two problems arise:

   – In the first place, the limited amount of data available about the firms concerned prevents a satisfactory valuation of them. This uncertainty leads would-be buyers to reduce their offers, sometimes to levels lower than the public authorities originally fixed. The transfer process is then blocked.

   – Second, it is essential that the information, even if merely fragmentary, be accessible to all. A major risk of the private sale lies in the inadequate information available about the real financial situation of the firms concerned. Inconsistent information of this kind, whether deliberate or not, discredits the whole procedure.

The difficulties encountered during the Philippines' private transfer programme show the importance of evaluating the firm's real situation and also of the other factors surrounding the transaction (financial guarantee, the minimum number of offers for the procedure to be valid). Reports of the transfers of Nonoc Mining and Industrial Corp. and Paper Industries Corp. during 1989 reflect the limitations of privatisation procedures by means of direct transfers to private buyers. In the case of the nickel mining and processing firm Nonoc, the two offers proposed at the beginning of 1989, both below the government's minimum price ($300 million), were rejected because they did not comply with the rules relating to deposits by way of guarantee. In the case of Picop, the largest Philippines paper company, the transfer operation failed twice without any offers having been received[27].

iii) The excessive concentration of privatised firms in the hands of a few powerful financial groups (consortiums of local conglomerates or expanded to include foreign financial partners) is a major risk of private sales. The example of Chile at the time of the privatisation operations between 1975 and 1981 is particularly revealing. At that time, the two main private conglomerates, Vial and Cruzat-Lorrain, closely linked with the military junta in power, benefited considerably from the transfer operations. What is more, they obtained favourable financial terms and had massive resort to international borrowing to finance these acquisitions. The nationalisation movement in 1982-83 demonstrated that excessive concentration of capital was not viable. When this was broken up from 1985 onwards, the reprivatisation movement of the firms nationalised three years earlier learned lessons from the first wave of privatisation. In this perspective, priority was given to allotting a percentage of equity to the general public or employees when state-owned enterprises were privatised by direct transfer.

*C) Staff buy-outs*

This procedure, practised to a differing extent in the various developing countries in our sample, includes two modalities leading to employee shareownership (whether by executives, managers or employees): on the one hand, acquisitions of a majority holding financed from the employees' own resources or by debt secured over the firms' assets and, on the other hand, certain percentages of capital earmarked for employees in the context of a public offering or private transfer.

1) Cases where staff are the main actors in the buy-out

Only four staff buy-out operations, in the strict sense of the term, have taken place. Moreover, staff buy-outs only concern small public enterprises. In the developing countries, injection of cash by employees is a major obstacle, as their financial resources are insufficient and access to the capital markets is still extremely limited. On the other hand, in the industrialised countries, buy-outs by staff and management have increased (leveraged management/employee buy-out, US Employee Stock Ownership Plan programme). The possibility of raising the funds needed for buying out their companies on the capital markets, using the company's assets as security, enables staff to mobilise substantial financial resources and thus be viewed as credible purchasers.

In Chile, the buy-out of ECOM, a small microcomputer firm, was facilitated by a bank loan over ten years, covering 90 per cent of the cost of the operation ($1.5 million), with the loan secured over the assets of the privatised company. In this case, the public holding company CORFO (Corporacion de Fomento de la Produccion de Chile) acted both as the lending organisation and as the transfer authority (as ECOM was one of its holdings). Similarly, this type of financial assistance played a major role in the buy-out of EMEL, a company created following the partial fragmentation of ENDESA, a Chilean public enterprise involved in electricity production and distribution. Another case, in Tunisia, was the buy-out of SOTUVER. Buy-outs by staff or by trade unions — an example of the latter took place in Mexico in 1988, with the transfer of Grupo Textil Cadena to the union CTM (Confederacion de Trabajadores Mexicanos) — open the way to restructuring the enterprise, taking account of employees' interests insofar as possible.

2) Employee shareownership as a complementary procedure

In view of employees' limited financial resources, procedures that introduce partial employee shareownership seem best suited to the developing countries. Since 1987, Bangladesh, which has one of the lowest levels of wealth per inhabitant, has reserved 15 per cent of the capital of firms transferred for employees (34 per cent being sold by public offering). Minority shareholding by employees facilitates socially delicate transfers (reorganisations that involve redundancies and substantial wage cuts). When the transfers of the telecommunications firms, Compania de Telefonos de Chile or Telephone Company of Jamaica, earmarked part of the capital for employees, this was a signal to their employees that the privatisation of the enterprise would not be to their detriment. Similarly, the fact that the miners union was a member of the consortium chosen to take over the mining group, Mexicana des Cobre, was significant from two viewpoints: both the union's intention to represent the employees in the new division of capital, as privatisation was seen as inevitable, and the desire of the consortium and in all likelihood the government, to involve the workers' representatives so that the restructuring policy was worked out in an efficient and concerted manner. In Chile, in about one-quarter of the transfer operations, the government has encouraged employee participation in the firm's capital. Although it is generally less than 10 per cent, in some cases the employees' share is much more substantial (29 per cent in the case of Industria Azucarera Nacional, 41.5 per cent in the case of Acero de Compania Pacifico, etc.).

## D) Unsubscribed increase of capital

An increase of capital that is not open to subscription by the majority public sector shareholders opens the division of the capital to private investors. Accordingly, like a partial transfer, it leads to a dilution of the state's holding. In common with the other transfer techniques, however, this procedure comes up against the fact that many would-be purchasers lack financial resources. Two factors distinguish an unsubscribed increase of capital from a partial transfer operation: the determination of the price of the private holdings and the impact on public finances.

### 1) The price of private acquisition of shares

The increase of capital has the advantage of avoiding the evaluation both of assets and of the financial value of the transfer of capital. The acquisition price is directly based on the size of the capital increase and the percentage of the new share issue subscribed for by the private investor. However, the operation does not avoid the risk of undervaluation of the firm, in the form of a significant underpricing at the time of the transfer. The inadequate capitalisation of public enterprises in the developing countries (low level of equity in comparison with operating losses or profits) is an obstacle to this procedure. Indeed, an increase of capital that has a high relative value (compared to the initial equity) but a low absolute value (compared to the financial sums engaged) is liable to result in the private sector's obtaining a majority holding in return for a relatively limited financial commitment.

By way of example, the 50 per cent increase in the capital of SITEX, the Tunisian textile firm, was essentially subscribed for by the American-Canadian group Dominion Textile. This operation enabled it to obtain a dominant position in the new division of capital, for about 6 million Tunisian dinars. In comparison, SITEX's turnover amounted to 53 million dinars in 1988, and the net profit to 5.1 million dinars[28]. Assuming the private shareholder receives his dividends on a *pro rata* basis of his share in the capital (in this case 33 per cent), the American-Canadian group would receive 1.7 million dinars in the first year, a return of nearly 30 per cent. This situation results from the low level of capitalisation of the company's profits prior to the increase of capital[29].

The application of these procedures is thus limited by state-owned enterprises' reduced equity resources as well as by the government's financial inability to increase their authorised capital in advance. These two limitations help to explain why this method of diluting the government's holding is so seldom used (only four operations identified; the two operations in Tunisia are presented in detail below, "Three case studies")[30].

2) The impact on the budget

An increase in capital generates no income for the state. Public ownership in an enterprise can therefore be transferred to the private sector without any direct financial consideration to the state. However, this procedure is not entirely neutral at the level of public finances. The injection of fresh money by the private purchaser, through subscription to the capital increase, finances both the firm's recapitalisation and the investments in modernisation that it needs in order to develop. By thus replacing the state in financing the firm's activities, the private sector enables the government to reduce its injections of capital and subsidies to finance investments. This underlying reduction in transfers to the former public enterprises has a positive impact on the government's budget.

In view of the private sector's acquisition of equity in the public enterprises, the unsubscribed increase in capital confirms the reinforcement of the private sector's role in financing investments. This gradual dilution of state holdings has the parallel result of reducing the state's importance as financial backer of the business. This withdrawal from the management and financing of the firm's operations is generally speeded up subsequently with a partial transfer to the private purchaser.

### Strengthening the role of the private sector

Leases and management contracts aim to increase the role of private investors and managers, without necessarily leading to the transfer of ownership of the firms or activities concerned. The basic principle underlying them is the need to improve the firms' management on criteria of efficiency. Resort to management transfers is, as E. Berg and M. Shirley stressed as long ago as 1987, "amazingly low"[31]. In our sample, we noted only 49 operations of this type out of a total of 255, that is about one-fifth of the privatisation operations. The advantages attributed to these mechanisms, their flexibility and the impact of competition between potential lessees and managers during the tender stage, do not seem so obvious if one regards the facts. This stems from the problems of defining the modalities of each operation and of supervising the application of such contracts.

### A) Leases

These grant the lessee full operational and financial control of the assets essential to the firm's activity, for a given period. In consideration, the private lessee undertakes to pay an annual rent to the state, however the financial situation develops. The lease is one of the vectors of "effective privatisation". For the public authorities, it is an attractive procedure in that i) it frees the state from responsibility for the enterprise's operating and investment costs, ii) it generates a stable income, iii) it encourages competition between different potential lessees, iv) *in fine*, it retains public ownership over assets whose value increases with the improvement in management and in the financial results.  In addition, it avoids the threefold problem posed by transfer procedures in developing countries, lack of financial resources on the part of purchasers, the problem of fixing the transfer price, and obstacles of a legal nature (existence of non-transferable assets, mainly land).

This procedure has however been little used (17 operations have been identified), with the exception of Jamaica (9 operations) and Malaysia (6 operations), and has centred on the agricultural and services sectors (tourism, transport, telecommunications).  It is particularly appropriate when the public enterprise is liquidated or split up and the assets are easily transferable (coaches in the case of Jamaica Omnibus system, audiovisual space and tourist complexes in Jamaica and Malaysia).

The main problems relate to the renewal of the lease, the changeover from lease to transfer, and state control before, during and after execution of the lease.

i)  In theory, the renewal of the lease, after the expiry of the initial term, allows the state to renegotiate its terms with all the potential contractors (including the previous lessee) from a position of strength.  This periodic competition is a guarantee of satisfactory behaviour on the part of the lessee chosen.  Nonetheless, it is clear that the outgoing lessee has a decisive advantage (current investments, experience, inside information), thus limiting the government's choice at the time of renewal.

ii)  The lease may be the forerunner of a transfer[32].  Under these circumstances, during the term of the lease, the lessee-purchaser has an opportunity to assess the state-owned firm's viability and to make an offer based on his knowledge of the firm's financial situation and potential.  The lessee has a considerable advantage over other potential buyers and also over the state.  Indeed, if the lessee does not divulge all the available economic and financial information about the company, the state may assess incorrectly the actual value of the firm concerned and thus underprice the company substantially.

iii)  Accordingly, the state has to exercise effective control over the behaviour of a lessee responsible for managing and financing the enterprise he is running.  This strict control must be carried out in the light of the obligations undertaken.  Supervision of this kind, which is a necessary complement to a very precise preliminary definition of the terms of the lease (which should be made very difficult to amend), considerably reduces the flexibility of such procedures.  It also underlines the problems that grants of leases cause in the medium to long term.

## B) Management contracts[33]

In spirit these are somewhat different from leases. In the short term, management contracts strengthen the role of the private sector by entrusting to it, if not the right to derive profit, at least responsibility for the activities of the privatised firm. They focus their action on improving the management and making potential entrepreneurs compete on criteria of efficiency. Management contracts have been used twice as often as leases — in 32 privatisation operations as against 17, in particular in Jamaica (14), Morocco (7), Ghana (6) and Malaysia (5) — mainly because of greater interest from private entrepreneurs in this type of procedure. This interest is grounded in two considerations that distinguish the lease from the management contract:

In the context of management contracts, the government continues to make financial provision for the operating costs and investments. The private contractor has no responsibility for this at all, and this is crucial when the public enterprise concerned either suffers heavy losses or undertakes a vast modernisation of its production methods. As no financial responsibility is transferred to the private sector, even if the firm is henceforth managed on private sector principles, management contracts cannot culminate in "effective privatisations".

In addition, the state pays the private managers to manage the operation in compliance with the terms of the contract and, generally, to improve the financial results. This resort to specific skills represents a cost for the state, but this is most likely to be set off by the reduction in losses incurred by state-owned firms under private management.

In the privatisation of 12 hotels owned by the Jamaican government (National Hotel and Properties), management contracts were an interim step prior to their final transfer to private owners. Although it does not necessarily lead to transfer, the management contract, by introducing a new management team, seeks to remedy the problems ensuing from inadequate management skills. For example, the management contract relating to certain activities of the Jamaican sugar group National Sugar Company was aimed at ending a period of inefficient management which had led to total disorganisation. Accordingly, the major British sugar group Tate & Lyle was appointed to take charge of its management and reorganisation for a ten-year period.

The Malaysian approach is somewhat different. In this case it was not merely a matter of entrusting the operation to private entrepreneurs, but also the construction of new networks. Four contracts were concluded for the construction and management of three new motorways and two new power stations. The granting of the larger of these contracts (500 km motorway crossing the peninsula from north to south, at a price of more than $1.3 billion) revealed the political limitations of tender procedures. The party in power in Malaysia had an indirect holding in the company that was awarded the contract. Some felt that this choice showed the lack of independence on the part of the authorities in charge of the tender procedure.

At the level of investments and social welfare, the risks of conflict between the state and the new managers should be borne in mind. For example, as the managers know that part of the firm's investments are financed by the state budget, they will tend to overinvest in order to increase productivity rapidly and thus improve the firm's results. Similarly, the managers may achieve the company's recovery at the employees' expense (massive redundancies, wage reductions). In both these cases the financial or political cost for the state is likely to be extremely high. Management contracts should therefore precisely define the objectives and extent of the powers granted to the future management team, so as to prevent any problem as regards the interpretation of the contractual clauses. It is difficult, however, to draft a standard contract applicable to all sectors and situations; contracts have to be drawn up case by case, which complicates these procedures still further and slows their implementation.

In no case is transfer of management a panacea, enabling governments to avoid the constraints caused by financial evaluation, the narrowness of the capital markets and the limited number of potential buyers. Neither is it a last resort in the face of inability to transfer ownership in public enterprises. In the developing countries, no procedure is simple to implement. The increase of operations combining a number of methods underlines the governments' preference for *ad hoc* procedures in transferring of management or ownership. This particularly pragmatic approach to privatisation reflects the diversity of individual and sectoral situations, as well as the peculiarities of each developing country. Pragmatism, however, is not a substitute for the theoretical framework of rules that is essential for the rational and objective conduct of privatisation.

### Three case studies

Three examples of privatisation are presented in detail. Our aim is to illustrate the relationship between the implementation of the process and the objectives pursued. Our illustration refers to three countries in our study (Malaysia, Jamaica and Tunisia), using three different techniques (one private sale of equity combined with a lease, one transfer by public offering and one divestiture by means of an increase of capital) in three different sectors (port services, finance, textiles).

### A) The privatisation of Port Kelang (Malaysia)

The privatisation of Port Kelang, the first experience of this type in Malaysia, had two aims: to affirm the government's commitment to strengthening the private sector in the Malaysian economy, and to convince the public of the value of this type of process.

1) Selection of the enterprise

The choice fell on the container terminal at Kelang, the largest port in Malaysia, through which 80 per cent of its foreign trade passes. The port was managed by a public enterprise, the Kelang Port Authority (KPA), under the aegis of the Ministry of Transport but autonomous financially. The container terminal, representing part of the port activities at Kelang, had four advantages:

i) Its activities had been highly profitable since their installation in 1973.

ii) The future private company was to benefit from a natural monopoly in the supply of its services.

iii) The Kelang port installations had a national reputation, yet they did not belong to an economically strategic sector.

iv) The operation of the installations was deemed fairly inefficient, in comparison with large foreign ports.

2) The preparatory stages

The privatisation of part of the activities of Port Kelang called for a long preparatory process, which revealed that the various administrative bodies appointed to carry out the privatisation were unable to complete their task effectively. An *ad hoc* committee grouping local skills (under the direction of a Malaysian merchant bank, Aseam Bankers) as well as foreign ones (in particular, the auditing firm Price Waterhouse and the British merchant bank Kleinwort-Benson) was formed to define the legal and financial framework of the privatisation. The experts' report, completed in December 1984, contained the following recommendations:

i) Creation of Kelang Container Terminal (KCT), an autonomous company grouping all the container-storage activities, to be held at the outset by KPA. The aim of this legal provision was to reduce the administrative procedures and make a share issue possible.

ii) Lease between KCT and KPA relating to the site of the container-storage activities. In this case Malaysian legislation prohibited the privatised company from owning the land on which the activities were situated.

iii) Sale of 51 per cent of the shares in KCT to a private partner.

iv) Public offering of a percentage of the KCT shares within two years following the privatisation.

3) Modalities of the privatisation

Four offers to buy the firm were considered. The Malaysian government, advised by international experts, accepted the offer of a newly created company, KTK, a joint venture between a Malaysia transport company, Kontena Nasional (80 per cent shareholder), and an Australian conglomerate, P & O (20 per cent shareholder). The Malaysian authorities hoped to attract foreign skills and capital, by means of the privatisation programme. The presence of the Australian conglomerate enabled KTK to become the majority shareholder of KCT, with a 51 per cent holding. In addition, the purchasers signed a 21-year lease with KPA for use of the non-transferable assets (land and buildings).

The future of the workers employed in the storage company prior to the privatisation also had to be negotiated. The Malaysian authorities considered this factor crucial, as they wished to demonstrate that privatisation operations would not go ahead to the detriment of the workers. The 801 employees voted massively to join the privatised company, after obtaining adequate guarantees which led to a new legal arrangement (amendment to the 1980 Pension Act).

4) Conclusions

The privatisation of part of Port Kelang's activities, presented as a success opening the way to rebalancing the public and private sectors, teaches the following lessons:

  i) The firm's productivity seems to have improved significantly. In the 18 months following the privatisation, the hourly container-handling rate increased by 40 per cent (rising from 18 containers to 25). In the same period, storage time was considerably reduced, from an average of 12 days to 3-4 days. The productivity and improvement targets appear to have been achieved[34].

  ii) It is debatable whether KCT was really privatised, given the weight of public institutions in the final distribution of the capital. In fact, 82 per cent of the Malaysian purchaser, Kontena Nasional, is held by a government organisation whose aim is to promote the position of the Bumiputras (ethnic Malays) in the national economy. The total public holding in KCT's capital therefore amounts to more than 75 per cent. Moreover, although it had a minority holding of 10 per cent in KCT, the Australian multinational succeeded in imposing an Australian management team and operational director. This reaffirms the need for an in-depth study of the division of the capital between public and private shareholders, and of the relationship between ownership and management (see above, "The concept of privatisation: definition and justification").

  iii) The privatisation required the help of many local or foreign intermediaries, both public and private, and entailed several legal arrangements. The slowness of the procedure, more than three years overall, exemplifies the disadvantages of *ad hoc* practices.

iv) The hiving off of the container-storage activities, which were the most profitable, poses a threat to the financial situation of the residual public enterprise, KPA. Accordingly, subsidies will be needed to keep KPA afloat.

## B) The privatisation of National Commercial Bank of Jamaica

At the beginning of 1986, the conservative government of Jamaica had already negotiated with private partners the transfer of the management of several hotels, the sale of close to 32 000 hectares of land and leases for most of the rural organisations involved in marketing agricultural products. Nonetheless, as decisive legislative elections approached, the government wished to give a new boost to the privatisation programme. For this reason, the privatisation of the National Commercial Bank (NCB) — both the size of the transaction and the methods employed — was a turning-point in the process of rebalancing.

### 1) Privatisation by public offering

The Jamaican government, advised and supported by USAID, the US development agency, demonstrated its intention of convincing the public of the merits of its privatisation programme. In opting for a public offering on the stock market, Prime Minister Seaga and his main adviser, R. Downer (managing partner with Price Waterhouse, Kingston), aimed to achieve three objectives:

i) By transferring 51 per cent of the capital in the largest Jamaican commercial bank, the idea was to pursue government withdrawal from economic and financial activity. Moreover, the NCB, nationalised in 1977 by the previous government, had less satisfactory financial results than the large private Jamaican bank NBS.

ii) The operation counted on a strong mobilisation of national savings for investment in a financial product (the share) that was new for a large fraction of the Jamaican population. This hoped-for participation by small savers was facilitated by three clauses in the public offering:

a) Only Jamaican citizens were eligible to purchase shares in the privatised company (warding off criticisms of possible majority shareholding by foreign interests).

b) No Jamaican citizen would be allowed to own more than 7.5 per cent of the total capital, so as to avoid too great a concentration of capital and to encourage democratisation of the ownership.

c) Specific measures aimed at small subscribers and NCB employees (facilities for payment, priority distribution of shares to small investors) were to help make the NCB transfer financially attractive.

iii) The introduction on the stock market of part of NCB's capital (during the initial phase the state retained 49 per cent of the capital, although it waived the voting rights attached to this holding) would increase the capitalisation of the Jamaican Stock Exchange by nearly 10 per cent. This transaction involving 30.6 million shares and $16.5 million would make the stock market — which up till then had opened only four hours a week — more dynamic and would increase opportunities for private firms to obtain direct financing.

To achieve these three objectives, NCB had the necessary characteristics for attracting potential shareholders: a good reputation and a healthy financial situation. In parallel, the attractive terms of the public offering (in particular as regards the share price) expressed the government's will for the public sale of NCB to succeed even at the expense of the expected profitability from the transfer operation.

2) A complex but rapid procedure

The public offering is a risky gamble in a medium-income developing country where the savings rate is low and the stock market insufficiently developed. Moreover, despite the lack of preparatory work, the government hoped to complete the procedure rapidly. Accordingly, the government asked the British bank N.M. Rothschilds, which had underwritten the public offering of British Telecom in Great Britain, and the accounting firm Price Waterhouse to take part in drafting the NCB privatisation plan. Within three months the modalities of the public offering (valuation of the assets, share pricing and marketing of the operation) had been defined. In less than ten months, all the stages leading to the transfer of NCB had been completed.

---

**Timetable of the main stages of the privatisation**

*February 1986*    Government decision to privatise NCB

*March 1986*    Formation of the *ad hoc* committee chaired by Downer

*June 1986*    Decree transferring NCB shares to the portfolio of National Investment Bank of Jamaica in charge of the transaction

*August 1986*    Start of work by the British advisers

*November 1986*    Issue of report on the modalities of the public offering

*December 1986*    15-day advertising campaign publicising the public offering

*23 December 1986*    First transactions on the Jamaican Stock Exchange

---

## 3) The lessons learned from the public offering of NCB

The Jamaican government presented the transfer operation as a major success. First of all, the return of NCB to the private sector demonstrated popular support for the privatisation operation. Indeed, the offering was oversubscribed by more than 170 per cent. Sixty-three per cent of the company's capital was allotted to small shareholders and employees. The government's main objective, democratisation of the ownership, was achieved, as the bank now had more than 24 000 shareholders. In addition, the government took into account the fact that with 49 per cent of the capital, and facing a fragmented group of private shareholders, it would remain NCB's main shareholder: to demonstrate its intention to grant wide autonomy of decision to the private shareholders, it waived the voting rights attached to its holding.

Next, the success of the public offering made possible an appeal to the capital market to mobilise domestic resources. This finding led the government to privatise another major Jamaican enterprise by public offering a few months later, though it did not achieve the same success. This time the public offering related to 100 per cent of the capital of Caribbean Company. Only 72 per cent of the capital was subscribed for, and from the first few days the share price dropped well below the initial price of the offering.

The Caribbean Company experience highlights the problems that arose during the NCB privatisation but were hidden at the time owing to the success of the operation. NCB was a financially solid public enterprise (receiving no public funds and even paying tax on its profits), operating in a competitive environment (not benefiting from any specific legal protection). The impact on the public deficit and on competition could therefore only be marginal. Further, it was clear that its shares had been underpriced at the time of the public offering, as the first quotations showed a 68 per cent rise in the price. All these factors demonstrate that the success of the NCB privatisation was difficult to repeat, especially in the case of a firm that had experienced financial difficulties in the past.

Nonetheless, the conservative government's victory was above all ideological. The success of Manley's centre-left party in the 1988 legislative elections did not call his predecessor's privatisation programme into question. In fact during 1989 the new administration even seems to have increased the rate of privatisations, particularly in the tourist sector.

### C) Privatisation of the Tunisian textile sector

The textile sector accounts for about 30 per cent of the Tunisian manufacturing industry. It comprises six large firms — before privatisation, two were in the private sector and four (SITER, SITEX, SOMOTEX and TISSMOK) owned by the public holding company SOGITEX (Société Générale de Textile) — and numerous small private firms. The fundamental principles of the Tunisian privatisation programme — to increase the private sector's involvement in the effort to modernise public enterprises and to treat operations on a case-by-case basis — found a favourable field of application in the textile sector.

## 1) Modernisation of the textile firms

The desire to modernise the various segments of the public sector textile firms (denim cloth, spinning, weaving, finishing) emerged at the start of the 1980s. The Tunisian textile industry's growth and development were in fact limited by its outdated machinery and manufacturing processes. The grant of a large loan ($18.6 million) by the World Bank in 1981 enabled the subsidiaries of SOGITEX, in conjunction with the Tunisian government, to make the first investments in modernisation. The funds lent were invested principally in SITEX ($14.4 million for purchasing looms) and to a lesser extent in SOMOTEX and SITER.

These massive investments were intended to make the public enterprises more dynamic so as to attract local or foreign private investors. In fact, as from 1986, the Tunisian government wanted to reduce direct government intervention in the running of firms in this key sector. It was not a matter of calling into question the modernisation efforts undertaken, since the new private investors were to replace the state or the World Bank in financing the modernisation programme. Privatisation by diluting the government's holding in the companies concerned was viewed as a means of transferring the financing and subsequently the control of the operation to private investors (generally former partners).

## 2) Privatisations on a case-by-case basis

By the beginning of 1990, the state's divestiture of SITEX and SITER was virtually completed, that of TISSMOK well advanced, and that of SOMOTEX (and the other clothing manufacturers owned by the holding company SOGITEX) projected.

The privatisation of SITEX is an example of the acquisition of control by a private enterprise, in this case an American-Canadian firm, following a subscription of an increase of capital, and later by the purchase of part of the public holding. In December 1986, the Canadian group Dominion Textile, a technical and trading partner with SITEX since 1974, subscribed for the bulk of the 50 per cent increase in the capital. It thus became the shareholder of reference, with nearly one-third of the capital. International Finance Corporation (IFC), an affiliate of the World Bank, held 10 per cent; STUSID, a Tuniso-Saudi development bank, about 20 per cent; and SOGITEX retained 26.4 per cent. The substantial increase in capital increased SITEX's equity, and hence its *capacity for self-financing the additional investments needed for its modernisation*. In 1989, SOGITEX withdrew totally from SITEX's capital by assigning its holding to the Canadian group, STUSID and SITEX itself (which holds these shares as a nominee while waiting to transfer them to small investors or employees of the firm). It is interesting to note that at first the Tunisian government wished to divest its holding through the stock market. However, the Canadian group offered to purchase part of the equity at 30 per cent above the market price. The government opted for strengthening Dominion Textile's percentage, revealing the pragmatic nature of the privatisation procedure. Now the American-Canadian group holds 44 per cent of SITEX's capital and, with the support of the IFC, controls the operation and the investment programme.

The case of SITER is somewhat different. In December 1987, the company increased its capital in order to finance the continuation of its modernisation programme. SOGITEX subscribed as majority shareholder, ending up with an 88 per cent holding in SITER. It then assigned 25 per cent of the capital to the French Group DMC, 10 per cent to the IFC and about 25 per cent to Tunisian development banks, keeping 29 per cent. The choice of DMC was due principally to its capacity to provide technical assistance and management, making it a most desirable industrial and trading partner. The involvement of DMC was in the context of the GRIP (Guaranteed Recovery on Investment Principal) proposed by the IFC. Under this agreement, the private investor contributes the funds, and the IFC invests in its name, bearing the risk of loss in capital, for whatever reason. At the end of the guarantee period, during which the dividends are shared, the private investor either becomes the outright owner of the shares or withdraws, receiving the whole of his initial capital. The aim of this procedure is to attract foreign private investors by safeguarding them against the principal's risk of loss. Offers by Tunisian operators to purchase SOGITEX's minority holding were still under study at the beginning of 1990.

The privatisation of TISSMOK has proved more difficult, since unlike SITEX, which was in profit before private partners took control of it, TISSMOK has suffered very heavy operating losses. For example, in 1988 alone, its losses amounted to nearly 10 per cent of its turnover and 40 per cent of the subscribed capital[35]. In view of the company's financial situation, stock level and inadequate modernisation, the private textile group BACOSPORT refused to take over the 44.5 per cent held by SOGITEX.

3) Conclusions

Privatisations in the textile sector were rapid for three main reasons:

i)  The financial results of the public enterprises were significantly lower than those of the large private companies (Lee-Cooper Tunisie, BACOSPORT). Accordingly, they seemed less able to finance their modernisation in this key sector of the Tunisian manufacturing industry. Although the privatisation programme is not completed, the textile sector is largely dominated by private firms, which in 1988 made nearly 70 per cent of new investments.

ii) Employment is the Tunisian government's primary objective. Political hesitations about privatisation, owing to likely redundancies of surplus staff, diminished when the public authorities considered the beneficial effects in the medium term of modernisation and strengthening the role of the private sector. For example, in three years BACOSPORT created 700 jobs, a 50 per cent increase in its work-force, whereas the public enterprises were laying off their staff or having difficulty in keeping them on.

iii) The privatisations of SITER and SITEX led to the strengthening of foreign investment, as the authorities had greatly hoped. This has changed from technical and commercial partnership to direct shareownership. Moreover, they can be classed as "effective privatisations", as the two conditions for this — the application of private rationality and the buyers' financial liability — are fulfilled.

## Microeconomic and empirical analysis of the privatisation operations

Are particular sectors of activity affected in priority by the privatisation process? Are these sectors competitive, or are they oligopolistic, even monopolistic, as the theory of privatisation implies (whether the public enterprise has market power)? Does the designation of "strategic" sectors in all the developing countries correspond to a minimal or ideal concept of the size of the public sector? The answer to all these questions presupposes a sectoral analysis of the privatisation movement. The analysis is divided into two parts: i) the sectors concerned by transfers of management and ownership, ii) the "strategic" sectors excluded from the privatisation process.

### Sectoral analysis

The sectoral analysis of privatisation entails a study of the former distribution of public enterprises per sector of activity and the relative position of each sector of activity in the respective national economies. For example, privatisations in the United Kingdom affected the banking sector only marginally because public involvement is very limited in this sector; this is not the expression of a political will to keep it from privatisation, as too cursory a comparison with the many operations carried out in the French banking sector would lead one to think. A comparable sectoral approach should be applied to our sample countries (see Table 11).

*A) The uneven sectoral distribution of privatisation operations*

1) The agricultural sector

To date, the agricultural sector has been relatively little affected by privatisation movements. A few small agriculture-based food-industry firms (Morocco, Chile and Jamaica) and certain large farms (Ghana, Chile) were privatised by transfer. In the case of larger public agricultural enterprises, the need for complete management and operational reorganisation has usually led the authorities to opt for transfer of management (*cf.* the example of the National Sugar Company in Jamaica). It seems, however, that in agriculture, more particularly in the case of export products, priority has been given to *internal restructuring* of the public presence (liquidation, merger of numerous paragovernmental marketing, inspection and export- promotion bodies). The Ghanean cocoa production and distribution network provides an illustration of this approach.

2) The industrial sector

To date, three countries — Chile, Bangladesh and Mexico — have significantly reduced public involvement in the industrial sector.

In Chile, the privatisation movement has concentrated on large public enterprises (gas production, COPEC; the iron and steel industry, CAP; cement works, POPAILCO) and the electricity production and distribution companies (more than half of all operations). In the two other countries, privatisation has been carried out by divesting numerous small enterprises. In Bangladesh, most often there have been reprivatisations of small units in the traditional industrial branches. In the key textiles sector, opened to privatisation in 1980, 22 of the 53 firms, accounting for 42 per cent of the production capacity and about 30 000 employees, were divested in 1982-83 (Lorch, 1988). In Mexico, the divestiture affected about 30 per cent of the public manufacturing and mining sector value-added achieved by public enterprises[36]. In the case of Mexico, however, two comments must be made. First, the figures presented above reflect not only the impact of the transfers of public enterprises but that of a process known as *desincorporacion*. Accordingly, other rebalancing methods (liquidation, merger, transfer) are taken into account. Next, since mid-1988, when these estimates were drawn up, several major transfer operations have taken place (Mexicana del Cobre at a price of $680 million at the end of 1988).

It should be noted, however, that industrial structures are not developed to the same standard in the various sample countries. In some countries, such as Bolivia, Ghana and Morocco, a major percentage of industrial sector activities is still in the area of mining and the processing of agricultural, mineral or energy commodities. As these are the main, or even the only generators of foreign currency, the public enterprises in these sectors are not concerned by the privatisation process. As they

Table 11

PRIVATISATION OPERATIONS: SECTORS CONCERNED

| | AGRICULTURE | | INDUSTRY | | FINANCE | | TRANSPORT | | TELECOMMUNICATIONS | | TOURISM | | MISCELLANEOUS | |
|---|---|---|---|---|---|---|---|---|---|---|---|---|---|---|
| | Transfer | Management | Transfer | Management | Transfer | Management | Transfer | Management | Transfer | Management | Transfer | Management | Transfer | Management |
| GHANA | 1 | 1 | 3 | 5 | | | | | | | | | | 1 |
| MOROCCO | 6 | 2 | | | | | | | | | | 27 | 1 | |
| TUNISIA | 2 | | 12 | | | | 1 | | | | 9 | | | |
| BOLIVIA | | | | | | | 1 | | | | | | | |
| CHILE | 5 | | 16 | | 16 | | 2 | | 4 | | | | | |
| JAMAICA | 8 | 6 | 9 | | 1 | | 2 | 1 | 2 | | 9 | 6 | 1 | |
| MEXICO | | | 14 | | 13 | | 2 | | 1 | | 28 | | | |
| BANGLADESH | 30 2 (since 1987) | | 475 7 (since 1987) | 1 | | | | | | | | | | |
| MALAYSIA | | | | | | | 4 | 3 | 1 | 1 | | 1 | 3 | 1 |
| PHILIPPINES | 2 | | 4 | | 5 | | 1 | | | | 3 | | 1 | |
| FRANCE | | | 4 | | 7 | | | | 3 | | | | 1 | |
| UNIT. KINGDOM 2 | | | 26 | | | | 7 | 1 | | 5 | | 1 | 10 | |

150

Table 11 (continued)

| | |
|---|---|
| Morocco: | *Tourism:* 27 hotels, of which 17 belong to the Office National Marocain du Tourisme (ONMT). |
| Tunisia: | *Industry:* SITEX; *Tourism:* SIITT (including hôtel Tanit), Hôtel Hannibal, Hôtel international. |
| Chile: | *Agriculture:* INFORSA & SUDAMERICA, INDUS, IANSA; *Industry:* ACERO DEL COMPANIA PACIFICO, COPEC, ENDESA, SOQUIMICH; *Finance:* six banks (including BANCO DE CHILE, BANCO DE SANTIAGO) and ten insurance companies (including AFP Provida, AFP SANTA MARIA); *Transport* 2 airlines (LANCHILE et LADECO); *Telecommunications:* COMPANIA DE TELEFONOS DE CHILE, ENTEL. |
| Jamaica: | *Agriculture:* NATIONAL SUGAR COMPANY, WEST INDIES PULP AND PAPER; *Industry:* CARIBBEAN CEMENT COMPANY, SEPROD; *Finance:* 1 bank, NATIONAL COMMERCIAL BANK OF JAMAICA; *Telecommunications:* TELEPHONE COMPANY OF JAMAICA; *Tourism:* 12 hotels, including the ROYAL CARIBBEAN. |
| Mexico: | *Industry:* MEXICANA DEL COBRE, TEREFTALATOS MEXICANOS, DIESEL NACIONAL, VEHICULOS AUTOMOTORES MEXICANOS; *Finance:* 14 banks (including BANAMEX, BANCOMER, SERFIN); *Transport:* 2 airlines (AEROMEXICO and MEXICANA); *Tourism:* 28 hotels belonging to the chain NATIONAL HOTELERA. |
| Bangladesh: | *Agriculture:* DHAKA VEGETABLE OIL INDUSTRIES, ZEAL BANGLA SUGAR MILLS; *Industry:* EASTERN CABLES, KOHINOOR CHEMICAL. |
| Malaysia: | *Industry:* LABUAN-BEAUFORT POWER INTERCONNECTION; *Transport:* MALAYSIAN AIRLINE SYSTEM, PORT KELANG CONTAINER TERMINAL, NORTH-SOUTH HIGHWAY; *Telecommunications:* JABATAN TELEKOM NEGARA, TV3; *Other:* SPORT TOTO. |
| Philippines: | *Agriculture:* BUKIDNON SUGAR CENTRAL MINING, PHILIPPINE COTTON CORPORATION; *Finance:* 5 banks, PHILIPPINE NATIONAL BANK, PHILIPPINES BANK, COMMERCIAL BANK OF MANILA, INTERBANK; *Tourism:* CEBU PLAZA HOTEL. |
| France: | *Industry:* SAINT GOBAIN, ELF, CGE, MATRA; *Finance:* 7 banks, including SUEZ, PARIBAS, SOCIÉTÉ GÉNÉRALE, CRÉDIT COMMERCIAL DE FRANCE; *Telecommunications:* HAVAS, TF1. |
| United Kingdom: | *Agriculture:* BRITISH SUGAR; *Industry:* BRITISH PETROLEUM, BRITISH GAS, BRITISH AEROSPACE, ROLLS-ROYCE, AMERSHAM; *Transport:* BRITISH AIRWAYS; *Telecommunications:* BRITISH TELECOM, CABLE & WIRELESS; *Other:* 10 water distribution compagnies. |
| *Note:* | This list shows the principal privatisations, selected on the basis of the turnover of the firm concerned, the transfer price and the importance of the firm in the sector. In going beyond the simple quantitative presentation of the table, it delimits more precisely the sectors that are most affected by privatisation. This table is based on the information on the Annex 2. |

belong to sectors deemed "strategic" for the national economy, these enterprises are instead restructured and remain under public ownership and control (see the restructuring of COMIBOL and YBPB in Bolivia).

3) The financial and banking sector

In our sample, only one country out of two has undertaken a privatisation programme in the financial and banking sector. These operations were carried out exclusively by means of transfers (public offering or private sale).

In Chile and Mexico, many financial and banking institutions were returned to private ownership as early as 1985-86[37]. In both these countries, the banking sector had been nationalised in 1982: in Chile, to limit the consequences of the collapse of the banking system, and in Mexico as a result of a decision by President Lopez Portillo in the last few months of his term of office. The rapid reprivatisation of these nationalised enterprises enabled the authorities to affirm their commitment to privatisation operations. Moreover, as their main priority was to make the process sustainable, they resorted to public offerings in the case of the main financial and banking institutions. In the Philippines, the privatisation programme mainly concerned the public financial and banking sector, which in 1984 represented 66 per cent of all public sector value-added (Manasan & Buenaventura, 1986). The sales of the five major banks were thus the main transfers that took place in the context of this programme. The most extensive privatisation programme was carried out in Chile, where many banking institutions (6), insurance companies (8) and pension funds (2) were transferred to the private sector, considerably reducing the weight of public financial institutions.

4) The transport sector

The transport sector is essential for the national economy yet is not always deemed "strategic". As its enterprises are attractive, owing to their oligopolistic or monopolistic position and their potential profitability, it has provided a favourable area for an ever-increasing number of privatisation operations. They have been concentrated on air, road and sea transport; the age and deterioration of the rail networks and the massive debt of the railway companies have caused the rare attempts at privatisation in this area to end in failure. Malaysia has not found a purchaser for its national railway company, KTM, despite the token price of one ringgit[38]. However, nearly half the privatisations in this country involved the transport sector. These operations consisted of partial transfers or transfers of management, the Malaysian government always retaining a minority, or even a majority, of the capital of the privatised companies.

The transport sector is viewed very differently from one country to another. Whereas Chile and Mexico privatised their main airline companies (respectively, Lanchile and Ladeco, Mexicana and Aeromexico), the Philippines and Morocco classed their national airlines as "strategic" enterprises.

5) The telecommunications sector

Although viewed in a very different way, the telecommunications sector is comparable to the transport sector. Ghana, Morocco, Tunisia and Bolivia view it as strategic, whereas the others have already undertaken privatisation operations (Chile, Jamaica) or are in the course of doing so (Malaysia, Mexico). The need to extend and modernise the telecommunications networks in the developing countries, combined with a relatively non-competitive market structure, gives a glimpse of a potential for very high profitability. Accordingly, the transfer of public enterprises in this sector attracts technology and capital from foreign companies hoping to take advantage of the opportunities offered by the privatisation (Australian partners in the case of CTC, Spanish in the case of ENTEL in Chile, British in the case of TOJ in Jamaica).

6) The tourist sector

In Morocco, Tunisia, Jamaica and the Philippines, tourism is an essential sector, generating substantial foreign-currency earnings. In these four countries, many hotels have been transferred to private investors or managers. In a highly competitive sector, the performance of the undynamic state-run hotel chains was far and away inferior to that of the private sector. The possibility of splitting up the tourist companies into independent entities (as was done in Tunisia, with SHTT) enables separate sales of assets to take place (hotels and tourist complexes). The transfer operations or transfers of management accorded (mainly in Morocco and Jamaica) appeared all the more attractive in that the profitability of the acquisitions seemed assured, even in the short term.

B) Progress in completing the privatisation programme and sectors concerned

The sectoral study of the privatisation operations shows that there is a relationship between the type of sectors affected and the extent of the privatisation process. Two phases of privatisation can thus be defined:

1) During the first phase, transfers of ownership or management affect nationalised public enterprises haphazardly (the nationalisation of a bank entails that of the industrial and financial holdings in its portfolio) and/or as a result of the economic situation (rapid increase of the public sector resulting from a critical economic or political situation) (Saulniers, 1988). Most often, the programmes start either with reprivatisations, which express the political authorities' intention to reverse the rapid growth in the number of state-owned firms, or with privatisations in those sectors where direct government intervention in productive activity seems

neither necessary nor justified. Chile after the fall of Allende in 1973 and again since 1985, Bangladesh since 1973, only two years after its independence, and Mexico as from 1982, after the successive presidencies of de Echeverria and Lopez Portillo — all adopted this first step[39]. As an illustration of the second approach, the first privatisations in Ghana, Morocco and Tunisia were in the agriculture-based food industry, small-scale industry and tourism sectors (see Table 11).

2) The achievement of a full-scale operation is a turning-point in the privatisation programmes, and is presented as such by the authorities. Most often it has affected the financial and banking sector: in Chile, the transfer of AFP Provida in 1985; in Jamaica, that of NCB in 1986; in Mexico, that of BANAMEX in 1987; in the Philippines, that of PNB in 1989. This shift initiated a phase of privatising sectors of activity that, often since independence, had belonged to the traditional area of government intervention (sectors involved in import substitution, which boost the rest of the national economy) and had fairly uncompetitive market structures. The sectors combining these characteristics — air transport, telecommunications and modern industries (production and distribution of electricity, mining and chemicals) — became prime targets for privatisation.

Only Chile and, to a lesser extent, Jamaica, Mexico and Bangladesh, started to implement this second phase. It calls for both the definition of an overall privatisation programme, specifying in advance the sectors concerned and the privatisation methods, and the determination of the sectors the government deems "strategic". None of these privatisation processes, however, apart perhaps from the Chilean programme, fundamentally called into question the original functions of the state (defence, justice, health and education). The pursuance of the programme on new grounds accordingly calls for serious reflection on the residual size of the public sector at the end of the privatisation movement. This type of organisation and planning contrasts with the pragmatism and *ad hoc* procedures noted at the time of the first privatisation operations. In 1989, three other countries, Ghana, Morocco and Malaysia, presented detailed plans regarding the continuation of the privatisation programme and, hence, regarding the relative position of the public sector in the economy. This type of presentation is likely to accelerate the rate of privatisations over the next few years.

### The "strategic" sectors

The "strategic" sectors are omnipresent in the study of privatisations, although they have not been precisely defined. They are sectors in which it is deemed essential that the state have a priority or even exclusive right to intervene in the production or distribution of certain goods and services. This assessment differs from one country to another but is also often liable to alteration. For example, in 1982, with the adoption of its New Economic Policy and the renewal of the legal structure of privatisation, Bangladesh reduced the number of strategic sectors from 19 to 6. Although lists are not available for all the developing countries in the sample, it is possible to draw up a comparative table of the strategic sectors (see Table 12). They can be divided into two groups: utilities and vital sectors. After a brief presentation, the political significance of strategic sectors will be considered.

## A) Public utilities and vital sectors

The following are generally classed as public utilities: production and distribution of drinking water, electricity, transport (rail, sea, road and air) and telecommunications. The weight of investment in development and modernisation, lack of certainty as to the profitability of the operations, quality constraints and non-competitive market structures are all reasons put forward by governments for excluding these sectors from privatisation. This approach is not unanimously accepted, however. Chile has departed from this line the most spectacularly by divesting a fraction, often a majority, of government holdings in enterprises in these sectors.

The "vital" sectors of the economy are those which, it is argued, should always be under public ownership, for reasons of national independence. These are the main export sectors, sources of foreign currency and budget income. Privatisation is deemed inappropriate for the major public companies exploiting national natural resources. Phosphates in Morocco and Tunisia; oil in Mexico, the Philippines, Chile and Bolivia; copper in Chile and Bolivia; cocoa in Ghana; and forestry in Bangladesh — all these production networks and their derivatives (e.g. the Mexican or Philippine petrochemicals industry) are destined to remain in the public sector.

It is particularly important to emphasize that the financial and banking sector is not included in the strategic sectors. This represents a considerable change from the positions defended in the 1970s by certain development economists, mainly Latin Americans associated with CEPAL, who advocated state control over the collection networks and financial intermediation channels. At present, there is a reduction in direct government intervention in the banking and financial sector and a tendency towards more liberal regulations (relating to credit and debit interest rates and credit policies), whilst indirect control (through the Central Bank) is being strengthened.

## B) Ideal or minimum size of the public sector: a global standard definition?

The presentation of the strategic sectors of activity in the developing countries leads to three important comments:

i) Although in certain cases the number of strategic sectors is extremely small, these restrictive definitions leave very wide scope for intervention by the entrepreneur state. The largest public groups come under the umbrella of the "priority or exclusive sectors" (to use the Mexican

*Table 12*

## THE STRATEGIC SECTORS

| | Water & Electricity | Transport | | | | Post & Telecom. | Services | Export Products | Industry |
|---|---|---|---|---|---|---|---|---|---|
| | | Road | Rail | Sea | Air | | | | |
| GHANA | X | X | X | X | | X | X | Cocoa, oil, gold | |
| MOROCCO | X | X | X | | X | X | | Phosphates | |
| TUNISIA | X | | X | | | X | | Phosphates, oil | Fertilizers |
| BOLIVIA | X | | X | | X | X | | Copper, oil | Mining Heavy industry |
| CHILE | | | | | | | | Copper, oil | |
| JAMAICA | | | | | | | | | |
| MEXICO | X | | | | X | | | Oil | Petrochemicals Agricultural equipment Fertilizers |
| BANGLADESH | X | | X | | X | X | | Forestry | Armaments Nuclear power |
| MALAYSIA | | | | | | | | Oil | Heavy industry Automobile industry |
| PHILIPPINES | | | X | | | | Financial and social services | Oil | |

156

*Table 12 (continued)*

*Commentaries on each country:*

**Ghana:** List of 22 "core state-owned enterprises" that cannot be privatised, including Volta River Authority, Ghana Water and Sewerage Corp., Electricity Corp. of Ghana, Ghana Oil Co., Ghana Railway Comp., State Gold Mining Corp., COCOBOD, Ghana National Petroleum Co., Posts and Telecom Corp., State Transport Corp., City Express, GHAIP.

**Morocco:** Only six public enterprises, among the most important in the country, are officially deemed strategic (Office National d'Eau Potable, Office National de l'Electricité, Office National des Chemins de Fer, Royal Air Maroc, Office Chérifien des Phosphates, Office National des Postes et Télécommunications).

**Tunisia:** No list as such, but reference to strategic sectors (in particular, Société Nationale d'Exploitation et de Distribution d'Eau, Société Nationale des Chemins de Fer Tunisiens, Société Tunisienne d'Electricité et du Gaz, Compagnie des Phosphates de Gafsa, Groupe Chimique, Société Tunisienne des Industries de Raffinage), as against the competitive sectors (tourism, textiles, manufacturing).

**Bolivia:** Reference to strategic sectors is set out in the Development Plan 1976-80. Eight public enterprises are concerned, including Empresa Nacional de Electricidad, Lloyd Aereo Boliviano, Empresa Nacional de Ferrocarriles, Corporacion Minera de Bolivia, Yacimientos Petrolíferos Fiscales Bolivianos, Empresa Nacional de Telecomunicaciones.

**Chile:** The draft bill of August 1986 defined the conditions for government intervention very restrictively (thus defining the scope of Article 19 of the 1980 Constitution). This essentially concerns two enterprises: Corporacion del Cobre (CODELCO) et Empresa Nacional de Petroleo (ENAP).

**Jamaica:** Enterprises divided into three categories: a) privatisable within three years, b) strategic enterprises, c) no decision on their future.

**Mexico:** Definition of sectors exclusively reserved to the state or reserved in priority to the state. State involvement in these sectors is expressly mentioned in Articles 25, 26 and 27 of the Constitution. The list can nonetheless be altered (*cf.* PROFANICE, *The Plan: Progress Report*, 1985).

**Bangladesh:** The official list of six reserved sectors, published in 1982 in the context of the New Industrial Policy (NIP), is considerably more restrictive than the list of January 1973 (19 sectors). In addition, strategic enterprises will only be transferred partially (previously the state retained 100 per cent fo the capital).

**Malaysia:** No list defining the strategic sectors. Under the global plan of action of September 1989, however, the state's majority holding in Petronas (oil), Proton (automobile), HICOM (heavy industry), MAS and MISC (air and sea transport) would not be affected. Many operations have concerned these sectors, but the state either keeps a majority holding or arranges a transfer of management, in order to keep control *in fine*. Privatisations envisaged for 1990-91: STM (telecommunications), SLM (electricity), KTM (rail transport).

**Philippines:** List presenting different plans for each of the 296 public enterprises (135 privatisations, 65 liquidations, 15 mergers, 58 reorganisations/consolidations and 38 to be retained in the public sector). Main enterprises: Metropolitan Waterworks and Sewerage System, National Power Corp., Philippine National Railways, Philippine National Oil Corp., Development Bank of the Philippines, Land Bank of the Philippines, Social Security System.

terminology). In Bolivia the seven strategic sectors contain the eight largest public enterprises in the country. The same observation applies to Morocco.

ii) Certain countries, such as Ghana, Mexico and Bangladesh, have expressly laid down limits on privatisation. This does not mean, however, that the size of the public sector cannot be reduced by other rebalancing methods. Even when protected from privatisation, public enterprises operating in the strategic sectors are subject to restructuring, or even to partial or total liquidation. The examples of COMIBOL and YBPB in Bolivia, PEMEX in Mexico, PNOC in the Philippines and OCP in Morocco show the desire to modernise and revive financially and economically enterprises and sectors that are to remain under public control and ownership.

iii) The determination of strategic sectors is a genuine global standard definition of the ideal size of the public sector at the end of the privatisation programme, that is, in a relatively distant future. The slow progress of privatisation, owing to the problems of completing the preparatory stages (audit of the public firms, legal and organisational questions) and the economic, legal and financial constraints imposed by the developing countries, is constantly stretching the end of the process to an ever more distant horizon.

By defining the residual size of the public sector, even if that definition is not final, the developing countries define the hard core of direct government intervention in economic activity. The importance of the strategic sectors in most of the developing countries, with the notable exception of Chile, seems to include a new relationship of strength within a rebalanced mixed economy. In this perspective, a larger and more dynamic private sector will exist alongside a refocused and modernised public sector (see Chapter 5).

# NOTES AND REFERENCES

1. With the notable exceptions of Heald (1985) and Yarrow (1985).

2. See Ross (1973), Nalebuff & Stiglitz (1983), Arrow (1985).

3. At the level of managers' behaviour, the restoration of private management incentives (better remuneration, prestige), as distinct from public sector management's lucrative sinecures, will have less impact than the re-establishment of constraints (lower remuneration, dismissal). The credibility of the constraints is based on the principal's ability to reduce the distortions of information perpetuated by public sector managers in their desire for "a quiet life".

4. On the other hand, a liberal regulatory framework will lead to the question of the consequences of applying private rationality in non-competitive situations.

5. Malaysia is a perfect illustration of this idea. Parapublic institutions and development banks with public capital take part in transfer operations by buying substantial shares of privatised companies on behalf of the Malaysian ethnic group, the Bumiputras. In another register, in Morocco, the large private group Omnium Nord-Africain (ONA), one of the main companies involved in the Moroccan privatisations, is held in part by the royal family.

6. See Vuylsteke (1988, p. 165) for "preference shares" held by the Malaysian state in the capital of MAS and MISC in Malaysia. Often used in the privatisations in the United Kingdom (particularly British Telecom and Jaguar) or in France (Elf, Havas, Matra), "golden shares" enable the state to retain, in certain exceptional circumstances (the national interest, decisions relating to certain of the firm's assets), a right of consultation, or even a right of veto. At the beginning of 1990, when Jaguar was sold to the North American group Ford Motors, the British government did not use the right of veto that the "golden shares" gave it in theory.

7. "Techniques of Privatization of State-Owned Enterprises", Volume 3, *Inventory of Country Experience and Reference Materials*, R. Candoy-Sekse, World Bank Technical Paper, No. 90, Washington, D.C., 1988.

8. Presuming that the problems of separation of managers and shareholders are resolved by the privatisation, which remains very theoretical.

9. Some consider that many public firms in the developing countries benefit from greater autonomy of management than their private counterparts. The state may intervene in management decisions in certain cases at its discretion but would not exercise constant supervision of the firm's activities, unlike the shareholders of private firms.

10. The government is an institution that aims to maximise the income from the sale of its assets and that co-operates of its own accord with the private buyers. The unions seek to preserve the level of employment within the firm. The decision to privatise is therefore accompanied by negotiations, the results of which influence the operation of the firm and, in consequence, must be borne in mind by the parties involved (Bös, 1987b).

11. Unfortunately, it is virtually impossible to compare the cost of acquiring or owning nationalised enterprises and the costs engendered by other forms of redistribution (subsidy, regulation).

12. The condition of parity of value requires the public buyer to pay the same price for the whole of the capital of a firm as would a private buyer.

13. The same reasoning applies in the case of additional budget expenditure derived from the income from the transfer. Nonetheless, any increase in current expenditure encroaches on the state's budgetary position in that this income is transient, entailing in the long run a loss of well-being for the community.

14. With the neo-classical theory that there is no premium for state-held resources ($\lambda_g = 1$), social welfare is not dependent on the transfer price. It is a neutral financial transfer between the purchaser and the government whose amount is of little importance. The only important matter is the difference between the social welfare derived from private or public operation of the enterprise.

15. See the article in *Politique économique*, August-September 1985.

16. This evaluation of the two components of social welfare (monopolist profit and consumer surplus) presupposes a linear demand curve. One thus obtains the rules for fixing prices and quantities applied by a monopolist seeking to maximise his profit. It is then possible to express the monopolist's profit as a function of the parameters of demand and of the percentage reduction of the costs, and the consumer surplus as a function of the new prices and new quantities (Jones *et al.*, 1988, p. 80).

17. The British example of privatisation of public companies in a monopoly situation reveals the difficulty of achieving an efficient regulatory system. The many proposals relating to supervision contained in the Beesley report in 1980 and the Littlechild report in 1982, followed by the setting up of OFTEL (regulatory body for telecommunications) and Mercury (potential competitor of British Telecom), only partially resolved the problems posed by the privatisation of British Telecom in 1982.

18. In Great Britain and France, the public offering with resort to the stock market has become the most favoured procedure for achieving their vast privatisation programmes. The privatisation of all the major industrial and banking groups (Saint-Gobain, CGE, Société Générale, Paribas and Suez in France, and British Telecom, British Gas, British Petroleum, British Airways and Trustee Savings Bank in Great Britain) was carried out by means of a public offering.

19. See the examples in 1985-86 of the reprivatisation of the banks Banco de Chile and Banco de Santiago, and the pension funds AFP Santa-Maria and AFP Provida.

20. E.g. the Malaysian government holds 62 per cent of the capital of MAS after the partial public offering; the Philippine government, 70 per cent of the Philippine National Bank; and the Mexican government, 66 per cent of the banks BANAMEX and BANCOMER.

21. *Rebalancing the Public and Private Sectors in Developing Countries: the Case of Jamaica,* OECD Development Centre, Technical Paper, Paris, 1991.

22. *Asian Wall Street Journal,* 28-29 July 1989.

23. Although Great Britain has a very powerful financial and banking sector, the transfers there have clearly shown two factors: i) shares are considerably underpriced at the time of public offerings (about 35 per cent of the transfer income in the case of British

Airways, British Telecom, Rolls Royce and TSB), ii) the costs inherent in the technical realisation of the operation are between 3 and 11 per cent of the total cost of the transfer. In the case of British Telecom, the loss of profit for the British Exchequer amounted to more than £1.5 billion (£1.3 billion from the underpricing and £265 million for the costs of implementation), or 40 per cent of the total transfer! *Cf.* Chapter 7 of J. Vickers & G. Yarrow (1988, pp. 171-85).

24. *Financial Times*, 21 September 1989.

25. Of which about $860 million in respect of Chapter 19 (conversions of debts into foreign investments) and $340 million in respect of Chapter 18 (reserved to local operators). Note of the French Embassy in Chile, November 1989.

26. Economist Intelligence Unit, *Philippines Report*, No. 1, 1990.

27. See respectively Economist Intelligence Unit, *Philippines Report*, No. 2, 1989, and *Financial Times*, 6 October 1989.

28. *Maghreb Développement*, "Le Textile en Tunisie", No. 10, 1989.

29. Certain financial restructurings reduce the authorised capital at the outset in order to absorb losses, and then go on to increase the capital. Under these circumstances, the capital does not increase substantially afterwards, but the financial situation is reorganised and the state partially divested (e.g. Fluobar in Tunisia, cited by Vuylsteke, 1988).

30. Public offerings are often accompanied by the issue of new shares. These increases of capital are the corollary of such transfer operations and are not closely akin to the procedure described in this paragraph.

31. *Divestiture in Developing Countries*, World Bank Discussion Papers, No. 11, 1987.

32. Leases may refer expressly to a subsequent opportunity for the lessee to purchase the firm or its assets (Vuylsteke, 1988).

33. Great Britain and France have resorted to transfers of management only twice, the firms concerned being among the smallest privatisations carried out.

34. Figures extracted from M. Asli, "Case Studies: Malaysia", in *Management Dynamism in State-Owned Enterprises in Asia*, Asian Productivity Organization, Tokyo, 1989, pp. 161-98.

35. *Maghreb Développement*, 1989, *op. cit.*

36. These figures taken from Villareal (1988) do not take into account the national oil company, PEMEX. If PEMEX is included, the impact of the *desincorporacion* is reduced considerably, affecting only 0.5 per cent of public sector value-added in mining industry and 10 per cent in manufacturing industry (Villareal, p. 130, 1988).

37. With this difference, however: in Chile, the whole of the capital of the institutions concerned was transferred, whereas in Mexico, the transfers involved only 34 per cent of the capital.

38. Economist Intelligence Unit, *Malaysia*, No. 2, 1988.

39. During the respective presidential terms of office of de Echeverria and Lopez Portillo, between 1970 and 1982, 258 public enterprises were created, almost two-thirds (65.1 per cent) of the total number created since 1934. *Cf.* Casa & Peres (1988, p. 36), cited by Michalet (1989, p. 28).

*Chapter 4*

# THE IMPACT OF PRIVATISATIONS
## (OR THE NECESSARY INTERACTION WITH OTHER FORMS OF REBALANCING)

The privatisation process, an essential component of rebalancing policies, will be judged by the extent to which it achieves its two final objectives: improving public finances and increasing the allocative and productive efficiency of the economy. These macroeconomic impacts will reflect developments in the financial and competitive situation of each privatised enterprise. To assess the impact of privatisation, we must describe the analytical frameworks needed for interpreting the conclusions drawn from prospective and retrospective observation of the financial results and market structures of privatised enterprises. The first section of this chapter will assess the impact on public finances. The following section, adopting an identical methodological approach, will evaluate the impact on economic efficiency. Lastly, the social consequences of privatisation should be assessed, since this question is of prime concern for the governments of developing countries. Throughout, it will be demonstrated that privatisation is complementary to the other elements of rebalancing (mainly liberalisation and restructuring).

## The impact on the state's financial burden

The theories of development economics in vogue at the time of the creation and subsequent reinforcement of the public sector advocated that priority be given to the achievement of quantitative economic objectives. The financial cost of achieving such objectives was viewed as a minor factor in the light of the effects on economic independence and development. When the tightening of government financial constraints, following the breakdown in 1982 (see Chapter 2), led to research into the main factors responsible for the state budget deficits, criticisms were levelled at public enterprises, basically owing to their poor financial results. The state could no longer afford the operating subsidies and injections of capital needed for running them. In this context, privatisation looked like a miraculous method that would not only reduce that financial burden but also procure additional tax revenue.

In order to make a correct assessment of the budgetary impact of the privatisation operations, a detailed analytical framework will first be presented. This will be followed by an empirical application, particularly at the level of the development of financial relationships between the state and the privatised enterprises, which will enable general conclusions to be drawn relating to the impact of privatisation on the public finances.

### The analytical framework of the impact on the budget deficit

Evaluating the impact of privatisation on the budget is no easy matter. It calls for consideration of the many parameters that will be changed in both the short and the long term by privatisation operations. In order to make a satisfactory evaluation, a two-stage approach is required. First, the impact of transfer operations will be assessed in a very simplified framework. Next, the theoretical assumptions should be taken one by one, in order to provide a detailed interpretive grid. We should note that the various studies on the budgetary impact of privatisation deal only with operations involving transfers of shares or assets. Such transfers of ownership generate tax earnings, which are viewed as the sole factor that helps to alleviate the budget deficit. This analytical framework will be extended to include transfers of management and subjected to empirical applications in the following subsection.

#### A) The impact on the budget in a simplified framework

This framework of reference, deliberately describing an extreme situation, introduces nine restrictive hypotheses (see Heller & Schiller, 1989, p. 758). In order to measure the intrinsic effect of the income from transfers of ownership, no savings can be made in subsidies or injections of capital. In addition, by assuming stability over time of the privatised firm's financial results, the static framework eliminates any resultant financial effect (reduction or increase of state payments to the public enterprises or of taxes paid by the public firms). In this context (see Table 13), and if the evaluation of the assets is correct and complete, resulting in an undiscounted transfer price, the impact of privatisation on the public finances is nil. This lack of impact results in intertemporal arbitrage, as the income from the transfer is equal to the actualised value of the future profits of the former public enterprise.

The government's budgetary position is not changed, although during the fiscal year when the transfer takes place, the income from the sales of shares or assets will reduce the apparent budget deficit (Mansoor, 1987, p. 50). All other things being equal, the counterpart of this provisional reduction in the deficit will be the elimination of annual financial transfers from the firm to the state in subsequent years. It is here presumed that the public enterprises are operating at a profit and that no enterprise pays corporation tax. In other words, the state's net wealth is not affected by the privatisation. It is merely the substitution of one physical asset by a liquid asset of the same value.

Some people take the view, however, that public enterprises earning profits, apart from those operating in the primary products sector, do not pay dividends to their sole shareholder or principal, the state. Instead, they accumulate and capitalise their net profits, thus increasing the value of public assets from year to year. This results in a much higher transfer price at the time of the transfer of ownership. The state therefore has to balance the advantages of obtaining income from the transfer in the short term against the enhancement of its stock of assets. This decision will depend both on the state's budget situation and on a comparison of the return on the capital accumulation of the public enterprises with that derived from the financial investments of the income from the transfer.

### B) The impact on the budget in a less restrictive framework

When the hypotheses set out above do not apply, the impact on the public finances may be evaluated by the aid of a new analytical grid, synthesised in five points.

### 1) Financial relationships between the state and the public enterprise are not solely restricted to transfers of profits

In addition to simple gross transfers from public enterprises to the state, the study should examine net flows, taking account of transfers from the state to public enterprises in the form of subsidies or injections of capital. This approach has the advantage of assessing the impact on the budget whilst taking into account not only the income resulting from the transfer operations but also the savings achieved by the state in meeting the public firms' financial requirements. The impact of privatisation on operating subsidies and injections of capital is particularly important, as these transfers are a heavy burden on public finances.

   i) The reduction in operating subsidies presumes that financial responsibility for the firm will be taken over by the private purchasers and that there will be an improvement in the privatised firms' financial results (mainly in the case of public enterprises operating at a deficit). However, there are three reasons for caution:

   a) Privatising the profitable activities of an enterprise and maintaining deficit activities in the public sector may put an end to an internal network of cross-subsidies. Once the privatisation is completed, the direct burden on the budget is likely to be increased by grants of additional subsidies.

   b) Subsidies for certain goods or services are justified on the grounds of redistribution or national independence, which are not the objectives of the managers of the privatised firm. A more selective subsidy policy will be adopted once the privatisation is completed (the total

*Table 13*

**MAIN HYPOTHESES**

| | |
|---|---|
| 1. | Public enterprise in profit |
| 2. | The transfer price of the firm is equal to the full market value of the assets |
| 3. | Agreement between the state and the private purchasers on the cash-flows generated after privatisation |
| 4. | No tax on corporate profits |
| 5. | Integral transfer from the state to the enterprise |
| 6. | No financial transfer from the state to the enterprise |
| 7. | No change in the financial results following the privatisation |
| 8. | No change in the state's income or expenditure |
| 9. | Full information on prices and markets |

*Sources:*    Heller & Schiller (1989).

elimination of subsidies would indicate that these aims had been abandoned, a decision that is politically difficult and costly from the social point of view).

c) Private purchasers will tend to lobby the government actively in an attempt to obtain either continued financial aid from the government or the grant of increased protection (Heald, 1988, p. 77).

ii) Similar reasoning can be applied to injections of capital. The savings achieved by the state in this area depend on the actual financial involvement of the private sector in strengthening the equity capital of privatised firms. At the time of the transfers of ownership studied in the sample countries, the private purchasers generally assumed responsibility for the growth and management of the equity capital needed for the firm's development. It should be emphasized that the state will have provided at the outset for the *reconstitution* of the equity capital, by reorganisation of the liabilities and by massive injections of capital.

iii) If corporate profits tax is taken into account, the market valuation of the firm will be different. The transfer price will then correspond to the actualised value of the post-tax profits of the privatised company. If a different tax regime applies to public enterprises and privatised firms, the additional income received by the state following privatisation (as a simplification, the public enterprise was exempt from tax) would lead to a lower actualised value, and hence a lower transfer price. Strictly speaking, the situation of the public finances will be improved if the sum of the value of the taxes henceforth paid by the privatised firm and the income derived from the financial assets purchased by the earnings from the transfers is higher than the taxes and transfers that the public enterprise would have made (Mansoor, p. 51).

2) It is not certain that the income from the transfer and the actualised value of future cash-flows will be equal

*The market's assessment of the value of the firm's assets* may be mistaken, as the financial markets are insufficiently developed and the instruments of analysis and evaluation are inadequate. Moreover, the characteristics of the microeconomic environment granted to the enterprise by the state (particularly regulatory, contingent or liberal measures) are factors of uncertainty that complicate the calculation of the actualised value of the firm's future cash flow.

The *transfer price fixed* may not reflect the full value of the assets. Private purchasers' aversion to risk is exacerbated by the fact that the information regarding the actual value of the assets may be fragmentary. The maximum price they will offer for the whole or part of the capital of the public enterprise will therefore be reduced (Mansoor, 1987, p. 51). The political desire for transfer operations to succeed in difficult circumstances and the notion that the cost of capital is higher for private purchasers than for a sovereign state (Rosa, 1988) result in a transfer price that is lower than the realisable value of the firm's assets. From this point of view, privatisation by transfer reduces the state's net wealth, as today's gain does not compensate for the future loss of income. Such decisions may nonetheless be taken by governments prepared to bear the opportunity cost engendered by transfer of ownership, for financial (fiscal crisis) or political reasons[1].

### 3) Use of the income from the transfer

This should be taken into consideration in order to assess the impact on the budget in the medium term. The IMF considers the income from a total or partial transfer equivalent to reimbursement of a loan[2]. As Mansoor notes (1987, p. 48), "this is the counterpart of classing nationalisation as a loan". This kind of approach therefore presupposes a certain utilisation of the income from transfers. Other things being equal, the sale of shares or assets will reduce the state's overall debt (and, in consequence, financial costs in subsequent years) by the amount of the income from the transfer. Under these circumstances, the state's budget position will be unchanged.

If the state increases current budget expenditure and/or reduces tax rates, the budget deficit for the year of the transfer will not be affected by the privatisation operation, but it will increase in subsequent years. Thus, in order to compete with other methods of privatisation, transfer of management will need to provide a satisfactory return on the financial investments made by the state in the public enterprises concerned. Otherwise, simply at the fiscal level, the retention of the assets or shares of public enterprises will yield less income than a transfer of ownership coupled with a rational use of the income from the transfer.

### 4) Public enterprises in deficit

Public enterprises operating at a deficit will be privatised at a price that reflects their value at liquidation (Heller & Schiller, 1989, p. 761). Nonetheless, radical solutions, which advocate liquidation of public enterprises that would be unviable without continual massive subsidies and/or the maintenance of strong protectionist measures, come up against three stumbling-blocks:

i) The public enterprises incurring the highest deficits are often the sole suppliers of essential public services. It is therefore difficult to conceive of their simply being put into liquidation.

ii) The solution of selling off the enterprise by transferring the assets to the private sector poses two problems: the residual responsibility for the firm's liabilities and the unlikelihood of the state's obtaining a return on its earlier investments, owing to the low value of the transfer.

iii) It is difficult to determine a positive transfer price for the most heavily indebted public enterprises.

Under these circumstances, liquidation or privatisation is not a satisfactory alternative to the problems of public firms operating at a deficit, and the way is thus left open to other methods of rebalancing. Economic restructuring and financial reorganisation of public enterprises should therefore be viewed as complete solutions on their own, which do not lead inexorably to privatisation.

5) Changes in the financial results after privatisation

In a static framework, the impact of privatisation on the budget deficit will be nil, or even negative. In a dynamic perspective, the achievement of a positive impact will depend on an increase in tax revenue resulting from an improvement in the privatised firms' financial results. In this case, the privatised enterprises will also reduce the financial burden on the state budget (operating subsidies if the public firm was in deficit or, more certainly, injections of capital).

This increase in operating profits should not however be obtained at the expense of competition and, *in fine*, of economic efficiency. The state should not place privatised enterprises in a non-competitive situation in order to make them attractive and by this means seek to maximise the income derived from the transfer in the short term (Commander & Killick, 1988, p. 119). Only if the role of market forces is strengthened will full advantage be gained from the transfer of ownership rights and increases in economic efficiency be achieved, thus ensuring in the medium term improvement in the firm's financial results and a recovery of the state's fiscal position.

Mansoor's article in 1987 checked the general optimism of bilateral and multilateral organisations as regards privatisation in general. His conclusions, which were very cautious as regards the impact of privatisations on the budget deficit, had two major consequences: i) they had a strong, even excessive influence on the literature in this field (Hemming & Mansoor, 1988; Cook & Kirkpatrick, 1988; Heald, 1988; Heller & Schiller, 1989); ii) they showed that only a privatisation process that is carried out satisfactorily from the points of view of domestic and foreign competition, the characteristics of the public firms concerned (in profit or in deficit) and the use of the income from the transfer, is likely to produce a sustainable positive effect on the public finances.

*Empirical application and assessment of the impact on the budget*

The aim of the above discussion was to point out the possible direct and indirect effects on the state budget resulting from a transfer operation. We now intend to supplement the theoretical arguments with an empirical application based on the experiences of the countries in our sample. The conclusions drawn will clarify the likely impact on the budget of privatisations in the developing countries.

*A) Financial situation of the privatised enterprises*

The study focuses on three factors: the state-owned enterprises' financial results prior to privatisation, the development of financial relationships between the state and the privatised firms and the relation between profits realised and the competitive situation. As the main privatisation operations are relatively recent and accounting methods in state sector companies inadequate, few data are available regarding the development of privatised companies' financial results. On the basis of such fragmentary information as we have, we shall attempt to reply to the following questions: a) What is the financial position of privatised enterprises? b) Is it possible to privatise or transfer a public enterprise in a deficit situation? c) What are the criteria on which the state bases its decision to privatise or rehabilitate one particular enterprise or another?

1) Privatisation mainly affects profitable firms

In the sample countries, as a general rule, the enterprises privatised to date were profitable even before their transfer to the private sector. This general comment should not lead to an underestimation of the variety of financial situations. On the basis of this criterion, it is possible to define three types of privatised enterprises: intrinsically profitable firms, firms that require an active restructuring policy prior to their transfer and firms in deficit.

i) Intrinsically profitable enterprises

In the ten developing countries studied, we are bound to observe that prior to their privatisation, a large number of public enterprises had satisfactory financial results and excellent prospects of growth and profitability. Most often these firms had the advantage of favourable operating conditions, especially in the form of limited domestic or foreign competition and/or a buoyant market (banks, telecommunications, tourism). Moreover, the largest privatisations, on the criteria of the turnovers of the enterprises concerned or the total transfer price, have involved intrinsically profitable firms.

A whole range of privatisation techniques has been used. The main operations involving a public offering have concerned the following profitable firms: the Mexican banking organisations, Banamex, Bancomer and Serfin and the Jamaican bank NCB; the companies MAS and MISC in Malaysia. Private sales have concentrated on the telecommunications sector (in Chile, CTC, ENTEL; in Jamaica, TOJ), airline companies (Lanchile and Mexicana) and tourist and hotel complexes. Management transfers have taken place in the case of road construction and operation or electricity companies in Malaysia or Chile, activities that are bound to be profitable even in the short term.

ii) Restructuration of the enterprise as a preliminary

Other firms with a poorer financial situation have been massively restructured prior to their privatisation. The results are then much more fragile. To facilitate the privatisation of Philippine National Bank, the Philippine government undertook a major reorganisation of the bank's financial situation. On the one hand, most of the bad debts owed by other public enterprises ("non-performing assets") were removed from its balance sheet, resulting in a 70 per cent reduction in the value of its assets (from 78 billion Philippine pesos to 24 billion pesos). On the other hand, a recapitalisation scheme (12 billion Philippine pesos) was undertaken. From 1987, PNB's results showed a significant improvement (net profit of 1 billion pesos as against a loss of 1.1 billion in 1986). The final objective, the partial transfer of the bank by a public offering, was thus able to take place in July 1989[3].

There are many such examples of restructuring/reorganisation with a view to privatisation. In Chile, the effort to maximise the income from the transfer of privatised enterprises is based on two stages: as a first step, the public authorities direct the economic restructuring and financial reorganisation of the enterprises; they are then transferred gradually in blocks of shares or assets in order to raise the price of the last tranches of capital transferred to the private sector[4]. In a different way, Bangladesh has stated specifically that the privatisation programme adopted in June 1987 would affect only restructured and profitable firms.

iii) Enterprises in deficit

Lastly, some firms in deficit have been privatised in the countries in our sample (in particular, certain reprivatisations by means of transfers of enterprises in the textile sector in Bangladesh in 1982-83)[5]. None of these enterprises, however, was a "budget-hungry" public firm, one of those that incur heavy operating losses and require substantial financial transfers from the state (in the form of subsidies or injections of capital). The only notable exceptions are the management transfer of National Sugar Company in Jamaica, and particularly the transfer of the Mexican airline company Aeromexico, which had lost $130 million from 1986 to 1988 and which had incurred losses for 11 consecutive years since 1973[6].

171

## 2) Privatisation or retention of public firms in deficit

Why are there so few privatisations of public firms with substantial deficits, when these are the very firms that impose the most onerous burden on the national budget? This question is embarrassing for the advocates of privatisation, who most often justify such operations by the positive impact they are supposed to have on the government's budget. At this level, we should therefore consider the possibility of privatising a firm in deficit.

### i) Assessment of the firm's future results

The transfer of a public enterprise in deficit is theoretically possible in that the valuation of an enterprise is based not on current but on future financial results. The potential private purchaser will calculate the net actualised value of the future cash flows of the firm he is interested in acquiring. The amount of these cash flows will depend on the firm's operational plans and any benefits, such as restrictions on competition and tax advantages, granted by the state at the time of privatisation. The private purchaser will offer a purchase price (or payment of a rent) for the firm to be transferred (or leased), on the basis of this valuation. If the buyer's offer is higher than or equal to the minimum price deemed acceptable by the government, the privatisation will go ahead. If the proposals do not satisfy both parties, the privatisation will not take place, except in the form of a management contract[7]. Depending on the firm's financial viability, the state will either continue restructuring the enterprise or put it into liquidation.

### ii) Taking the net assets into consideration

A further factor, the book value of the net assets, is also integrated into the valuation procedure. The net assets are a measurement of the difference between the enterprise's total assets and total liabilities. It enables account to be taken not only of future *cash flows* but also of the *stock* of accumulated debts as a ratio of total assets. This factor is particularly pertinent, since many public firms in the developing countries have both an exceptionally high level of debt (investments are financed by bank borrowing rather than from equity capital) and limited assets (low volume of equity capital, accumulated losses carried forward on the balance sheet). Moreover, the high level of indebtedness makes the enterprise more fragile in two ways:

a) great vulnerability to fluctuations in interest rates, which determine the amount of financial costs;

b) an unfavourable debt-equity ratio from the viewpoint of contracting new loans to finance investments in the firm's development and modernisation.

The potential buyers' caution is further accentuated by the fragmentary nature of the financial data available about most public enterprises.

This financial assessment of both *cash flow and stock* helps to explain the lack of enthusiasm for the purchase of certain public enterprises shown by private buyers, both national and foreign (*cf.* the difficulties surrounding the transfer of the Malay railway KTM, or the Philippine electricity production company MERALCO). Economic restructuring and particularly financial reorganisation (reduction of public firms' debt and the increase of their equity) are preliminaries to the success of any privatisation operation. Accordingly, the transfer price has to include the cost of investments in modernisation and recapitalisation carried out by the state prior to the privatisation. A transfer price based exclusively on the firm's financial results might thus prove too low in the light of the value of the net assets and might be seen overall as a bad financial deal for the government.

3) Privatisation or retention of profitable enterprises

With the return to profitability, the public enterprise will become attractive to private buyers, and the state will then have to decide whether to keep control of it. The decision to privatise a profitable public enterprise is based on two arguments: i) a balance of the relative advantages and disadvantages over time, with a preference for the present, ii) the gains in efficiency derived from private operation and management.

i) Preference for the present

In theory, public firms that make net profits will pay a dividend to their sole shareholder or principal, the state, or transfer the net profits directly into the state coffers. Whatever form they take, these financial transfers correspond to a yield on the capital invested by the state, in the form of injections of capital or operating subsidies. The state thus collects its income in instalments over time. Assuming a full and correct assessment both of the net actualised value of future income and of the value at the time "t" of the transfer, the decision whether to transfer has to balance today's advantage against tomorrow's disadvantage. Strictly speaking, these two measures are equal, but two factors will finally incite the state to opt for privatisation.

a) When the public finances are in crisis, the state will show a preference for the present, in other words, will hope to obtain transfer income today rather than annual cash transfers in subsequent years. Its rate of preference for the present is then higher than the market actualisation rate[8].

b) In reality, profitable public enterprises accumulate their profits, thus increasing the value of the assets held by the state. The transfer enables a financial gain to be made, since the low rate of return generally derived from the operation of the public enterprise will be lower than the return the state can obtain either by investing the income from the transfer or by paying off some of its debts.

The developing countries in our sample, apart perhaps from Chile, are characterised by substantial budget deficits. This situation favours behaviour that has a strong preference both for short-term improvement in the financial results of public enterprises (transfers of management) and also for transfer income here and now. Accordingly, the state tries to carry out privatisations rapidly, even if this reduces the income from the transfer. However, the problems of valuation and the factors of uncertainty as regards the performance of privatised enterprises considerably complicate the arguments for and against transfer.

ii) Economic efficiency derived from private rationality

Owing to the problems of evaluation and balancing the relative advantages and disadvantages, the procedures for privatising profitable firms seem to have developed more on pragmatic or ideological grounds than on a simple financial calculation. Transfers to the private sector allow advantage to be taken of all or any of the following: the transfer of ownership rights, reduction in political interference, widespread use of private management criteria and the elimination of the advantages and restrictions that falsify competition between public and private enterprises. In addition, there is likely to be a reduction in the difference between the profits realised by the public enterprise and the potential profits realisable. When there are comparable private competitors the difference is all the more easy to estimate. By way of example, the privatisation of the National Commercial Bank in Jamaica was helped by the presence of another bank, of similar size, but with better financial results, the Bank of Nova Scotia[9]. The tourist and hotel complexes (Morocco, Tunisia, Jamaica) or certain small firms in the competitive sector (fishing, agriculture-based food industry, small-scale industry) are evidence of the major improvement to financial results that can result from privatisation operations.

This conversion to private management objectives and criteria does not mean that the trend towards the privatisation of profitable firms is boundless. The "strategic sectors" group public enterprises whose earnings are an important source of income for the national budget. Accordingly the largest contributors, mainly national enterprises operating in the primary products export sector (oil, phosphates, copper), are excluded from the privatisation process.

The over-representation of profitable firms among the first privatisation operations is evidence of the behaviour of the actors involved in privatisation. On the one hand, the government will wish to start off the process with attractive firms, in the hope of developments on two fronts: a) that the restructuring will bear fruit and other public firms will become attractive, b) that the triggering of the process will lend credence to the government's commitment and bolster the confidence of local and international investors. On the other hand, at the same time, private investors will remain very cautious in the face of the dual risk that the purchase of a public enterprise represents: a) the microeconomic risk inherent in the firm's position, with apprehension being reinforced by uncertainty, b) the macroeconomic risk linked to the country's economic, political and social situation.

*B) Assessment of the real impact on the budget*

1) The conduct of the privatisation

The local or foreign potential private buyers' assessments of the value of "privatisable" firms are directly influenced by the macroeconomic and microeconomic environment prevailing at the time of the privatisation operations. Such assessments determine the private buyers' interest and the success of the operation.

In order to maximise the potential income from the transfer, governments have to control the rate at which the privatisation programme is carried out and take advantage of a favourable macroeconomic climate. Short-term constraints (financial crisis, pressure from international organisations), however, may speed up the transfer programme at an inappropriate moment[10]. Indeed, the private investors' appraisals and, accordingly, the purchase prices they offer, will depend on their view of the country's macroeconomic situation. If they have high expectations, purchase prices will be revised upwards, improving the financial terms of the operation for the government. On the other hand, a "sluggish" macroeconomic climate, combined with chronic political instability, will raise the country's level of risk, turning major local and international investors against the privatisation operations.

Thus Chile, which has not experienced any major fiscal imbalance since 1985, has been able to apply a partial and progressive transfer policy to public enterprises. This approach has the advantage of benefiting from the increase in profits realised by the privatised enterprise, so that an increasingly high transfer price can be asked as each partial transfer takes place. In the case of Chile, this staggering of partial transfers has been facilitated by a favourable macroeconomic climate between 1986 and 1989. More recently, the recovery of the Mexican economy, which started after the election of President Salinas in 1988, considerably improved the expectations of international investors. This strong attraction has enabled the privatisation programme to be speeded up appreciably since 1988[11]. In contrast, in the Philippines, the aggravation of the economic crisis and political uncertainty have considerably slowed down the privatisation programme, and even blocked it at the end of 1989. The aversion to risk has led investors to turn their backs on Philippine enterprises available for privatisation, however low the prices asked when compared to the potential assets value, and whatever the financial or regulatory benefits granted to the potential purchaser.

Table 14

## ASSESSMENT OF THE IMPACT OF THE PROGRAMMES FOR PRIVATISATION AND RESTRUCTURING OF THE PUBLIC SECTOR

| | Criteria for assessment of privatisation | Criteria for assessment of restructuring | Criteria for assessment of overall impact |
|---|---|---|---|
| GHANA | 11 enterprises out of 235 | Major restructuring of Ghana Cocoa Board<br>14 plan contracts and performance agreements<br>10 liquidations | Transfers to the budget reduced from 1% of GDP in 1987 (- 30%)<br>Transfers to public enterprises represent 8% of state expenditure in 1986 |
| MOROCCO | 14 enterprises out of 688<br>(41 transfers of minority holdings including 11 held by the Office of Industrial Development) | Undertaken in October 86<br>Liquidation of Office Chérifien des Exportations<br>Major restructuring of the tourism sector<br>Office Chérifien des Phosphates<br>Demonopolisation of urban transport in Casablanca (1985), Rabat (1986) | |
| TUNISIA | 24 enterprises out of 600<br>(from a sample of 10 enterprises transferred belonging to the industrial sector, the price. 28.1 million dinars, and 3 500 jobs). | Many liquidations in the following sectors: electricity (COGELEC), tourism (SHHT) automobile industry (STIA), heavy industry (SOMINE)<br>Restructurings of the three largest public enterprises:<br>SNCFT, CPG and Groupe Chimic;<br>of the dairy industry (SOTULAIT), and pharmaceuticals (PCT)<br>Introduction of programme contracts, management contracts | Gross transfers from the state to the public enterprises rose from 9.8% of the GDP in 1981 to 12.2% in 1984 then fell to 6.3% in 1988 |
| BOLIVIA | 1 enterprise out of 58 | Restructurings of YPFB (Oil company)<br>COMIBOL (Mining company)<br>Winding up of Bolivian Development Corp.<br>Reorganisation of the Central Bank | The part of the public enterprises in the public sector consolidated budget fell from 62% in 1984 to 54% in 1989 |

176

Table 14 (continued)

| | Criteria for assessment of privatisation | Criteria for assessment of restructuring | Criteria for assessment of overall impact |
|---|---|---|---|
| CHILE (since 1985) | 38 enterprises from all sectors<br>114 000 new shareholders<br>Income from assets transferred by CORFO: $918 million - $1 billion (depending on source)<br>Positive budget impact for 1986-89 of an annual amount of $210 million ($ 87).<br>negative for 90-97 by an amount of between $100 and $165 million ($ 87) | Restructurings in the context of subsequent privatisation: autonomy of management, new management objectives (maximisation of profit), strict control of debt levels, similar taxation to that applied to private enterprises, reform of pricing (energy and telecommunications sectors) | The financial results of the public enterprises improved considerably (producing an operating profit of 13% of the GDP in 1986 as against 5.6% in 1981) |
| JAMAICA | 45 enterprises,<br>Income from transfer 1987-88: $89 million plus $32 million from the transfer of CC and the hotels in 1988<br>According to the budget report in April 1987, $11 million income from leases<br>$10 million income from savings on losses<br>$22 million income from transfers | Reorganisation of the sugar (NSC) and banana (Banana Co.) industries, and the parastate entities in the agriculture sector<br>Reform of public pricing as from 1983, in order to attain rates of return for public assets of between 3% and 5% | Difficult to measure; the objectives fixed as regards return on assets were not achieved |
| MEXICO | According to the Pichardo Report in July 88, 116 enterprises out of 1 214 were transferred for a total value of $419 million<br>Two major transfers since, Mexicana del Cobre and Aeromexico for approximately $1 billion | 138 liquidations out of 258 envisaged (main liquidation: Fundidora Monterrey)<br>102 extinctions<br>63 mergers and 23 transfers | Marginal contribution of the transfer income to the budget deficit ($419 million representing 3% of the deficit for 1987 alone)<br>Reduction of about 30% of strategic presence in the mining and manufacturing sectors (apart from PEMEX) |
| BANGLADESH | More than 500 enterprises transferred since 1974, at a total amount of $35 million (estimate based on 437 enterprises)<br>Including 22 textile enterprises for $1.2 million<br>Since 1987, 9 enterprises for a total of $7.2 million | Restructuring of production and distribution of fertilizers (reduced role for the Bangladesh Agricultural Development Corp.)<br>Massive restructuring in the industrial sector of 6 large public enterprises (BJMC, BTMC, BCIC, BSEC, BSFIC, BFDIC)<br>Injection of capital and debt/equity swaps ($240 then $93 million over the periods 81-85 & 86-88)<br>Increased management autonomy<br>Control of debt levels | Results of the industrial public enterprises deteriorated during the 1980s. For the 6 large industrial groups, the virtual balance of the accounts (average fiscal year 82-85) gave way to a deficit of 150 million aka (average fiscal year 87-89)<br>Net transfers from the state to the public enterprises increased rising from 0.8% (fiscal year 86-88) of GDP to 3.2% (fiscal year 89) |

177

Table 14 (end)

| | Criteria for assessment of privatisation | Criteria for assessment of restructuring | Criteria for assessment of overall impact |
|---|---|---|---|
| MALAYSIA | 22 enterprises out of 943 (including 888 subsidiaries) Sales of shares in public firms amount to $240 million The savings in expenses on infrastructure (a privileged sector for privatisation) amount to $1.5 billion | Restructuring of the cement and iron & steel industries Recapitalisation of KTM (railways), and NEB (electricity) | In 1987 the non-financial public enterprises produced a surplus of $80 million |
| PHILIPPINES | 16 enterprises out of 245 (including 149 subsidiaries) ($ 400 million derived from the operations From January 1987 to the end of 1989, 181 non-performing assets were transferred to the private sector for a price of 10 billion pesos Target for 1990 : 8.4 billion pesos | Efforts at restructuring of enterprises listed as "privatisable": Nonoc (mining enterprise), Philippine Airlines, Manila Hotel Gradual divestiture of the banking sector Mid-1988, 30 public enterprises were liquidated Opening of fertilizer industry to imports, industry dominated by the public producer (Philphos) | Difficult to measure owing to the instability of the process of reforming the public sector |

178

However advantageous the conditions linked to financing the operation (debt-equity or debt-assets swaps, payment in instalments) or to the repatriation of the profits, these are not sufficient to influence the behaviour of those investors who are in a position to choose between different countries. Assessment of the macroeconomic risk is the main criterion of their investment decision.

2) Volume and under-valuation of transfer operations

Apart from Chile and Jamaica, and to a lesser extent Bangladesh and Mexico, the volumes of transfers have been relatively low (see Table 14). This reflects the limited number of transactions carried out but above all the limited size of the firms concerned by the privatisation process.

In order to measure the importance of the income from transfers, it is necessary to assess what percentage of the total budget earnings this income represents. In Jamaica, the transfer income for the fiscal year 1987-88 (which included the major transfer of Caribbean Cement) was nearly 9 per cent of the total budget earnings. In Bangladesh and Mexico, transfer income has remained less than 5 per cent of the annual public deficits. In 1988 the transfers of Mexicana del Cobre and Aeromexico, at a total of close to $1 billion, represented only 6 per cent of the annual budget deficit for 1988, $16.8 billion. In Chile, transfer income represented an average of only 4 per cent of tax revenue over the period 1986-87. In the other sample countries, transfer income was marginal compared to the total national budget income and deficit.

In Jamaica, transfer income in 1987-88 was more than the public deficit. Chile, which has undertaken the most extensive transfer programme since 1985, recorded a significant budget impact per budget year between 1986 and 1989, estimated, in 1987 dollars, at $210 million[12]. This positive flow more than covered the budget deficit for 1986 ($194 million in 1987 dollars). Nonetheless, the counterpart to this positive impact will be an annual loss of profit over the period 1990-97 of between $100 and $165 million in 1987 dollars. This kind of development illustrates the dual movement of apparent improvement in the budget situation for the years when major transfers take place followed by deterioration in future budget situations.

To assess the impact of transfers on public finances, it is important to consider the transfer price in relationship to the actual value of the assets transferred. Underpricing at the time of the transfer will lead to a reduction in the state's net wealth, even if its income increases in the short term. In both developing and developed countries, most transfer operations have been considerably underpriced (see Chapter 3, "Transfers of public enterprises"). Accordingly, leaving to one side the resultant effects on the financial results of the enterprises transferred, the intrinsic impact of the transfers on the national budget is bound to be negative.

179

The government therefore bears the cost of the transfer of state-owned assets to the private sector. This short-term loss, although counter-productive from the viewpoint of reducing the state's financial constraint, has to be put in perspective. The positive effect of transfer operations in fact appears in the medium term with the state's release from financing the firm's activities and also with the improvement in the firm's financial results.

3) Taking transfers of management into account

The impact on the budget of transfers of management cannot be neglected. However, it is worth specifying the repercussions that leases and management agreements have on public finances.

Leases have a threefold effect on public finances. First, the state receives annual rents from leasing the assets that it owns. Second, the lessee assumes financial liability, which means that the operating subsidies or injections of capital are considerably reduced, or even eliminated. This elimination of a major part of the government's financial transfers to the now privatised firm will relieve the national budget. Lastly, the expected improvement in these firms' operating results should increase tax receipts in future years (ensuing from corporate profits tax or transfers of profit from the enterprise to the state).

Management contracts produce a positive effect only from the third point of view. Their primary objective, in fact, is to create conditions whereby the privatised companies' financial results can be improved. To this end, the government recruits outside skills and seeks to reduce public interference in decisions connected with the firms' operation and management. As the state continues to cover the privatised firm's financial requirements, however, no savings in subsidies or injections of capital can be achieved. Nevertheless, this method is of interest when firms with a substantial deficit, which could not be transferred to the private sector by other procedures, are affected by the restructuring undertaken by the new private managers.

Unfortunately, the data available are not sufficient for assessing the likely developments of privatised enterprises' financial results. This lack of information results from the combination of three factors: lack of data about the financial situation of public enterprises, low transparency of the accounting methods of firms in the developing countries and the recent nature of the privatisation operations. Such financial information would enable the debates relating to the budgetary impact of transfers of ownership and transfers of management to be settled (in order to decide whether the theories regarding property rights are valid) and the degree of inefficiency of the public enterprises to be determined[13].

One can however cite the case of Jamaica, which has had wide recourse to management transfers and has published certain data about this. It seems that the reductions in losses and the rent from leases were significant when compared to the amount of income from transfers (see Table 14). Under these circumstances, the overall impact of privatisation on the public finances depends, according to the technique used, on three main factors: the savings in subsidies and injections of capital (transfers and leases), additional tax revenue or transfers to the budget (transfers, leases and management contracts).

The impact of privatisation on the public finances seems relatively marginal, although it is difficult to conclude without knowing precisely *the development of the firms' financial results, the extent to which the assets were undervalued and the discount applied to the transfer price.* Five conclusions can be drawn from this brief study:

i) The reasoning must be based on trends in the public finances over several fiscal periods and not on annual budget deficits.

ii) The impact on the budget depends on the development of the privatised firms' financial results. If there is no such development, the impact will be nil or even negative.

iii) The impact of privatisation is low in absolute value. This situation ensues less from specific constraints affecting developing countries than on the fact that privatisation is not a satisfactory solution for public firms with very heavy deficits.

iv) Financial performance should not in any circumstances be improved at the expense of ompetition on the markets and/or behaviour aimed at achieving economic efficiency.

v) In view of the minimal impact of privatisation on the state's tax position, the pursuance of operations must be justified by other objectives: increase in the privatised firms' economic efficiency, state divestiture of sectors where its intervention is deemed inadequate and redistribution of wealth between the state and the new shareholders.

## The impact on economic efficiency

This study centres on changes in the privatised enterprises' relatively uncompetitive market structures, for two main reasons. First of all, these are the market structures (monopoly, oligopoly) most often affected by the privatisation process. Next, apart from the difficulties that privatisations of competitive public firms come up against (Chapter 3), the process becomes still more complicated when the operations concern an enterprise in a monopolistic situation. In fact, the basic question is whether privatisation will result in the strengthening of domestic or international competition. This development is a preliminary step to any sustainable change in behaviour by the privatised enterprises in the direction of greater economic efficiency. The privatisation of enterprises in an oligopoly or monopoly situation presents both an opportunity to increase the play of market forces in the sectors in which improvements in efficiency are potentially very high, and a risk of having private rationality applied in situations that are hardly competitive at all.

As in the previous section, we shall start with an analytical presentation of the complex relationships between privatisation and economic efficiency. We shall then discuss the conclusions regarding the impact of privatisation on economic efficiency, despite the difficulty of assessing precisely competitive conditions in the developing countries.

### *Privatisation, competition and economic efficiency*

The relatively inefficient behaviour of most public sector firms at the level of minimising costs and the capacity to determine coherent pricing signals leads to the following two questions: In the developing countries, are bureaucratic failures more important than market failures? To what extent and by what means is privatisation in a position to affect economic efficiency?

There are two levels of reply to the first question.

- In the first place, the literature on the comparative performance of public and private firms[14] suggests that, although the results would seem to favour the private sector, there is no decisive evidence as regards the impact of the ownership of the enterprise on its economic performance (return on labour and capital, minimisation of costs). In fact, none of these studies is able to compare two enterprises, one public, the other private, with an identical regulatory framework, in the same sector of activity and in the same country. The results are therefore considerably weakened and cannot provide a satisfactory justification for privatisation.

- The second level of reply is to distinguish, among the various public enterprises, those firms whose existence is supported by the theoretical corpus of public economics (public goods and services, presence of external factors, natural monopolies and increasing returns) and those created on the basis of different considerations (national independence, redistribution, lack of a private sector capable of financing and providing for the production and distribution of certain essential goods or services). It is worth recalling that the second group represents a major percentage of state sector enterprises in the developing countries.

In the first case, market failures make it impossible to determine equilibrium prices and quantities by means of the market and thus achieve Pareto optimality of the first order. In these borderline cases, the public enterprises make up for market mechanisms by adopting different production and pricing rules, which should lead to a "second best" resource allocation in the economy. In public intervention of this kind, however, the achievement of allocative efficiency is not conditional on that of full productive efficiency, unlike situations that fulfil the conditions for Pareto optimality[15]. This does not contradict the search for better utilisation of the resources made available by the firm.

Public enterprises in the second category may be subject to the same requirements as regards allocative and productive efficiency as private enterprises. They have to adopt behaviour that is at least as efficient as that of private sector firms[16]. Subject to this proviso alone, which assumes in theory that X-inefficiency does not exist (Liebenstein, 1966), public sector firms avoid the privatisation knife.

For both types of public enterprise, improvement in productive efficiency (minimisation of costs for a given output level) and allocative efficiency (re-establishment of pricing signals equalising the marginal producer processing rate and the marginal consumer substitution rate) must accordingly be sought (Kay & Thompson, 1986, p. 21).

A general analytical presentation of the relationships between privatisation and allocative and productive efficiency is therefore essential. This approach is based on the behaviour of private purchasers and contractors. The adoption of private rationality is not in itself enough to improve allocative and productive efficiency. Indeed, there is nothing to imply that the aim of maximising profits is linked to behaviour involving minimising production costs or the fixing of optimum price from the allocative viewpoint. Accordingly, the changes that help to achieve optimal private management (transfer of ownership rights, strengthening of competition and regulations) need to be determined.

Particular attention will be paid to interactions among privatisation, competition and regulation (see Diagram 1). The discussion will also take into consideration certain individual cases (natural monopolies, cross-subsidies). In the absence of solid empirical verification, the main interest of this discussion lies in the analytical framework that ensues from it. Thus, the interpretations proposed on the basis of the available factors will be based on progressive reflection.

## A) *Search for greater efficiency by means of transfer of ownership*

Because it affects both ownership rights and market structures, transfer of ownership is at the heart of the debate relating to the economic efficiency of privatisation operations. In the first case, it strengthens the power of private shareholders and private rationality in the firm's operation and management. In the second, the transfer of a state-sector enterprise may increase or reduce the number of agents authorised to produce or distribute the goods and services sold by the firm transferred. The respective impacts of private rationality and market competition on the allocative and productive efficiency of the economy remain to be determined.

## PRIVATISATION, REGULATION AND ECONOMIC EFFICIENCY

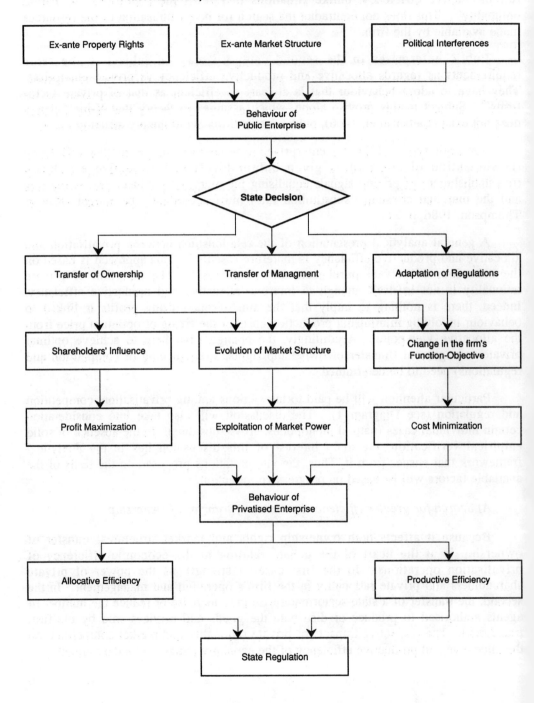

## 1) The transfer of ownership rights

One of the foundations of the transfer of ownership of a firm is the change in ownership rights. According to A. Alchian and his disciples[17], "the public enterprise is vowed to inefficiency owing to the very fact that its owners, the electors, have neither the motivation nor sufficient means to impel it to efficient management. Indeed, unlike the private shareholder, the citizen-shareholder cannot sanction bad management (no stock market involvement), any more than he can benefit directly from good management (there are no dividends and no capital gains)" (Pestiau, 1987, p. 1191). The difference in behaviour between the private and public manager is based mainly on the separation of ownership and control (an extreme example of which is the wholly state-held firm), on the information at the shareholders' disposal and on the effectiveness of the procedures for purchasing enterprises on the capital markets.

The reintroduction of a system of constraints and incentives is supposed to change managers' behaviour significantly. The control of behaviour and results on two levels is likely to be more restrictive than control exercised by the state[18].

i) Private shareholders, financially concerned by the development in the firm's operating results, exercise constant pressure on the managers by insistent demand for information about the firm's financial situation.

ii) The capital and stock markets provide both opportunities for hostile takeovers of the firm (an operation that is presented by the would-be purchaser as defending the shareholders' interests in view of the difference between potential and actual profitability) and the spectre of insolvency as the ultimate sanction of inefficiency. In addition, the obligation on the part of the management to produce results (comparison of financial performance with the targets assigned by the shareholders and with that of other private companies) and the threat of their being ousted are guarantees that private management will maximise the shareholders' utility function. At the same time, the transfer of ownership rights permits an increase in the managers' autonomy and re-establishes a system of incentives for them, linked to the firm's results (remuneration, share in the capital). Such constraints and incentives contrast with the presumed position of managers of public enterprises: divergence between the aims of the state and the aims of the managers, inequality of information to the detriment of the state, unlimited public funding (public enterprises do not file for bankruptcy).

Several comments on the impact of the transfer of ownership rights on economic efficiency are called for:

a) As Pestiau quite rightly points out, "to date there are no studies, at the empirical level, confirming the theory of ownership rights" (1987, p. 1197).

b) In the developing countries, transfers usually involve only a fraction of the capital, the state remaining the shareholder of reference. This considerably restricts the scope of the transfer of ownership, notably as regards the duality of objectives (social in the case of the state, financial in the case of the private shareholders), the takeover of the firm and the autonomy of the decision-making process. Eckel & Vining consider that gains in economic efficiency are proportional to the percentage of the private share in the firm's total capital (1985, p. 93). A semi-public company is situated midway between the efficiency of a firm wholly owned by private shareholders and the relative inefficiency of a firm wholly owned by the state. The simplicity of the argument refers to the problems of defining privatisation and the debates regarding the difference between transfers of ownership and transfers of management (see above, "The impact on the state's financial burden"). Eckel & Vining's study (1982, 1985), in restating the arguments of the proponents of the theory of ownership rights, involuntarily provides an explanation for the limited impact on productive efficiency of partial transfers, a particularly frequent scenario in the developing countries.

c) In the case of public offerings that disperse the capital among thousands of small shareholders, but also in view of the unlikelihood of hostile financial raids and the lethargy of the stock markets in the developing countries, the managers of large privatised enterprises are not subject to effective control from the shareholders or the capital markets. The gap between ownership and management is therefore only partially bridged. Under these circumstances, the management team may continue to pursue management objectives different from those of the shareholders (maximisation of profit is not necessarily sought). The impact on productive efficiency is therefore not as obvious as theoretical analysis envisages.

2) Transfer of ownership and competition

Over and above the mere transfer of ownership rights, transfer operations affect market structures. This effect is the most important, as market competition is the key to allocative *and* productive efficiency (Yarrox, 1985; Kay & Thompson, 1986; Domberger & Pigott, 1986; Hemming & Mansoor, 1988). Under these circumstances, it is essential to analyse the behaviour of the privatised enterprises on the basis of changes in competitive situations.

In the simplest case, the public enterprise already operated on a competitive market, and the transfer operation enables advantage to be taken of the strengthening of private rationality under pressure from the capital markets (ownership rights) and above all from the products market. Assuming that the transfer does not significantly change the market structures, the operation will have a positive impact on economic efficiency.

In the case of other market structures, the problem arises of the conflict between the application of private rationality and the non-competitive situation. If the imperfectly competitive market structures that prevailed prior to the transfer are reproduced afterwards, this will reduce the gains in efficiency drawn from the operation. The impact is likely to be positive as regards productive efficiency (rationalisation of production processes resulting in better use of resources) but negative as regards allocative efficiency (prices fixed by the enterprise higher than the optimum competitive price, resulting in a transfer of the consumer surplus to the producer).

Transfers of public or natural monopolies to the private sector without any change in market structure call for regulatory intervention by the state. Such attempts at regulation seek to avoid the application of private rationality solely for the benefit of the purchaser of the monopoly, and to the detriment of all the other economic agents. The privatisation then transforms the monopolistic public enterprise into a regulated monopolistic private enterprise. This leads at best (if the new regulations adopted are efficient) to a simple transfer of ownership rights, and at worst (if no specific regulations are adopted or if they are inefficient) to an exploitation of the firm's monopolistic power for private ends. The examples of OFTEL and OFGAS (supervisory bodies created following the transfer of British Telecom and British Gas) in the United Kingdom showed that it is particularly difficult to regulate the behaviour of the newly privatised private monopoly[19].

Insofar as possible, the transfer process should encourage, if not the break-up of monopolies, at least the diversification of the sellers. One is bound to note, however, that after the transfer of ownership, these types of market structure develop very unevenly from the viewpoint of strengthening competition (see the following sub-section). In certain cases, transfer operations have strengthened industrial and financial concentration and thus oligopolistic market structures. Moreover, many transfers of monopolies have been carried out without opening the market structure up to domestic or international competition. Under these circumstances, the transfer of monopolies is highly unlikely to yield substantial improvements in terms of economic efficiency, as Yarrow (1985), Hemming & Mansoor (1988) and Heller & Schiller (1989) reckon. In both scenarios, often noted in the developing countries, the intrinsic impact of transfer on competition, and thus on efficiency, is nil or even negative. In these fairly uncompetitive market structures, the gains in productive efficiency due to the transfer of ownership rights alone are not likely to compensate for the losses in allocative efficiency.

Thus, insofar as the transfer process will not result in strengthening competition (comparisons of market structures before and after transfer), the state will introduce new regulations, during the transfer operation (as in the case of transfers of public or natural monopolies) or subsequently[20]. This complex process of liberalisation/reregulation by the state is essential because the privatisation renders the old regulations obsolescent. The new regulatory framework is now aimed at controlling the profit maximisation behaviour adopted by the privatised enterprise, in order to avoid the exploitation of market power, left intact by the process of transfer of ownership[21]. Reregulation is also necessary in the privatisation of public enterprises that have important environmental effects (pollution, infrastructure), in order to preserve the conditions for achieving the maximum level of efficiency.

On the basis of the examples of opening monopolies to competition (in the case of natural monopolies, see above, the transfers of management), it seems that the introduction of a competitor or the adaptation of the regulations are not satisfactory solutions. The opening up to foreign competition should be done gradually, so that newly privatised former monopolies are given time to adapt. In addition, the national competitor must be credible (unlike Mercury in the United Kingdom), in other words, must have the means to create a genuine alternative in the supply of certain goods and services.

Consequently, the development of the market structure — over which the state has a definite influence, in that it chooses the buyer and fixes the conditions of competition — should be marked by a reinforcement of market forces. Indeed, it appears doubly paradoxical that the proponents of the transfer of state-owned enterprises:

i)   attribute the expected improvement of efficiency solely to the effects of transfers of ownership, whilst neglecting the main determinant of efficiency, competition;

ii)  advocate regulatory intervention as a means of remedying the lack of specific actions in the context of the transfer process, whilst criticising the inefficiency and excessive costs of such intervention.

## B) *Search for efficiency through transfer of management*

Transfers of management also aim to steer the privatised firm's behaviour towards private rationality, in other words, the maximisation of profit. Efficient behaviour by the firm after transfer is thus indissociable from market structure. Transfer of management proves particularly suitable, as compared to transfer of ownership, when defects in public management are manifest and the existing market structures are only slightly competitive, or even monopolistic. More generally, the transfer of management has three advantages:

i) Provided the manager is selected on objective criteria and the contractual terms are defined unambiguously, the transfer of management will provide the state with two guarantees.

First, the contracting firm undertakes to pursue the objectives assigned by the state, bound by the clauses of the management contract or leasing agreement determined by the government. In theory, the transfer of management is an effective way of "standardizing" the firm's behaviour. The state's attitude or its capacity to impose certain clauses on the other contracting party (price fixing, quality control) bears the most weight. When the existing market structure is relatively uncompetitive, the impact on allocative efficiency is potentially great, as the firm cannot exploit its market power by means of discriminatory pricing.

Second, the contractor devotes himself to increasing his profits to the maximum, once the contractual terms have been drawn up. This attitude should result in behaviour aimed at minimising costs. When carried out under optimum conditions, the transfer of management has a strong impact on allocative and productive efficiency, because it has a direct influence on the behaviour of the privatised enterprise.

ii) It opens to competition market structures for which the expected gains in economic efficiency are substantial. In the case of a natural monopoly, the technique of franchising[22] even looks like the only viable option for privatisation (Demsetz, 1968). The tender process places various firms in direct competition one with the other as they compete to win the contract or franchise, depending on the existing market structure. This introduction of competition in the course of transferring the management and/or operation affects neither ownership rights nor the existing market structures.

iii) When the contract expires, this gives rise to a new tender process. If he is to obtain renewal of the contract or franchise, the contractor selected previously is well advised to meet his obligations. In addition, the renewal of the contract represents an opportunity for the state to redefine its objectives.

The transfer of management does give rise to certain problems, however. The performance of the contract and its renewal can call for substantial government involvement. For example, the drawing up of a medium to long-term contract may be problematical: technological upheavals or unforeseen price variations may arise that run counter to certain terms of the contract. Similarly, short-term or open-ended contracts reduce procedural pressure on the contractor's behaviour, thus increasing the risks of mediocre efficiency. State control then appears inevitable, since factors such as sunk costs or access to extra information often give the first contractor a decisive advantage. When the contract is renewed he finds himself in a position of strength, and the tender process is more closely akin to a renegotiation of the contract. This need for control by the state removes the advantages of the system as regards its flexibility and its impact on the behaviour of the contracting firm.

Three conclusions emerge at the end of this brief presentation of the relationships among privatisation, competition and allocative and productive efficiency:

i) The role of the state in the privatisation process is pre-eminent and is situated at two levels:

    a)   In determining the methods of privatisation (choice of the procedure and of the purchaser/contractor) and the nature of the privatised firm's microeconomic environment, the state has to foster the emergence or reinforcement of competition (diversification of producers or decision-making entities).

    b)   The success of the first intervention governs the occurrence of the second. If the privatisation leads to strengthening market competition or the achievement of efficient behaviour, the subsequent need for regulation will be reduced.

ii) Maximising the income from the transfer to the detriment of the development of competitive market structures is not in any circumstances an acceptable option for transfers of ownership. Such an approach considerably limits the gains in economic efficiency.

iii) Insofar as privatisation operations affect sectors whose structure justifies public intervention, public enterprises will give way to regulated private enterprises.

### Changes in the competitive position of privatised enterprises

Two general characteristics of public enterprises in the developing countries must be borne in mind throughout this study about market structures:

i) A substantial proportion of the state sector is made up of public enterprises that were granted an oligopolistic or monopolistic market structure by the government when they were created or nationalised.

ii) The national public enterprises, most often specialised in a single production and distribution network, rank among the largest in the country.

The number of large public enterprises in an oligopolistic or monopolistic position poses the problem of their transfer to the private sector on the basis of the considerations set out in the previous subsection.

## A) Characteristics of market structures and the privatisation process

i) Many privatisations of public and natural monopolies have taken place, most often by transfer of ownership (sale to the public, transfers of shares). It is difficult, however, to estimate how large a proportion of the total number of firms privatised were in a monopoly position prior to privatisation. Much more significant is the fact that these transfers from the public to the private sector are the most important operations as regards both the *financial sums involved* and the *firms' strategic or economic importance*.

In Malaysia, for example, virtually all the firms privatised enjoyed a monopoly position in the operation and supply of goods and services (air, sea and road transport and telecommunications, TV3 and STM). In Chile, the regional electricity production and distribution entities, two airline companies and three telecommunications enterprises (Telex Chile, CTC and more recently ENTEL), all in a national or regional monopoly position, were affected by privatisation. It is also worth citing the two Mexican airline companies, Mexicana and Aeromexico, and the Jamaican telecommunications company, TOJ.

One attraction of monopolistic firms for potential buyers resides in the prospects of high profitability in view of the lack of domestic competition and protection from foreign competition. However, the firm's monopolistic position is not the only necessary precondition in the eyes of potential purchasers. Its profitability prior to privatisation or the possibility of realising satisfactory financial results in the short term is a much more fundamental criterion of assessment. Attempts at privatising firms in a monopoly situation but whose financial position was poor (e.g. KTM, the Malaysian railway company) have not succeeded.

ii) One cannot however reduce the privatisation movement to a simple transfer of large monopolistic firms from the public sector to the private. In Ghana, Morocco, Tunisia, Mexico and Bangladesh, most of the firms privatised were of a modest size, operating on markets that were in the main competitive (agriculture-based food industry, small-scale industry, tourism). In Bangladesh, the large number of reprivatisation operations by the transfer of small firms, about 550 between 1975 and 1986, has reduced the percentage of state-held assets from 85 per cent to 45 per cent of total assets (Pirie, 1988, p. 316).

In addition, medium-sized industry (cement, automobile construction, paper and mining) generally has an oligopolistic structure. As the firm has a certain degree of market power, the transfers of ownership that have taken place should be studied in depth. Indeed, owing to the privatisation process, sectoral, financial and decision-making concentration is liable to

191

be strengthened. Such a development would run counter to the government's aim to take advantage of privatisation operations to strengthen competition on the markets both directly (intrinsic effect on market structures) and indirectly (parallel measures, liberalisation).

*B) Characteristics of transfers of ownership and market structures at the end of the process*

A retrospective analysis of market structures will assist in defining a fundamental point in the debate on the appropriateness of privatising enterprises in a non-competitive situation. The occurrence of privatisation depends in part on the achievement, once the transfer to the private sector is completed, of a market structure strengthening the play of competition. In the case of each market structure (monopoly, oligopoly, competition), this step, linking privatisation with competition, will help to decide whether the operation will be implemented. Owing to the changing structure of markets, no reply can be given in advance for any of the three scenarios envisaged. Thus, one cannot decide whether the privatisation of a particular firm is valid or inappropriate, until the possibilities of the competitive situation's being changed by means of the privatisation process have first been studied.

1) Public and natural monopolies

In the developing countries, most of the public sector firms in a monopoly situation are public monopolies rather than natural monopolies. The concept of public monopoly is based on a state-instituted absence of national competitors involved in the production and distribution of certain goods and services, and, as a general rule, on protection from foreign competition. The natural monopoly corresponds to a very precise configuration in which the existence of a single producer is justified by the characteristics of the cost curve, the admission of a competitor engendering a suboptimal situation. The telecommunications sector is one of the rare illustrations of this theoretical concept. On the other hand, airline companies are examples of monopolies whose existence is essentially dependent on political and other non-economic factors. As by statute they are the only national suppliers of this type of service, they also benefit from selective protection from foreign competition.

This differentiation is essential to an accurate assessment of possible changes in market structure and the introduction of competition. In fact, it is generally observed that many privatisations affecting monopolies have only marginally strengthened competition. In none of the operations has the enterprise been broken up into competing entities or a private competitor introduced alongside the privatised monopolistic enterprise (e.g. Mercury, competitor of British Telecom in the UK). Rightly sceptical, in the light of the results of such measures, or not wishing to reduce the market power of the firms concerned by adopting appropriate privatisation techniques, the governments of the developing countries have taken measures aimed at liberalisation and opening up to international competition on a case-by-case basis, particularly in the case of the airline companies. This change in the regulatory framework, which exposes privatised companies in a monopoly situation to pressure from foreign competitors, accordingly gives priority to the indirect method of promoting competition.

## 2) Oligopolistic situations

Privatisations of public sector firms in an oligopolistic or fairly non-competitive situation lead to concern about the movement towards concentration. It is with this type of market structure that the impact of concentration on domestic competition is the most negative. The risk of strengthening market power by means of privatisation is genuine, owing to the combination, in the developing countries, of three factors:

i) the lack of enthusiasm on the part of foreigners at the time of certain minor privatisations, or even, in certain cases, legal provisions limiting their involvement in operations to prevent their taking over;

ii) the limited number of local buyers (nationals or foreigners already established there) who are credible both at the level of financial resources and as regards their plans for developing the enterprise (industrial and commercial experience, contribution of technological know-how);

iii) lack of transparency of the procedures for transfer of ownership (private sale of assets or shares) or transfer of management (selection of contracting parties).

These three characteristics of privatisation procedures lead to the increase of industrial, economic and financial concentration, already well established in the developing countries. This trend, which is counterproductive to the governments' initial plans as regards the strengthening of competition, is found in several countries.

In Chile, between 1974 and 1982, privatisation operations virtually systematically benefited the two industrial and financial empires linked to the military junta in power, VIAL and Cruzat-Lorrain. These had been gradually strengthened during the first privatisation period, but the collapse of the Chilean economy in 1982 called the essential part of that development into question. In Mexico, owing to the high concentration of capital and the restriction of foreign investors to acquisitions in certain sectors (in particular the automobile industry), the privatisation operations greatly benefited the large private industrial groups. For example, after the acquisition of GARCI-CRESPO, the VISA group was in a monopoly situation on the mineral-water market. The number one in cement, Cementos Mexicanos, by acquiring three cement works previously belonging to the public sector, increased its control over the Mexican cement market. Similarly, the VITRO group acquired Prodomex, which placed it in a duopoly situation alongside GUSSA in the sale of household linen (Michalet, 1989, p. 55). In Morocco, the leading Moroccan and

African financial and industrial group, Omnium Nord Africain, strengthened its dominant position in sugar refining by acquiring the main Moroccan refinery, Consumar, in 1986. The fears that national or foreign enterprises already present on the market will strengthen their position by means of the privatisation process are therefore not unjustified.

This risk of concentration results as much from the constraints that of necessity exist in the developing countries as from the state's deliberate policy[23]. One method of reducing the propensity to strengthen the financial and industrial groups is to transfer the control of the companies to as wide a shareownership as possible. However, transfer by public offering is difficult to envisage for modestly sized companies. The only possibility of linking privatisation and the promotion of competition then lies on a firm commitment by the state to diversify the decision-making units for each market, in particular when choosing the purchasers or contractors. It therefore would seem desirable for the public authorities to give financial encouragement to buyers other than the firms already present on the market, if necessary bearing the financial cost of this diversification.

3) The transition from public to private

Whatever the enterprise and market structure concerned, the transfer to the private sector eliminates certain advantages and constraints previously granted to or imposed on public sector enterprises. Among the advantages, it is worth noting those relating to financing the enterprises (unlimited funding, state-guaranteed loans, injections of capital), advantages that in any case became hypothetical in view of budget constraints. It is much more risky to conclude that protection against domestic or foreign competition will be eliminated. Experience has shown that the privatisation process, as conceived and applied up to now in the developing countries, has related almost exclusively to the technical modalities and feasibility of transfers of ownership or management. Action in relation to the regulatory framework seems to have been situated in the main at the level of macroeconomic liberalisation measures. At the level of the lifting of constraints, privatisation is theoretically expressed by increased freedom and flexibility for the new managers as regards employment, pricing and equipment policy. The whole of this movement should put private and privatised enterprises on an even footing.

Privatisation in the developing countries is not intrinsically in a position to develop more competitive market structures. The objective constraints on the satisfactory progress of the privatisation process (limited number of potential buyers, large number of public sector firms with market power) are coupled with an ambiguous attitude on the part of the state. The government is more concerned with the effective achievement of the transfer or the lease than with market structures. Under these circumstances, privatisation is only marginally used as a vector in the liberalisation of market structures, although in theory the various privatisation techniques could carry out that task in part. Unless there is a parallel process of liberalisation (deregulation and/or reregulation), the effect of privatisation on allocative and productive efficiency seems particularly limited. As Kay & Thomson underline, only interaction between ownership and competition will result in economic efficiency (1986, p. 24).

## The social impact of privatisations

The positive effects of privatisation — accompanied by satisfactory measures relating to strengthening competitive forces and the regulatory environment provided by the government — on the budget deficit and on economic efficiency are not felt until the medium term. In view of the social constraints affecting most developing countries in the short term, it is important to measure the effects of the privatisation process on social structures.

It is not easy, however, to assess the social impact of privatisations. Two major problems come to mind immediately. First, it is difficult to assess the intrinsic social impact of privatisation compared to the relative social costs of implementing the other methods of reform (liberalisation, rehabilitation, liquidation). Second, the static effects that can be observed most easily (income distribution, employment policy, pricing of essential goods and services) are not sufficient for assessing the overall impact from the dynamic point of view. The acceleration of economic growth (although it remains to determine the extent to which this occurs in privatisation operations) and the use of the funds released by the transfers or lent by international organisations (multilateral or bilateral) are resultant social effects which it is impossible to neglect. Accordingly, we now intend to study all the questions relating to income distribution and redistribution raised by the implementation of a vast privatisation movement.

### Public sector enterprises and social objectives

#### A) An ill-defined raison d'être

In the developing countries, the finding that the public sector was potentially insolvent was the starting point of discussion focused on the privatisation of public sector firms. Unfortunately, the debate got under way before the ambiguity in measuring the performance of public firms had been removed. The advocates of privatisation have drawn up very critical assessments of public sector companies, based solely on financial performance, without taking account of the non-economic objectives pursued by such firms. Similarly, it is not enough to bear in mind — as the defenders of the public sector do — only the social objectives of public sector firms without questioning the extent to which these objectives are achieved and the financial costs involved. In between these two positions, the macroeconomic context, by reaffirming that the most important factor for the state is financial constraint, has made it necessary to weigh up the situation: the state is no longer in a position to bear the increasing budgetary burden of the very poor financial results realised by the public enterprises, especially as they appear incapable of achieving their social and non-economic objectives. In fact, the main element of disillusionment lies in their virtual failure to achieve the objectives, especially the social objectives, that are their *raison d'être*. The monopolisation of certain public goods and services, the surge in corruption and the increase in the granting of sinecures to individuals with close government contacts seriously call into question the operation of the public sector in many developing countries. This deep disillusionment is a key factor of the tendency to query the omnipotence of the public enterprises and the adoption of policies of privatisation and reform of the public sector.

The increase in the number of objectives of public sector firms has often been denounced. As instruments of government intervention and thus subject to constant political pressure, these firms are often assigned contradictory objectives. On the one hand, they have to aim for maximum economic efficiency in particular market scenarios; on the other, they have to respond to certain social constraints. The main social objective is to increase the level of social welfare by reducing economic and regional imbalances. Among these objectives of redistribution are keeping current levels of overmanning, paying overinflated wages and underpricing. Nonetheless, as a general rule, public enterprises seem to have failed to fulfil this social function relating to the interests of the community and social welfare satisfactorily, especially as regards the most underprivileged social classes.

*B) Social objectives carried out inadequately*

Public sector firms are concentrated in urban locations; overstaffing and high wages have involved a middle-class work-force; and some of the advantages have been misappropriated by the local élite[24].

For example, the paragovernmental institutions that market or export agricultural products, especially in Latin America and sub-Saharan Africa, have concentrated their attention and financial resources on export crops produced by large farms, paying little attention to food production for the home market and modest-sized farms. Further, in the developing countries where farming is the main means of livelihood, a genuine transfer has taken place between small farmers, penalised by low sale prices and heavy taxation, and the employees of public sector companies. In effect, the budget earnings derived from taxes on farming have been used partly to finance public firms' operating deficits, engendered by overstaffing and inflated wages. The question is whether public enterprises benefit only a few people: the managers and employees of the firm. Jones (1985), on the basis of studies carried out by Musgrave (1981) relating to the Bolivian mining company COMIBOL, concludes: "Up to the beginning the 1950s, COMIBOL was managed on the basis of the interests of its three capitalist owners; today the enterprise is managed on the basis of the interests of its 25 000 employees; when will it be managed on the basis of the interest of all the 5.5 million Bolivian citizens?" (1985, p. 338).

To change the subject, subsidies that lower electricity prices artificially in the developing countries will benefit the most underprivileged classes only marginally. The main consumers of electricity, and more generally of energy, are in fact the industrialists and high-income households. In the Bangladeshi clothing industry, the state in the 1970s sought to sell off goods produced by the public textile firms at prices lower than those charged by private local producers. This price difference did not benefit the consumers in any way, whether poor or rich, but was absorbed by the distribution channels. An identical development took place in the case of all the products subsidised by the State of Bangladesh, that is, on 75 per cent of public sector production (actual sale prices were between 80 and 400 per cent higher than the official prices). Accordingly, the social objective was not achieved by the public authorities, but the consequences of the underpricing on the public enterprises' financial results were immediate[25].

The analysis of the social impact of privatisation must bear in mind this social mission, which is very unevenly fulfilled by the public enterprises. It is on this basis that the net social costs of the privatisation operations need to be assessed. Moreover, the loss of a factor of intervention and distribution that results from the privatisation of a public enterprise does not necessarily indicate the abandonment of the social objectives adopted when the public sector firms were set up. Thus, bearing in mind the other means of redistribution at the state's disposal, especially taxation, privatisation will have negative net social results in only two circumstances:

i) if, following the privatisation, the state abandons the social objectives previously pursued and does not seek to replace the public enterprise by another form of distribution;

ii) if the supply of certain goods by the public sector was the most effective solution for reaching the underprivileged classes (Jones, 1985, p. 345; Van de Walle, 1989, p. 606).

These two eventualities are fairly unlikely, and consequently it is impossible to conclude *a priori* that privatisation has a negative social impact.

*The various levels of social impact*

*A) Economic efficiency and social gains*

If the privatisation contributes effectively to improving economic efficiency (obtaining the same level of output or provision of service at a lower cost), the consumer should benefit from a reduction in the price of the good or service for sale. This situation will result in an increase of real income for the consumers of this good or service. Nonetheless, the net social effects of the supply of goods by private entrepreneurs seem to be conditional, for three reasons.

First, "knowing whether the profits derived from the reduction in operating costs are transferred to the consumers or kept by the firm's new private owners, is dependent, as microeconomic theory implies, on the degree of competition to which the firm in question is subject" (Commander & Killick, 1988, pp. 99-100). Accordingly, privatisation may contribute to improving economic efficiency, but it does not lead to the distribution of the surplus generated.

Second, the reduction of production costs will in all likelihood be obtained from the dual effect of modernisation of production techniques and a reduction in wage costs. In other words, in part it is only a transfer of income from the former employees of the public firm to the consumers of the good produced.

Lastly, the state has often used public enterprises to supply certain goods (basic food products, water, petrol and coal) or services (rail and urban transport) at subsidised prices. Under these circumstances, privatisation leads not to a fall in prices but to savings in subsidies for the national budget. The government's possible use of these available financial resources for social projects (housing, education and health) should be considered before one makes a definitive judgment on the social impact of privatisations.

B) *Privatisation and employment*

One factor behind the public sector firms' poor financial performance is the overstaffing that they tolerate[26]. Overstaffing and higher wages than are accorded in the private sector are among the social objectives that the state imposes on its public enterprises. The impact of privatisation on employment is therefore measured by the reduction in overstaffing levels and the change in wage scales in privatised enterprises.

1) The significance of social constraint

There are many reasons for opposition by public-sector employees and trades unions, and this is a potential cause of blockage of the privatisation process. The factors are as follows: a) the certainty that the privatisation will lead inevitably to massive staff lay-offs and a fall in wages, b) the fear that the workers' benefits in employment rights and pension schemes will be called into question, c) the difficulty of finding other employment in urban areas already largely affected by unemployment and d) the lack of unemployment benefit schemes and the precarious situations of the employees laid off.

The governments of the developing countries are particularly anxious to demonstrate that the privatisation process will not harm public sector employees. In the developing countries, public employees represent a significant percentage of the middle classes, a social class whose support contributes to the longevity of democratic or authoritarian governments. The public authorities therefore pay close attention to the consequences of privatisations on public employment[27]. The state is aware of the imbalance in the jobs market, saturated by an inexorably and rapidly growing supply. Fearing the development of opposition movements on social grounds, it hesitates to follow the way of economic rationality, which requires the privatisation of certain labour-intensive public sector firms. Indeed, the financial costs (payment of redundancy premiums, pension premiums, financing of training programmes) and the political costs (opposition of social forces to privatisations, risk of social crisis) of massive redundancies are deemed prohibitive. The government rejects any arrangement aimed at achieving a balance over time between the elimination of redundant and fictitious jobs today and the creation of real jobs in the future (Jones, 1985, p. 340). Instead, it searches an optimal solution between the costs and the medium-term gains likely to result, on the one hand, from the reduction in staffing levels and wages, and, on the other hand, from the increase in productivity and economic efficiency.

### 2) The governments' cautious attitude

The developing countries in our sample have paid close attention to the problems of employment. In Jamaica, the two major transfers, National Commercial Bank and Caribbean Cement, did not engender waves of redundancies. In neither case were staffing levels excessive, and, in particular, the employees of the bank had adequate training and experience.

In Malaysia, from the beginning of the privatisation programme, the Confederation of Public Sector Trades Unions (CUEPACS) mobilised its forces, highlighting the risks of unemployment and deterioration in social conditions that threatened the employees of firms likely to be privatised. In order to disarm such critics, the Malaysian government advanced very precise proposals regarding the problems of transferring employees from the public to the private sector. These proposals were set out in the official report published in 1985, "Guidelines on Privatization". According to this report, private buyers had to agree to employ all the employees who chose to remain with the firm after privatisation. No dismissals are allowed (except for disciplinary reasons) for five years. In addition, the private buyers undertook to maintain the social benefits applied while the firm was in the public sector. The acceptance of such guarantees has become a condition *sine qua non* of transfer of ownership. At the time of the two major privatisations carried out in Malaysia, Port Kelang and Jabatan Telekom Negara, 99 per cent of the employees chose to join the privatised enterprise. It is impossible, however, to measure the impact of such obligations (which reduce the management freedom of the private purchaser) on the transfer price of firms (Nankani, 1988, p. 67).

In Bangladesh, the reprivatisation from 1985 on of some firms in the textile sector included a provision for keeping all the employees on for one year, a measure imposed by the government on the private purchaser. In fact, the cost of redundancy payments — compensation equivalent to several months' wages — limited resort to this type of procedure. According to the various estimates, in all the examples, the reduction in volume of employment was less than 10 per cent (Cowan, 1989, p. 45). Resolute opposition from the Bangladeshi unions and the endemic unemployment affecting the urban areas led the government to pay special attention to employment. A similar situation exists in Morocco and Tunisia, where job creation, mainly for young people in the urban sector, is the major social constraint of economic adjustment policy.

This desire to prevent privatisation from looking like a negative process from the employment viewpoint has compelled governments to take steps to ensure that the private purchasers comply with their undertakings and also to carry out drastic reductions in staffing levels during restructuring (see the following subsection). Large waves of redundancies thus occurred in the course of the rehabilitation and liquidation operations (see in Morocco, l'Office Chérifien des Exportations; in Bolivia, COMIBOL). In the end, the impact on employment is the same, but officially the privatisation is not in any way responsible for this development. Quite to the contrary, the aim of the privatisation is to create jobs to compensate for those lost in the restructuring.

Privatisation changes the relationships between managers and employees within the enterprise. In response to obligations considerably limiting the flexibility of employment, the new employers will seek to reduce wage costs by other means. For example, they will grant contracts of employment providing that the employee has the option, for the same job, of choosing between his wage level and job security. Similarly, they introduce wage scales that are dependent on productivity and, whilst maintaining the number of employees, seek to increase the level of employees' qualifications without increasing wage levels accordingly.

### C) Privatisation, provision of goods and services and pricing

The adoption of a new pricing policy after privatisation affects the division of the consumer surplus and the producer surplus for the goods concerned, together with the level of the relative prices. The increase in the price of a good or service results, in effect, in a loss of surplus for the consumers. Once underpricing is eliminated, the likely result of the application of private rationality following privatisation is a transfer of surplus from consumers to producers. The size of this transfer will be proportional to the increase in sale prices when subsidised prices change over to market prices. Let us consider the impact on the most underprivileged classes of a change in pricing and distribution of certain essential goods and services.

The rise in prices of essential goods entails a reduction in income for the poorest, since the elasticity of their demand compared to the price is nil. In the case of other goods and services, the elimination of subsidies and significant rise in prices may simply eliminate the demand of certain social classes of consumers for such goods. The social impact of privatisations seems very negative. Nonetheless, it has to be acknowledged that, with the exception of Chile, privatisation has not affected firms producing public goods or basic necessities. The spectacular increases in these prices thus seem less the result of privatisation than the consequence of policies aimed at restructuring the public sector or liberalising prices.

The provision of certain services, especially in rural or disadvantaged areas, is potentially affected by privatisation. The adoption of private rationality gives rise to the fear of a deterioration in the quality of service offered and also in territorial coverage. For example, transport firms are likely to stop operating on little-used and unprofitable routes. The same reasoning applies to the provision of water, electricity and telecommunications. A study of urban transport in Rabat, the capital of Morocco, suggests that privatisation/fragmentation/liberalisation resulted in a qualitative improvement in the service without reducing the number of destinations offered by the various companies (Damis, 1987). On the other hand, although the privatisation of bus operation in the region of Kingston (Jamaica) undoubtedly facilitated the increase in the number of private operators, the users suffered, mainly at the levels of comfort, adherence to timetables and the number of accidents (Mills, 1988, p. 394).

The state has three means of deadening the impact for the underprivileged classes of the changeover from subsidised prices to market prices for essential goods and services. It can restrict the behaviour of private buyers by regulatory action (price increase within a certain range), distribute an allowance or grant directly to the underprivileged members of society or pursue a policy of more selective subsidies (for specific routes, regions or social groups)[28]. These variants are potential answers to the failure of blanket subsidy policies. If they are to represent a genuine reduction in financial burdens, privatisation must be combined with the strengthening of competitive forces. The amount of the subsidy or allowance is proportional to the loss of surplus by the poorest consumers. If the privatised firm has the benefit of an oligopolistic or protected monopoly market structure, the market price will be situated below its level of competition. In other words, the less competitive the market structure is at the end of the privatisation, the higher will be the volume of subsidies or allowances.

By way of conclusion, it is worth recalling four essential points from our analysis of the social impact of privatisations:

i) Privatisation participates in the reformulation of social objectives and of the means of government intervention. It does not in any case signify the abandonment of these objectives, as they can be achieved more efficiently by other means (fiscal policy, direct redistribution to underprivileged groups).

ii) Transfer operations raise the problem of transforming potential public wealth into achieved individual wealth. Three groups seem to benefit, to varying degrees, from this transfer of assets: highly placed families with links with the national industrial and financial empires, ethnic groups and the middle classes (small investors, local entrepreneurs).

iii) The greatest losers in privatisation operations are those who had benefited the most from the operation of public sector firms: public sector employees and private entrepreneurs who obtained rich pickings in the lucrative world of public contracts.

iv) By imposing total reform of the management of public funds, government financial constraint encouraged the notion of profit as an indicator of the performance of public sector companies. This led to an implicit retreat from social objectives in the context of a general evolution towards strengthening private rationality. This also stems from the impossibility of giving a satisfactory content to the notion of social profit. Henceforth any reference to social profit looks like an argument aimed at masking the inefficiency of state sector enterprises. The "diktat" of financial performance, of which privatisation is only one of the causal factors, raises the problem of the original *raison d'être* of state-owned enterprises.

## Conclusion

The microeconomic and macroeconomic study of privatisation operations in the sample countries does not aspire to draw lessons that are applicable to every circumstance. On the basis of privatisation programmes that vary considerably from one country to another, it is clear that governments have not particularly encouraged the strengthening of competitive forces or the privatisation of firms in deficit. Above all, it seems that privatisation is not the appropriate method — in other words, the most effective method — of achieving the main objectives of rebalancing: improving the allocative and productive efficiency of these economies and reducing the financial constraint derived from public sector enterprises.

In the first case, progressive liberalisation and the splitting up of monopolies are the principal measures for submitting a growing proportion of the developing countries' economies to market forces. The fundamental problem is therefore the origin of non-competitive situations in the developing countries.

In the second case, economic restructuring and financial reorganisation undertaken by the state seem two conditions *sine qua non* of the achievement of "effective privatisation". Under these circumstances, it is worth considering whether the macroeconomic impact of privatisation is essentially limited to the transfer of profitable enterprises to the private sector.

Accordingly, privatisation should be viewed as facilitating the implementation and success of such policies. Without policies that open the way to domestic and foreign competition, transfers of ownership and management cannot on their own resolve the problems posed by the application of private rationality in a non-competitive environment.

This study of the financial, economic and social impacts has revealed two factors:

i) Privatisation as applied up to now in the developing countries depends as much on the objective constraints affecting the developing countries (at the level of purchasers, the technical modalities of implementing the operations) as on the government's attitude. This attitude should be pragmatic and should encourage transparency throughout the whole complex process of rebalancing.

ii) The rebalancing process cannot be limited to the application of only one of its components (liberalisation, restructuring, privatisation). To the contrary, a combination of all these modalities must be used when the vast process of state divestiture and growth of the private sector is being planned and implemented.

# NOTES AND REFERENCES

1.  It is highly unlikely that the state and the private purchaser will have identical expectations of the privatised firm's future cash flows. If they do, the exchange of assets will not take place unless the government agrees to bear the costs of the transaction, thus reducing its income from the transfer and its net *ex-post* wealth.

2.  See the IMF interpretation of "Government Finance Statistics".

3.  Economist Intelligence Unit, *Country Report on the Philippines*, Nos. 2 and 3, 1987, and No. 4, 1988.

4.  The reprivatisations of Chilean banking and financial institutions, in particular Banco de Santiago and Banco de Chile, are exceptions to this rule (the public offerings related to the whole of the capital, in order to emphasize the temporary nature of the public ownership, made necessary by the collapse of the financial and banking system in 1982).

5.  It should be noted that in the countries of sub-Saharan Africa (where virtually all the public sector was operating at a loss), a higher proportion of firms in deficit have been privatised, most often by transfer-of-management procedures.   As in our sample, however, firms operating at a serious deficit have not been affected by privatisation.

6.  *Financial Times*, 2 June 1988.

7.  The argument that the state would be able to transfer a firm in deficit by paying a private purchaser remains theoretical, to say the least.   Transfer of management is an answer to this problem, however, and in this context, the state will agree to pay the private managers for running the firm.

8.  This is a more convincing interpretation of $\lambda_g$, estimated by L. Jones *et al.* (1988) (see Chapter 3, "The concept of privatisation: definition and justification").

9.  *Rebalancing the Public and Private Sectors in Developing Countries:  The Cases of Bolivia and Jamaica*, OECD Technical Papers, 1991.

10. On the other hand, too slow an implementation of privatisation will lead potential private purchasers to question the credibility of the state's commitment and the future of rebalancing policies.

11. Two important transfers took place in 1988-89, Mexicana del Cobre and Aeromexico, and in all likelihood, Cananea and Telmex will be privatised in 1990-91 (*Euromoney*, March 1990).

12. Dagnino-Pastore, mimeo, 1989.

13. The comparison of financial results, like the measure of the relative efficiency of public and private enterprises, poses important conceptual problems.  The only way to make a perfect comparison would be to assess, other things being equal (especially the microeconomic and macroeconomic conditions of productive activity), the financial results realised by the privatised firm with those that the same firm would have realised

had it remained in the public sector. Because it is impossible to make this comparison, the closest combination is used: the results of the public firm compared to the results of privatised enterprises (in one country, in one and the same sector) whith a concomittant attempt to assess the impact of a changing environment (Galal, 1990).

14. See the works of Savas (1977), Caves & Christensen (1978), Borchedring (1982), Killick (1983), Millward (1982 and 1988).

15. Certain authors consider that the poor productive efficiency of public sector firms prevents them from fulfilling their role of cushioning the market in the area of resource allocation (Rees, 1984, pp. 15-16; Domberger & Piggott, 1986, pp. 147-48).

16. It should be noted that the behaviour of private sector firms is far from achieving full economic efficiency. The point of reference is therefore the behaviour of private firms, as observed in the developing countries.

17. For the pioneer presentations, see Alchian & Demstez (1972) on the behaviour of the "classic firm" (a single manager-shareholder) and Jensen & Meckling (1976).

18. The elector-shareholders' ownership is collective ownership, in other words, diluted, undivided and non-negotiable, which does not allow for effective management supervision. This results in higher costs and, in consequence, lower efficiency (Pestiau, 1987).

19. J. Vickers and G. Yarrow, "Privatization: An Economic Analysis", Chs. 8 and 9, 1988.

20. The definition of the term *regulation* is close to that of Yarrow, "any activity by a government or its agencies whose aim is to influence behaviour by means of establishing rules that guide or constrain economic decisions" (1985, pp. 343-44).

21. This question, centred on monopoly situations, has been dealt with in many theoretical studies, from those of Averch & Johnson (1962) on the "exact" rate of profitability of assets, to those of Littlechild (1983) on the rules of price fixing (RPI - X).

22. Here we are using the definition adopted by Pera (1989, p. 212): "franchising consists of granting the right to a natural monopoly to a firm that guarantees to supply the services demanded on the best terms, generally at the lowest price." See too Sharpe (1982) and Vickers & Yarrow (1985).

23. In certain cases — e.g. Mexico — the government uses privatisation as a means of increasing the size of national groups to make them more competitive on the international markets (critical size, economies of scale, dominant position on the national market).

24. On the urban bias of public enterprises, see Lipton (1977), cited by Van de Walle (1989, p. 606); for overstaffing and wages in public sector firms, Jones (1985), Commander & Killick (1988, p. 99) and Vernon (1989, p. 146).

25. These two examples relating to electricity and clothing are mentioned by Jones (1985, pp. 335, 343). In the case of Bangladesh, see Sobhan (1983), cited by Cool & Kirckpatrick (1988, p. 18).

26. We must point out, however, that public-sector firms have not created many new jobs, since as a general rule they have adopted very capital-intensive production techniques.

27. We are referring to employment in public-sector enterprises rather than employment by the central bureaucracy. In any case, the absorption of redundant employees from the public sector will not be an objective of the central government.

28. The implementation of a selective subsidy policy or a discriminatory pricing policy (different prices applied to social groups) raises insurmountable problems. By way of example, in the case of any consumption of a basic necessity, the enterprise and the state would need to be in a position to identify the social position of the consumer (whether or not he belonged to groups deemed underprivileged).

*Chapter 5*

# THE FUTURE OF REBALANCING

Forecasting the dynamics of rebalancing the public and private sectors amounts to asking whether the trend noted in all the sample countries since the beginning of the 1980s is really irreversible.

The very nature of the mixed economy implies constant tension between two apparently contradictory logics: on the one hand, the desire for efficiency, for economic reasoning, based on market mechanisms and the initiative of private agents; on the other, the pursuit — in the context of a medium-term plan within a regulated economy — of long-term objectives of development and national independence defined by the state backed up by a strong public sector. Over a long period, the countries in the sample have preferred the second stance. Naturally, the national mixed economy models have varied, and a classification has been used to comprehend the diversity of experiences. In every case, however, the state and the public sector occupy a pre-eminent position, while the public enterprises are considered to be the spearhead of industrialisation. The private sector plays a secondary role. Its position is defined as residual, in relation to either the strategic or priority functions accorded to the public sector (as in the case of Mexico, Chile before 1973, Bolivia or Jamaica) or the action to promote private initiative defined by the state (as in the case of Morocco, Tunisia and Ghana). In any case, it is never considered to be the basis of a development strategy.

It is precisely this concept that was called into question at the beginning of the 1980s. The adoption of programmes to liberalise the economy and reduce the scale of the public sector through the transfer of public enterprises to the private sector was evidence of a major turning-point in the concept of the functioning of a mixed economy. Here too, the scope of the movement was variable, but what is striking is that the countries in our sample changed direction at the same time. This simultaneity reflects the very serious constraints confronting these countries at the same period: the drastic reduction in financial resources caused by the withdrawal of the international banks, the deterioration in terms of trade, the rise of the dollar and interest rates. These countries found themselves unable to cope with the growing borrowing requirements of a public sector that had expanded considerably during the second half of the previous decade. It is undeniable that the choice of rebalancing was largely inevitable. That is the fundamental reason why, at the threshold of the 1990s, the question of its irreversibility is of prime importance.

The reply may be given in the form of an alternative. On the one hand, the rebalancing process is only an interlude linked to temporary economic difficulties; thus, when the financial constraints are loosened, the scales of the rebalancing process will tip in the other direction, resulting in a return to the traditional model. On the other hand, the turning-point of the 1980s was a decisive break with previous economic logic and hailed the advent of a market economy in which the economic role of the state and the position of the public sector were to be extremely limited. Such an approach is much too simplistic; the development of the rebalancing process will in all probability be much more complex. It is precisely this complexity which it is important to grasp in this attempt at futurology. It will be focused on two subjects. First, the necessary conditions for the irreversibility of rebalancing will be explored. Particular attention will be given to the opposition encountered by the privatisation and liberalisation programmes, which is one of the reasons why the rebalancing process has not been completed. This analysis will allow us to identify the mooring points which will appreciably reduce the risk of drifting back to the old model. Second, we intend to present the most likely characteristics of a renewed mixed economy model. It will be based on a new balance between the two sectors, which will be the outcome, though still an uncertain one, of the play of the contradictory forces that control the current development.

## Conditions for irreversible rebalancing

The rebalancing process is still incomplete. In trying to specify the conditions that will make it irreversible, one must first of all analyse the adverse effects and opposition that go hand in hand with the application of privatisation and liberalisation programmes. Second, it will then be possible to define the mooring points which ought then to guarantee that the choice of rebalancing will not be called into question again.

### *The rebalancing process is incomplete*

Privatisation and liberalisation policies are under way in all the countries in our sample. With the exception of Chile, however, nowhere have they reached the point of no return. On the one hand, the privatisation programmes are still at the embryonic stage; implementing them is generally more laborious than envisaged, and the first results have sometimes disappointed expectations. On the other hand, opposition to the new development model has not yet been totally conquered, and this is holding back the dynamics of the change.

## A) The effects of the privatisations are still uncertain

The results of the privatisation programmes in the countries that have carried out this policy the most enthusiastically — Chile and Mexico — are in part disappointing. In most cases, the handover from the public enterprises to private firms is far from completed.

In the few countries where privatisation operations on a reasonable scale have been carried out since the 1980s or earlier, as in the case of Chile, the first effects have often failed to live up to expectations, *inter alia* as regards the emergence of a competitive market dynamics. Transfers of ownership of public sector enterprises to the private sector have not always resulted in the expected improvement in economic efficiency.

In the first place, the enterprises selected as a priority for privatisation have nearly always been the most attractive in the public sector. Often basing their advice on the British experience (Croisset *et al.*, 1986; Bishop and Kay, 1989), government advisers have generally recommended the choice of the public enterprises with the highest profitability and the best development potential to inaugurate the new policy with the maximum chance of success. Although the question is very debatable, the sale price of these enterprises has, in most cases, corresponded to the lowest valuation in the range of estimates available. In view of the inevitable political connotations of these operations, the desire for their success has often won the day over concern for the state's financial interests. It is also true that the crisis in public finances resulted in a high increase in marginal utility for the state of the immediate cash revenues expected from these sales. Therefore the easiest transfers from the public to the private sector were given priority.

Second, despite efforts to increase the extent of popular shareownership in the long term, the shares of the privatised enterprises have gone into the portfolios of the richest strata of society. The lack of transparency of the offers for sale and the procedures for selecting the purchasers did not generally encourage dispersal of the securities. The consequent effects of privatisations on the development of the stock markets were therefore very limited. Often their main impact consisted of speculative movements that benefited only a well-informed minority.

Third, in the experience of the sample countries — limited, it is true, as Malaysia, Chile and Mexico are the main terms of reference — the transfers of public enterprises to the private sector do not seem to have been accompanied by a strengthening of competitive forces. It seems rather that the privatisation encouraged such features as industrial and financial concentration. This should come as no surprise, in that the private sector in these countries was very small at the outset and has subsequently developed on the fringe of the public sector. Accordingly, the number of potential national purchasers was very limited. Only a few large private groups, often conglomerates or family concerns, had sufficient capital at their disposal to enter bids in the privatisation campaigns. These groups naturally chose those public enterprises available for privatisation in sectors of activity closest to their own and whose potential they were well situated to judge. However, the consolidation of oligopolistic structures as a result of privatisation is perhaps only a minor disadvantage compared to the prospect of opening up the economy to international competition. In any case, to achieve a successful transformation of mixed economies, the governments will have rely more on the most dynamic local entrepreneurs than they did in the past, those entrepreneurs who are more attracted by the international market than by the domestic market and those who already have close relationships with foreign investors.

Fourth, particular attention must be paid to a type of adverse effect that may go hand in hand with privatisations: the triggering of financial speculation. The Chilean experience in its initial phase prior to 1982 is an example of this, but it is not the only one. Similar phenomena took place in Mexico in 1986-87. In the latter case this did not compel the state to renationalise the banking sector, as in Chile, but all the same it led the new president, Salinas de Gortari, to take coercive measures against a certain number of well-known businessmen. Such disadvantages are apparently difficult to avoid, but they demonstrate a certain lack of maturity on the part of the local private sector, which seems to be more interested in speculative financial operations than in earning interest on investments. This finding is bound to strengthen the opponents of change in their conviction that the withdrawal of the state and the public enterprises will open the door to unscrupulous speculators accustomed to investing their money abroad rather than in their country.

Finally, in the case of the public enterprises responsible for the public utilities and the supply of public goods and services, the privatisation process risks being even more laborious. The financial balance of these firms is precarious; as a general rule, it is they that weigh most heavily on the public sector deficit. In order to improve their financial situation, there have to be large price increases, with possible repercussions on the living standards of the most underprivileged members of society, and this may lead to serious social disturbances. Furthermore, the revaluation of electricity, gas or transport prices will have negative effects on the results of companies in the private sector. The valuation of enterprises providing public services is even more difficult than that of firms in the competitive sector and will certainly take longer. Substantial investments are required for modernising them. In addition, the trades unions are traditionally stronger in this sector than in private enterprises and will make it more difficult to implement necessary lay-offs justified by the traditional tendency towards overmanning. Obviously, these enterprises are not ideal candidates for privatisation programmes. There is no lack of arguments opposed to the idea of transferring natural monopolies from the public to the private sector (Yarrow, 1985). This means that privatisation will often take the form of a changeover from the status of public enterprise to that of a regulated private enterprise. This set of arguments militates in favour of keeping them in the public sector. Gains in efficiency may be achieved without transferring ownership, by the use of contractual management arrangements with private firms at the level of production or distribution and/or by programme contracts with the relevant ministries (Nellis, 1989).

*B) Opposition to rebalancing*

Before its positive effects start to be felt, there is a risk that the rebalancing process will have a negative impact on income distribution. First, the immediate consequence of liberalising mixed economies close on the heels of stabilization and structural adjustment policies may be to aggravate the situation of the poorest social classes. In addition, the privatisation movement may be reduced to a game for the rich and upper middle classes, whilst calling into question the established interests of certain privileged minorities such as holders of sinecures or rent-seekers — all the more so as the introduction of a stronger dose of liberalism will not necessarily be welcomed favourably in all the countries. Opposition of a different type, stemming from local culture, should also be taken into consideration. All in all, certain groups, in both the private and the public sectors, will fear the effects of rebalancing and try to block it or hold it up.

As regards the effects of liberalisation policies on redistribution, according to World Bank data (Kakwani *et al.*, 1989), between 1980 and 1987 the income per inhabitant fell in 44 developing countries out of 88; annual consumption per inhabitant fell by 1.8 per cent in Africa and by 0.8 per cent in Latin America between 1980 and 1984, subsequently rising by 1.4 per cent for the period 1985-87. In addition, budget reductions have affected public expenditure on education, health and welfare assistance. The deterioration in public well-being during the 1980s was punctuated by riots linked to the withdrawal of subsidies for popular consumer goods, as in Jamaica (1985), Morocco (1981) and Tunisia (1984). The consequences of the stabilization programmes for the poorest 30 per cent of the population, according to the World Bank criterion, or on the "most vulnerable" groups, according to UNICEF terminology, are a matter for concern on the part of the international organisations, as is evidenced by the 1990 World Bank report devoted to poverty. Programmes have been organised to help the most underprivileged groups, but their effectiveness is nearly always disappointing (Nelson, 1990). The poorest groups are not organised and have no means of bringing pressure to bear on governments; the governments in their turn take advantage of this to put back indefinitely the politically dangerous reallocation of the increasingly limited resources of the less underprivileged classes to the most underprivileged. They are generally much more concerned by reactions from the urban popular classes, basically made up of low-wage earners — most of whom work in the public sector — craftsmen and small traders. The urban population is the most immediately affected by austerity measures; it consumes the greater part of the subsidised goods, which are often imported; it benefits principally from public goods and services such as education and health; it suffers directly the effects of rises in public transport prices or rents and is the most closely concerned by the reductions in personnel in the bureaucracy and public enterprises. Certain measures in the rebalancing programmes therefore risk provoking violent reactions and leading governments to suspend the application of certain components of the liberalisation programme. The break with the populist tradition of the welfare state is very sudden. Under these circumstances, in the future social safety nets should be an integral part of rebalancing policies.

The public sector is a source of lucrative advantages for a number of groups belonging to the private sector (Glade, 1989). The rebalancing process may jeopardise these advantages. It will require private entrepreneurs to abide by market economy rules, of which they have had very little experience. Suppliers of goods and services to the public enterprises and the government are among the categories that benefit the most often from a privileged situation. With the application of more rigorous management criteria accompanying the change in status of certain of their customers, profit margins are likely to fall. Or, at least, to borrow from the logic of the theory of "rent-seeking" (Buchanan & Tollison, 1984), a larger part of the "rent" will have to be devoted to conserving the advantages acquired, when management and supply contracts are renewed with the new managers of the privatised enterprises. This new deal might result in alliances and coalitions being formed by groups opposed to the changes.

The prospect of both privatisations and restructurings worries consumers of goods and services supplied by the public enterprises. It has been underlined above that one of the main causes of their chronic deficits was the underpricing of their goods and services, the prices being imposed by the supervisory bodies. The inequality of terms of trade between the public and private sectors has often been justified by the aim of redistribution to the most underprivileged strata of the population. Delays in raising public prices to keep pace with market prices are applied to many types of goods, such as food and basic products, rail and urban transport and energy. These disguised subsidies make certain public enterprises play the role of producers of goods and services of public utility. This confusion between the notion of the public enterprise and the notion of public service is all the more detrimental in that personal income tax and corporation tax are low, and the institutional mechanisms that should enable preferences to be revealed are generally very limited. In the new economic logic, the restructured enterprises, and even more the privatised enterprises, anxious about their profitability, will no longer be in a position to agree to such practices. In order to anticipate the consequences of this change in the rules of the game, certain private sector pressure groups will be tempted to hold up privatisation programmes and/or endeavour to obtain financial consideration. In this case, the rebalancing process would result in a paradox: the state would continue to finance the private sector directly by means of subsidies or compensatory tax advantages, whilst it was supposed to be pursuing a privatisation policy in order to reduce public expenditure. In any event, the transition may well be difficult, both for the rent-seekers and for the state. Once again the unexpected combination of the interests of different social groups should be taken into account, since it may jeopardise the dynamics of the rebalancing process. A front that is hostile to change may group together large landowners and families in control of financial holding companies, backed up by the rank and file of agricultural labourers and low-ranking employees. In order to combat this situation, the state will have to rely — as it did in the case of the privatisation programmes — on the most dynamic local entrepreneurs, those who are directed more towards the world market than towards the domestic market. However, although growing strongly, this group is still at the embryonic stage in many countries; accordingly, its reforming influence is still limited.

A further question is the attitude of the employees and managers of the public enterprises, who are, finally, the most closely threatened by the rebalancing process. There is no doubt that the former are fearful for their future. Their level of pay is generally higher than in the other sectors, particularly in the public enterprises that exploit income derived from national resources of the soil and subsoil. Generally, pay levels in this sector were always more attractive than the pay offered by the administration, the customary reference of public sector employees. In addition, public enterprises have a structural tendency towards overmanning. Here too, the theory of rent-seeking may be applied. Lastly, since the unions in the sector are often well organised and powerful, it is clear that the purchasers of the public enterprises will have a long and difficult path ahead of them before they finally achieve the lay-offs required for a return to balance. In this connection, in several cases — Malaysia and the Philippines, for example — the state has made the purchasers undertake not to lay off workers without compensation. This clause entails additional cost that, in the end, the state is often obliged to bear in order to avoid the negotiation's breaking down.

The managers of the public enterprises are generally top civil servants, having entered the administration on the basis of their degrees, often obtained at foreign universities. They form a body of technocrats whose power is directly jeopardised by the rebalancing. Not only do they risk losing the substantial material advantages attaching to their position, but the choice of privatisation represents a sanction of their management in former years. Leaving to one side the opportunists who will try to obtain employment from the private purchasers by taking advantage of their inside knowledge of the enterprise, the common reaction of the majority might be to profit from the wind of change to demonstrate that they are capable of managing public enterprises efficiently. In this perspective, their aim will be, first of all, to prove that the public enterprises are necessary and irreplacable, by using the classic arguments justifying the existence of public enterprises — natural monopolies, external effect, strategic importance. Next, they will have to try to prove that the failures in the management of the public enterprises can be corrected once the major factor of "X-inefficiency" — political interference in day-to-day management — is eliminated.

At the end of the day, rebalancing will give them an opportunity to reinforce their power by enabling them to achieve greater autonomy from political control. Another paradox of the rebalancing policy: it is not impossible that the strengthened public enterprises will become a state within the state, once again escaping from the control of civil society in a certain fashion.

Lastly, the success of the rebalancing process will depend largely on an in-depth change in public mentality. By its very nature this question is a delicate one for an economist, since it forces him to leave his framework of reference — that of *homo economicus* — to take into account cultural factors that are foreign to his philosophy. Nonetheless, certain authors have quite rightly remarked that economic liberalism, which sprang from late eighteenth-century English thinking, has not been accepted spontaneously by every society, even those ordinarily classed with the group of developing countries. Thus H. Feigenbaum notes judiciously, "The concept of free enterprise, as developed in the England of the nineteenth century and transplanted to the United States, with its postulate of a competitive struggle for markets and drastic penalties for failure and with its emphasis on earning more and more for producing less and less, has never really been accepted in France." (Feigenbaum, 1985, p. 6). In place of this vision of the world, French ideology was based on the conviction that each individual had his place in society, that he should be able to produce enough goods and services to maintain his place there. In other words, the right to survival was based not on the capacity to realise a profit but on the correct fulfilment of a recognised social function. This ideal was no doubt more favourable to the development of a vast public sector than to that of a market economy based on competition. It is therefore not surprising that societies which have been outside the liberal current for much longer might have some difficulty in instantly making a radical ideological conversion. In this connection, C. Hamilton (1989) underlines that the notion of individualism, which is indissociable from economic liberalism, is absent from the culture of many countries, particularly in Asia, where the economic success of certain countries is nonetheless often cited as an example to those that are still attached to the 1950-60s model. The primacy of the community, of the group over the individual interest, makes it difficult to construct an economy based on the "addition of egoisms", to use Smithian terminology. Ignorance of providential intervention by the "invisible hand" is still very widespread and leads some societies to give priority to the role of a supervisory authority such as the state. The attachment to authority, to the hierarchy, to corporations is often the basis of the cohesion of nations that are today, willy-nilly, engaging in rebalancing policies. The importance of these factors should lead to a more cautious consideration of the depth of certain countries' commitment to economic policies, often inspired by foreign experts who tend to refuse to take particular national characteristics into account. In these cases, setbacks in the rebalancing process might easily be exploited politically by opposition movements in the name of the defence of traditional or religious values. The risk is certainly greater in the countries where the democratic institutions are fragile, where social inequalities are accentuated and where the leaders are not yet quite converted to the virtues of a liberal state that is poorer and weaker.

## The moorings of rebalancing

The rebalancing policies introduced since the early 1980s can result in an irreversible change in the operational rules of mixed economies. The combined play of liberalisation policies and privatisation programmes will produce sustainable effects only if the transfer of ownership of the capital of the public enterprises is accompanied by a strengthening of competition and if the disciplines to which the state and the public sector are subject fall into the context of a new development strategy. For this change to take root, two conditions must be fulfilled: the end of the state as "paymaster" and integration into the world economy.

### A) New operational rules

Rebalancing should be accompanied by the abandonment of the lax functioning of the mixed economy characteristic of the past thirty years — the term "functioning" (in French, régulation) here meaning the play of a set of economic and institutional mechanisms (Boyer, 1986). In other words, the constraints of economic calculation and of observance of the major balances — of the budget, the balance of payments, the currency — must be applied to those grandiose objectives, accelerated industrialisation and economic independence.

The analysis of the different national experiences shows that the mixed economy has generally been "balanced" by means of public financing. The operation in deficit of the public sector, aggravated by the wave of creation of public enterprises during the second half of the 1970s, was financed by domestic and foreign borrowing and by money creation. The central protagonist in the financial control of the economy, the state, was transformed into a "milch-cow". This function was all the more easily accepted when its implications for the taxpayers were negligible — as the state's main earnings came from taxation of foreign trade and revenues of the public enterprises engaged in exporting primary products. The monetary illusion hid the inflationary deduction from agents who had no opportunity to pass this charge on. The end of the period of easy borrowing from international banks, the collapse of traditional exports and the introduction of stabilization and liberalisation programmes under the auspices of the IMF and the World Bank, acting more and more often in conjunction with bilateral lenders, called into question the lax functioning of the economy. The disciplines introduced by the various conditions linked to the new loans reduced the state's room for manoeuvre: its traditional foreign resources had foundered, whereas the fight against inflation and the freeing of the exchange rates now prevented it from appealing to the Central Bank as it had in the past. The sale of part of the public sector enterprises produced a certain amount of financial income, but these resources, by their very nature, were non-renewable. In a word, the state could no longer fulfil the functions it had fulfilled in the past. It had become poor.

This development recalls the historical experience at the end of the absolute monarchies in eighteenth-century Europe, with the rise of parliamentary democracy, a parallelism that has been well captured by R. Goldscheid (in Musgrave & Peacock, 1964). The governments in the developing countries are being dispossessed just as the princes were in Europe two centuries earlier. In order to obtain the means they need, they now have to submit to rules fixed by the international bodies in control of the till. To a certain extent, the multilateral bodies play the same role *vis-à-vis* the states that the parliaments played to the monarchs. Economic liberalism is linked to forms of parliamentary democracy. At the present time, in the case of the less developed countries, control of the "prodigal state" is, in part, exercised by foreign institutions. The internationalisation of the procedures for controlling public financing — a process linked to the abandonment of the one-party system — would certainly be a key factor in rendering irreversible the changes in functioning of the mixed economy. It should lead to the end of a notion of economic management corresponding to what K. Popper defines as "methodological essentialism", a form of "utopian rationalism" where the end purposes of social organisation are fixed without any preliminary definition of the appropriate means of realising them and without any concern for the existence of a social consensus.

This new stance, linked to the radical change in the old method of functioning of the mixed economies, is bound to be strengthened by a stronger integration into the world economy.

*B) Integration into the world economy*

The irreversibility of rebalancing also depends on the modalities of the insertion of national economies into the world economy. The virtually exclusive dependence on primary products as a means of obtaining foreign currency calls for an effort at diversifying exports. For most of the primary markets, the current situation of surplus supply is on the increase. One cause of this imbalance is that over the past ten years or so, a growing number of producer countries have made efforts to increase their exports. It was aggravated by a structural reduction in demand for raw materials from the industrialised countries stemming from cheaper manufacturing techniques, the increase of synthetic substitutes and the adoption of protectionist measures. At the same time, the obligations linked to servicing debt continued to make the generation of foreign currency a prime objective. The stabilization and structural adjustment plans have pushed states to opt for a development strategy fueled by exports. The rebalancing process seriously calls into question the import substitution model that had been at the heart of the countries' economic stance for the past 30 or 40 years. Two major consequences should accompany this fundamental change in strategic policy and turn rebalancing into a permanent change.

In the first place, the commitment to export diversification calls for the identification of new comparative advantages. These will need to be defined upstream from the primary sector, mainly in the manufacturing and services sectors. There is no question here of considering what new products and services should be used as a basis for the new specialisation by our sample countries. What is important is to grasp the implications of these countries' new commercial policy for the rebalancing process. In view of the intensified competition on the world market and of the sample countries' delay in undertaking export promotion, the strengthening of competitiveness will become absolutely essential. The identification of gaps in the world market, the reduction of costs, the quality of products, flexibility of production, compliance with delivery dates — these principles, which have long been established practice for firms, are from now on extended to the states' industrial policies (Porter, 1990). The new doctrine is quite distant from the analytical tools of macroeconomics, which had been favoured in the import substitution models. Somewhat later in the day than the transformations in the European mixed economies during the 1960s, an open-economy industrial policy should be substituted for planning in the countries of the South.

In the second place, the integration of less industrialised economies into the world economy is going to take a number of different forms: it will be multidimensional. In some aspects, this new stance in development strategies, where the export of manufactured products has to occupy a central position, evokes the notion of the "new international order", which had some success in the mid-1970s. However, the resemblance is purely one of form: the modalities of integration into the world economy will be very different. The call for the new international order was an extension of the Latin American analyses that recommended the developing countries to produce and export manufactured products in order to avoid or reduce the effects of deterioration in terms of trade. In this perspective, the structure of trade was supposed to mirror the growing share of the industrial sector in the economies of the South, itself a result of the import substitution policy. Accordingly, the industrialised countries were asked to allow more manufactured products from the Third World to enter their markets more freely. In the new perspective, it is the competitiveness of the products that will give access to markets in both the North and the South.

This competitiveness may be based on advantages of cost or of differentiation, but in the long run it will be measured in comparison with competing products available on the world market. This means *inter alia* that products from export-oriented industries will have to comply with the same technical standards as those offered anywhere else, including by the most industrialised nations. To meet this challenge, firms of the countries from the South will likely have to work in close association with countries from the North. Direct investments and joint ventures are likely to increase. In the logic of the world economy (Michalet, 1985), the countries' specialisation will become increasingly dependent on the choice of localisation of productive activities made by the major firms in the context of their global strategy. The modalities of private international financing will be more closely linked to projects in the industrial or services sectors. All in all — and this is a central consequence for rebalancing — the integration into the world economy will be multidimensional. Contrary to the traditional notion of the international division of labour, it will concern not only trade in goods and services but also the productive process, through the delocalisation of production carried out by the companies from the North and flows of technology and funds. The result will be a strong trend towards standardization of activities and products. The rules of the game will become uniform and will be applied to every country, North or South. The notion of national independence — *a fortiori* that of nationalism — at the heart of the development strategies during the previous decades will have to be radically revised.

The impoverishment of the state and the close integration of national economies into the world economy are the two determining factors that should make the rebalancing process irreversible. Viewed optimistically, this development might lead to the reconciliation of economic rationality and development. In a historical perspective, the rebalancing phase — through its transformation of institutions, mentalities and economic logic — would begin a new period in the development dynamics of the countries that have adopted that route. Though forced at the outset, the choice of a new stance would have finally permitted the revelation of economic and social potential that might blossom in the context of a renovated mixed economy.

**The new balance of the public and private sectors**

The new balance of the public and private sectors will largely depend on the new stance of the development strategies. The changed orientation of the economic model from the domestic market to the international market involves a major change in the concept of the economic role of the state and in the management of enterprises, whether public or private. As import substitution gives way to export promotion, the primacy of national economic independence is replaced by that of international competitiveness.

The *rapprochement* of economic efficiency, provided by the private sector, and a development strategy defined by the state may give rise to a renovated form of mixed economy that will not fall into any of the categories used to analyse the national experiences: mixed economies dominated by the state, promoted by the state, or at the service of particular interests. The existence of mixed economies, however, will not be called into question. Naturally, the analysis below does not exclude the possibility that certain countries will convert totally to the market economy, on the heels of the present rebalancing experiences. They will not be the majority.

The argument will be grounded on two points: on the one hand, the real success of rebalancing will be based on the development of a private sector and not on its restoration; on the other hand, rebalancing will end not in total elimination of the public sector and state intervention but rather in their renovation. Once the rebalancing is completed, provided the opposition forces are defeated, the mixed economies will continue in existence, but they will have become radically different.

## The emergence of the private sector

It would be wrong to think that rebalancing means the return to an earlier balance that was destroyed. The historical background to the formation of the public sector of the developing countries studied shows that its expansion took place because private initiative was virtually non-existent. The public sector was also developed because the most widespread view was that the transplantation of the Western industrial model — the final objective, although it was sometimes disguised — would be achieved more rapidly if the state played the role that in Europe and later in the United States was played by the private enterprises and the market. This option was perhaps mistaken from the outset; perhaps it would have been preferable to wait for the spontaneous birth of a class of local entrepreneurs or the massive arrival of foreign investments. This kind of consideration falls well outside the scope of this work, as it raises the whole question of underdevelopment. To resume our narrower topic, the final goal of rebalancing is the emergence of a new class of entrepreneurs who are not afraid to face up to international competition. In order to grow strong and prosper, it is likely that they will form new alliances with foreign firms.

### A) The new entrepreneurs

The emergence of new entrepreneurs might be the final result of the withdrawal of state intervention and the reduction of the public sector. Paradoxically, by deciding to liberalise and privatise the state placed itself in a position to develop an autonomous private sector, thus reversing the substitutive function that it had fulfilled for decades in most of the developing countries. This turnaround has a sense of the grandiose, although the splendour of the sacrifice is somewhat tarnished by the weight of the constraints resulting from the crisis. Finally, by liberalising the economic environment and by privatising, the states were able to give decisive impulsion to a market economy based on profit seeking, competition and the pre-eminence of private investment. Nonetheless, even if this development progresses harmoniously, which is still not fully guaranteed at present, it will not lead to the "eviction" — returning to the use of jargon — of the public sector. It is still necessary, in fact, for private entrepreneurs to take over from the public sector. The rebalancing process will be a success if it offers an opportunity to a new local industrial class to gain momentum by confronting it with the demanding logic of the open economies.

The imperative of competitiveness lies at the heart of the positive integration of mixed economies into the world economy. It is mainly based on firms, supported by adequate industrial polcies defined by the state. It is in this longer-term perspective that the liberalisation and privatisation policies should be considered. The nations of Europe had a similar experience with the creation of the Common Market at the beginning of the 1960s. Subsequently, the increasing internationalisation of the economy widened the geographic framework of competition. Germany and Japan have shown themselves to be the best players, and it is not surprising that the "little dragons" of South-East Asia have modelled themselves on Japan, "the big dragon". There is no doubt that the developing countries currently starting to open their doors to the world economy have an interest in looking in the same direction.

Competition on the world market is intense; it will heighten still further with the arrival on the scene of countries that previously remained in the wings. The rules of the game for positioning oneself on the market are now well established: for a given product that corresponds to a gap on the world market, the costs must be reduced to the maximum by mass production (but must still comply with very high quality standards, following the "zero defect" principle), thus making it possible to benefit from economies of scale and/or to differentiate products through launching innovations, which calls for a considerable effort in research and development.

The internationalisation of competition has strengthened oligopolistic structures. The winning firms are those that attain the critical size and specialise in the production and distribution of a narrow range of products. From this viewpoint, the industrial concentration that accompanies some privatisation experiences may be going in the right direction. The notion of market power now has to be assessed in a context that extends beyond national boundaries. It is often necessary for a firm to occupy a quasi-monopoly position on its national market for it to attain the threshold of competitiveness on the world market, all the more so the narrower the original domestic market is. It must be stressed, however, that the firms' importance should not be measured solely on the basis of their total turnover. Accordingly, the transfer of public enterprises to local conglomerates will not necessarily imply the reinforcement of competitive advantage. The opening of borders will probably result in more than one dismemberment of family conglomerates set up under the shelter of protectionist barriers and captive markets. On the other hand, privatisation operations will have succeeded when they insert units from the public portfolio into existing private groups, strengthening the competitiveness of the latter by the addition of an extra trump card — technology, markets, financing, human resources. In addition, it must not be forgotten that the logic of internationalisation is transnational; it calls into question traditional national membership. Therefore, the firms of the developing countries will not be condemned to confronting international competition on their own.

## B) The new alliances

The transformation of national economies that is likely to follow the rebalancing process will encourage new alliances between national and foreign firms. The concept of direct international investment is changing. Traditionally, foreign direct investment took the form of a subsidiary controlled by a foreign firm on the basis of its holding all or a majority of the equity. On the grounds of the defence of national independence — a dominant concern before the change in the 1980s — this intrusion was viewed badly by the host countries and combatted by measures limiting or prohibiting the control of national entities by foreign economic agents in certain sectors of activity. The result of these regulations is debatable: in some cases, they discouraged the foreign investor, who took his money to countries where restrictions were less repressive; in others, the regulations were by-passed or amended. The foreign subsidiaries, for their part, pursued two main objectives. They produced goods either for the local market, by substituting direct production for the former exports which had been hampered or prevented by protectionist policies, or exclusively for export, by locating their factories in free industrial zones. In the first case they sometimes competed directly with local firms. In the second, they were simple enclaves within the host economy. Naturally, there are examples of joint ventures or "new forms of investment" based on a successful association between local and foreign firms, but these are not the norm even though they have become increasingly important during recent years (Oman, 1989).

The ideological reconversion towards foreign investments is a major characteristic of the 1980s. In the countries studied, rebalancing policies were generally accompanied by a revision of the codes applied to foreign investments: where there was an obligation to have a local partner, this was abandoned; the 100 per cent holding of the equity of a local company by a foreign investor was increasingly often authorised; and tender offers linked to the privatisation programmes did not exclude bids from foreigners *a priori*. In the logic of the world economy and rebalancing, the abandonment of the traditional mistrust of foreign investment should go much further. It might result in an increasing number of associations and/or partnership agreements between local private (or public) firms and foreign firms. Increasingly, access to the world market will be gained through international alliances between firms. Increasingly, large multinationals will abandon the principle of *internalisation* of their activities, which was the rule during the previous decades, and adopt more outward-looking structures, in networks, seeking independent partners on a contractual basis rather than on a basis of financial control (Michalet, 1989). Here too, the Japanese model is turning the organisation of enterprises and industries upside down (Aoki, 1986; Delapierre & Michalet, 1989). This trend may create new opportunities for firms from the developing countries wishing to confront the world market. The current transformation of entry barriers, increasingly structured on the basis of inter-firm alliances, will provide an opportunity for newcomers to take part in new groups in the course of constitution.

The changeover from multinational strategies to global strategies, to use the terminology of Porter (1986), will help to ensure that the change in strategy which is the basis of the rebalancing process is a success. However, the new opportunities offered by the globalisation process should not create the illusion that integration into the world economy will be easy. If the strategic partnership is based no longer on the vertical, centralised and closed structures of the hierarchical models (Williamson, 1981) but on co-operation between partners, the selection of these partners will be made on the basis of the competitive advantages that they are capable of demonstrating. The contractual relationship binding the partners implies a greater flexibility, and exclusion from the alliance on the ground of non-achievement will be the rule. Consequently, it is likely that only the most dynamic enterprises from the most industrialised countries of the South will be able to find a place in the globalisation process. Mexico, Chile, Malaysia and, to a lesser extent, Morocco and Tunisia are the best placed to take up the challenge. Bangladesh, Bolivia and Jamaica still have a long road ahead of them. It will therefore be essential for the industrial sectors excluded from this movement to engage in parallel actions. This situation may give the state and the public sector an opportunity to play a new type of economic role.

### The public sector's new role

Rebalancing and the opening up of economies may have two major effects. On the one hand, the public sector and, particularly, the public enterprises might be totally transformed. On the other hand, economic intervention by the state might follow a new trend.

#### A) Restructuring of the public sector

The historical background to the formation of the public sector in the countries in our sample led to the setting up of three distinct strata of public enterprises: first, those operating in the infrastructure, transport and public utilities sectors, together with the expropriated foreign enterprises in the export sectors; second, those created to respond to the desire for national economic independence under the leadership of the state; and third, a miscellany of entities from a variety of sectors whose presence in the public sector results from the rescue of private enterprises or from *ad hoc* initiatives whose main objective was to strengthen both the presence and the power of the government leaders. This last group became oversized during the second half of the 1970s following the improvement in the state's foreign earnings.

The easiest privatisations involve enterprises already subject to competition and belonging to the last stratum of the public sector. There is no special reason to keep these firms within the domain of the state, especially those that had become profitable once more, often owing to government action. Rebalancing then assumes the characteristics of a reprivatisation. This type of scenario corresponds to a minority of countries in our sample, those which already had a diversified economy during the 1960s and the 1970s, like Mexico or Chile. In the case of the public enterprises whose function is the supply of goods and services of public utility — those in the first stratum — privatisation is posed in different terms. The immediate application of private management criteria might result in a negative backlash. Their size, the weight of investments and the length of depreciation periods, the type of products, the need to combine a change in status with regulatory measures, the characteristics of natural monopolies or the production of public goods and services — all these characteristics make them unattractive for local or foreign private investments. Moreover, it should be borne in mind that most of the private local groups have limited technological skill and financial and managerial resources. The weakness of potential purchasers is a major handicap for the success of the rebalancing process. Accordingly, it should not be surprising that most enterprises of public utility remain in the public sector. Their public status is the complex result of the choice of an economic strategy where the desire to strengthen national sovereignty and the power of the state are intimately linked. In addition, these enterprises are often situated in advanced-technology sectors that call for substantial investment and are strongly dependent on foreign technology, which have generally been avoided in the past by local entrepreneurs more interested in immediately profitable activities. Privatisation of firms belonging to this group will therefore be an important test of the degree to which the states have converted to economic liberalism.

In any case, in the future the shape of the public sector will be substantially remodelled. Naturally, its boundaries will vary from one country to another: narrower than expected in some cases, wider in others, depending on current relationships of strength. The case of Mexico seems to indicate, following recent operations relating to public enterprises in the sectors defined as "priority" or even "strategic" (telecommunications, for example), that the private sector will be larger than had been envisaged at the start of the process. On the other hand, the slowness of setting up the privatisation programme in other countries, such as Ghana, Bolivia or the Philippines, seems to augur that rebalancing towards the private sector will be more limited.

The enterprises that retain their public status will in all likelihood be managed in accordance with criteria of greater efficiency. A number of factors lead to this conclusion. First, the nagging question of the crisis in public finances will not be resolved by the adoption of rebalancing policies. Accordingly, the main safeguard against the return to lax management of public enterprises is the inability most of the states to assume the burden of the deficit of public enterprises. Second, the current transformation has been (or will be) sustained by an increasingly large fraction of the technocracy, which might find that the new rules of the game are a springboard to increasing their expertise and authority. The fact that more and more young technocrats have been educated as economists or managers in the United States or

Europe makes it likely that they will be attached to the notion of rebalancing, all the more so as it may give them an opportunity to strengthen their authority against interference from the political sphere. Lastly, with the policy of opening up the economy to international competition, the public enterprises will have to prove their competitive capacity, not only in activities that place them directly in contact with foreign competitors but also in those upstream in the domestic industrial fabric, which will be more widely dependent on the private sector, but whose productivity will continue to depend on the external effects generated by the public sector.

In this new perspective, the public sector is changing its image: it seems no longer to be considered a burden on the economy and a haven of sinecures but is becoming the spearhead of the national economy faced by the challenges ensuing from integration into the world economy. Once again, the constraints deriving from competition are more effective as a means of improving firms' efficiency than are constraints relating to the status of ownership of capital. After rebalancing, both public enterprises and private sector firms are likely to be managed in a very different fashion.

*B) Export promotion*

The need for export promotion will dominate the new development strategies that will parallel and, possibly, speed up the rebalancing process. In order to keep on course, state intervention might take unusual forms. Clearly, there is no question here of drawing up a full list of the state's new role in open mixed economies. By way of illustration, however, we will deal with two possible stances.

The first follows the lines of integration into a world economy characterised by an oligopolistic type of competition. In this perspective, the analyses of comparative advantage and commercial policy derived from the Ricardian tradition would need to be seriously revised. On the basis of the laws of increasing returns and innovations, it can be demonstrated that selective protection of national markets is a means of promoting exports (Krugman, in Kierzkowski, 1984; Krugman, 1986). Indeed, the larger the local producer's market share, the more rapidly he will be able to grapple with the learning curve and thus improve his competitiveness. The recommendation of an export promotion policy is apparently in contradiction with the choice of free trade. However, a fierce proponent of free trade, C. Frischtak (1989, p. 16), supports it for three reasons: entry barriers are higher on the international market than on the domestic market (transport costs, marketing costs, quality norms); the attitude of local entrepreneurs who have remained apart from the international market for many years is parochial, and their reaction to new opportunities, even if these are more profitable, will be slow; export involves greater risk than sale on the domestic market. From a more general point of view, it is less and less arguable that international competition as taken into account in the international trade models no longer has anything to do with that which characterises the era of globalisation and the primacy of competitiveness (Michalet, 1989). In addition, the sudden opening up

224

of borders and the exposure of local industries to international competition, without any transitional period, may be counterproductive for the rebalancing policy. Indeed, in view of the low capacity for resistance of the present productive structures of the developing countries, it may provoke a terrified stampede back towards the protectionism of the past. The opponents of rebalancing would then be in a good position to advise the return to traditional policies in the name of safeguarding the national industrial potential ruined by the invasion of foreign products. If the main objective is indeed export promotion and no longer import substitution, there is no point in setting up a policy that involuntarily promotes imports. Japan has shown its ability in this connection, and, relatively speaking, it should be an inspiration for developing countries with a large enough local or regional market to serve as a springboard for certain products suitable for export.

The second stance is based on South-South export promotion. There is a growing gap between the technologies and products developed in the North and the absorption capacities of the countries of the South. The model based on the international product cycle (Vernon, 1966), which described a major movement of delocalisation of industrial sectors from the North to the South, has lost part of its pertinence. The sophistication of manufacturing techniques resulting from the installation of automated factories, flexible workshops permitting the substitution of economies of scope for economies of scale, the reduction of the ratio of wage costs to total costs and the increasingly sophisticated conditions of use of an increasing number of finished products are all factors that throw doubt on the continuation of a linear movement of renewal of comparative advantages. Integration into the world economy will increasingly take place in accordance with the partnership principles described above, but this process will not be applicable to all products. This sort of development is sometimes interpreted as strengthening a two-speed world economy, where the countries of the South would be marginalised, apart from those linked to firms in the "Triad" countries (Ohmae, 1985). This pessimistic vision affects the legitimacy of the rebalancing policies and instead encourages positions in favour of "separation" of the North and the South (Amin, 1985). In addition, it fails to take account of the new room for manoeuvre thus offered to the countries of the South to develop trade among themselves and create a parallel market for products and techniques suited to their capabilities. There is no reason to restrict the dynamics of competitiveness as referred to above to products and markets in the high-technology sector. The same principles might be applied to the production and sale of goods in the intermediate-technology range, for which there is an existing market and which the most industrialised economies are abandoning. In the case of products with a high technological content, the economies of the North tend to polarise their trade one with another, on the basis of intra-sectoral specialisation. It is possible to show that the theories used to explain export dynamics are fully applicable to South-South trade (Stewart, in Kierzkowski, 1984). For this new policy to materialise, however, it will no doubt be necessary for the states to define a framework appropriate to the new stance in foreign trade. By way of example, special financing modalities will have to be extended, such as compensatory measures; the creation or acceleration of monetary unions and regional common markets will also be on the agenda; flows of South-South investments will be encouraged to take over from investments from the North, in constant decline for about 15 years.

More generally, in the future, the determining factor of state and public sector influence will be less its size than its quality (Israël, 1990). In the new mixed economy, the state and the central government will need to have the capacity to define, set up and control macroeconomic and sectoral policies. This function calls for highly qualified personnel capable of adapting to change and thinking out new solutions. The lack of such staff was thought to have been one cause of the poor performance by public enterprises (Vernon, 1985). Moreover, the state will have to be capable of laying down the conditions for a genuine dialogue with the private sector, the importance of which will increase. Consultation with all the private agents should be substituted for the former situation, which often boiled down to more or less secret bilateral relationships with the most powerful groups, in which the state did not always have the greatest say. The public sector's change in attitude towards the private sector also implies that the latter will be reformed. The privatisation of the public sector should be coupled with "privatisation" of the private sector, whose representative institutions should accord more room to the small and medium-sized enteprises and no longer behave solely as pressure groups. The change in scale of the public sector and transformation of the rules of management of public enterprises will reduce opportunities for rent-seeking and will compel the private sector to adopt a new attitude towards the state. Increasingly, the state will be responsible for the economic and financial environment in which the activities of the private sector will develop. Following the initial processes of privatisation and liberalisation, it alone will be in a position to institute regulations strengthening the allocative function of the markets (Vickers & Yarrow, 1988). Finally, the public authorities will have to ensure that contracts are fulfilled; control the setting up of monopolies and cartels, and collusion between producers; ensure that the financial institutions comply with a certain number of prudential rules, thus avoiding the risk of crisis and ensuring investment confidence; lay down quality standards for products, etc. The new balance between the private and public sectors requires the installation of an environment that will prevent the market economy from being transformed into a free-for-all jungle, rapidly degenerating into the proliferation of informal activities.

In the end, rebalancing calls for awareness in two areas. On the one hand, the private sector has to understand that compliance with a set of rules is an essential precondition of the competitiveness and smooth running of the market economy. On the other, the state has to renounce the easy way of authoritariansm and proscribe petty and corrupt bureaucracy — which calls for a revaluation of the public function. Only if these conditions are fulfilled will it be possible to speak of a renovated mixed economy.

## Conclusion

The outcome of the "lost decade" for development, the 1980s, might be a total renovation of the functioning of mixed economies. It will be the product of a threefold change in the traditional model: conversion to the benefits of the international division of labour, first of all, with the adoption of development strategies directed towards an open economy and encouraging the promotion of non-traditional exports; second, conversion to the market economy, with the liberalisation of the economic environment and the reduction of the public sector; third, conversion to democracy, linked to the need to form new social and political alliances and to increase the participation of the whole of civil society in the successful completion of the rebalancing process. At present, however, none of these changes has definitively been accomplished. In order to become irreversible, they in fact call for a total break with a long tradition of "cronyism" and the indictment of rent-seeking situations that appear untouchable. The actions to be undertaken will be delicate and will have to affect both the public and the private sectors.

So far as the public sector is concerned, the renovation of the bureaucracy and the public enterprises is a necessary condition to enable the state to fulfil the new functions allotted to it in the context of a mixed economy open to competition. This renovation should result in the disappearance of the traditional "red-tapists" and "political" posts. The role of the bureaucracy will change from regulation and repression of private economic activities to promotion and dialogue. In this new perspective, it will no longer be used as a guaranteed outlet for new graduates and a temporary refuge for political personalities. At the same time, the restructuring and modernisation of the public enterprises, which will bring their management criteria more closely in line with those of private enterprises, will not be compatible with the customary play of political interference. On the one hand, the tasks allotted to the public enterprises will no longer be able to be increased to accord with populist electoral concerns. On the other hand, new managers will be selected no longer as the result of political or union influences but because of their skills, proved on the basis of their past performance.

The private sector, for its part, will have to complete as radical a metamorphosis as the public sector that it often used to mirror. Henceforth, local market shares — including public contracts — will be divided up between private producers and suppliers of goods and services on the basis of value for money. The corrupt practices of an underpaid bureaucracy and collusion with politicians in power are not the best ways of strengthening competitiveness. Confronted by public enterprises concerned with efficiency, the dismantling of protectionist barriers and the arrival of new foreign investors, the local firms will lose their monopoly positions on captive markets and will be forced to invest, innovate and manage better in order to survive.

In brief, for the rebalancing process to be sustainable, it has to be combined with the elimination of rent-seeking situations and "cronyism" in both the private and the public sectors. It will not be possible to achieve this result spontaneously in the various countries under examination until the governments have taken the initiative of rebalancing, somewhat constrained and forced by the crisis. The process undertaken mainly takes the form of a quantitive reduction of the relative weight of the public sector, coupled with measures for deregulating economic activity. This process whereby the state agrees to reduce its own power is laborious and incomplete. It is encountering opposition. It may lead to the emergence of new alliances and new divisions between existing social forces. In this case, the dynamics of the rebalancing process would yield disappointing results. It is therefore essential for the dynamics to go much further, for it to result in a qualitative change in the interplay between the private and public sectors — in other words, in a new economic rationality that would be imposed on private as well as public protagonists.

This perspective implies an in-depth change in behaviour, mentalities and organisations in both the public and the private sectors. If, at the present time, the break with past practices is not entirely completed in the countries in our sample, this means that the transition to a subsequent phase of the rebalancing process, not merely driven by the combined action of the national governments and the Bretton Woods institutions, is still uncertain.

# GENERAL CONCLUSION

In most of the developing countries in our sample, the shift towards rebalancing started in the early 1980s, about ten years ago. It seems too early to put forward any final conclusions. The process is far from complete in the majority of the countries and is still at the planning stage in the others. The dynamics introduced by the break with previous development strategies and models has led to a period of transition that is not yet at an end. It corresponds to a changeover from a mixed economy, based on strong direct and indirect government intervention aimed at achieving national independence, to an entirely different scenario in which private actors and market mechanisms are called to take over from government interventionism, in the context of an open economy. Completing a transformation of this kind is not a short-term process; hence its slowness and complexity should not be unexpected.

What is more, this transitional phase is marked by two ambiguities. On the one hand, criticism of the entrepreneur state and the welfare state began or intensified under the heavy pressure resulting from the economic crisis at the beginning of the 1980s. In all of our sample countries, the choice of rebalancing, far from being deliberate, was to a large extent imposed by the crisis in their public finances and by new foreign borrowing conditions. It was also actively promoted by the IMF and the World Bank through their increasingly co-ordinated stabilization and structural adjustment programmes. In certain cases, the change in stance coincided with an earlier desire for reforms, which the new economic climate provided the opportunity of realising. The second ambiguity is inherent in the implementation of the rebalancing process: governments found themselves in the position of having to restrain their own economic power, by deciding on economic liberalisation measures and, above all, by adopting programmes for the privatisation of state-owned enterprises. This helps to explain the vacillations both in decision making and in applying rebalancing policies effectively. This observation should not be too surprising: the study of the various national experiences has shown that rebalancing is a complex process, that is a source of contention and that it should not be applied uniformly in all situations.

*Rebalancing is a complex process.* At the beginning of this study it was stated that rebalancing is not merely a change in the relative proportions of the public and private sectors within a mixed economy. It integrates measures of economic and financial liberalisation: deregulation of prices, wages, customs tariffs and exchange rates. The dismantling of the managed economy is in effect a preliminary to the emergence of an economy governed by market forces. If no such reforms are carried out, privatisation operations lose much of their pertinence. The change in the ownership status of state-owned enterprises will improve the allocation of resources only if it is coupled with the strengthening and safeguarding of domestic and foreign competition. In addition, rebalancing calls for restructuring of the entities retained within the public sector in order to increase their efficiency and enable them to face the extra competition fostered by the opening up of the economy.

Accordingly, the choice of rebalancing represents a radical change in governments' development strategies. This remoulding of economic strategy will largely depend on the type of mixed economy prevailing initially. It will be all the more difficult where it has to be grafted onto a mixed economy dominated by the state. In this context, the growth of the public sector, accompanied by a whole battery of rules and regulations, will have discriminated against the private sector. In a mixed economy where the state played the role of promoter of the private sector, the transition will definitely be less problematic. In either case, the private sector in most of the countries will probably not be in a fit state or in a position to take over straight away. Rebalancing is thus the condition of the emergence of an efficient private sector and an open market economy.

*Rebalancing is a source of contention.* The new policy meets and will continue to be meet considerable opposition. Indeed, state divestiture and integration into the world economy, in accordance with comparative advantages and submission to the rule of international competitiveness, are extremely difficult since they radically call into question interests that various social groups have acquired over a long period. It is possible to pick out at least four sources of contention, which we shall present in order of their capacity to influence the progress of reforms.

First, high-ranking civil servants who occupied comfortable sinecures in the management of state sector and parapublic enterprises are worried about privatisation, restructuring or liquidation of the public portfolio, as each of these measures calls their established advantages directly into question. For less personal reasons, some high-ranking civil servants are not converts to the idea of transferring to the private sector profitable enterprises in the export sectors, which contribute substantially to national revenues. They are concerned by the prospect of the public sector's being reduced to a bare minimum, consisting of those public services with structural operating deficits (the railways, production and distribution of gas, electricity and water) — in other words, the enterprises for which the private sector is in no hurry to take responsibility. The fear of an aggravated crisis in public finances following the reduction in scale of the public sector is reinforced by anticipation of the reduction in tax and customs revenue that the liberalisation measures are bound to cause in the short term. In this perspective, the rebalancing process should also integrate an overall revision of tax systems in the developing countries. This clearly adds to its complexity.

Second, private suppliers of the state-owned enterprises and the government, as well as everybody benefiting from rent-seeking situations derived from excessive regulation, dread the elimination of the lucrative field of public contracts and the artificial non-competitive situations. By reducing the public sector, by making those enterprises whose public status is to be retained subject to the exigencies of efficiency and rigour, by increasing the role of domestic and foreign market forces, rebalancing will constrain such private entrepreneurs to give up a major part of their advantages. This new environment will also have a negative effect on private firms whose activities were particularly dependent on the supply of goods and services at subsidised prices.

Third, privatisation and restructuring worry public sector employees, who make up a substantial percentage of all employees in the countries in our sample. They are aware that their future is threatened by inevitable redundancies and note with alarm the current high unemployment rates and the inadequacies of the social security systems.

Last, the urban poor, growing inexorably more numerous as the rural exodus continues, apprehend the reduction or even the elimination of certain assistance programmes. Revisions of this kind, which are the most difficult to accept socially, will be imposed on the welfare state by the constraints of the new budgetary principles.

The indictment of traditional social policies might then give rise to unexpected alliances between the different losers from the change. For example, latent social discontent might be rapidly transformed into open social crisis and be exploited by certain government leaders opposed to the reforms, so as to slow or even block the dynamics of rebalancing. Consequently, the rebalancing process poses with new intensity the classic dilemma between efficiency and equity.

The main lesson to be learned from the opposition of the bureaucrats, profiteers and the underprivileged strata of society is socio-political. This resistance is due to the fact that the remoulding of economic development strategy represents a radical transformation. In other words, economic rebalancing must be accompanied by a rebalancing of political forces. A better representation of civil society in the political sphere, by widening democratic structures, is an essential component of the new policy stance. The socio-political dimension of the consequences of rebalancing reinforces the need for a process that is suited to the specific needs of each nation.

*Rebalancing should not apply uniformly in all situations.* If the movement initiated by the state is not to grind to a halt as soon as the first opposition is felt, it is essential that the first move be followed soon afterwards by private actors seizing the opportunities derived from the strengthening of the market economy opened to international competition. Under these circumstances, no rebalancing can be undertaken with reasonable chances of success in any of the countries unless attention is paid to the condition of the private sector, as well as to the objective conditions of competition and competitiveness prevailing in the economy before the process starts. The rate at which rebalancing is implemented will depend on the type of mixed economy in which it is to take place, the capacity of the private sector to drive development in a liberalised environment and the emergence of a competent technocracy with a mastery of the new development strategy. The process set off by the crisis of an omnipotent entrepreneur state and welfare state will be all the more likely to produce sustainable results if the turning-point of rebalancing corresponds to a new stage in the economic development of these countries. This choice, which at the outset is forced by the exigencies of the economic climate, would then merely accelerate a movement already under way.

The countries in our sample the best placed to round this corner are Chile, Mexico and Malaysia, definitely, and Morocco and Tunisia, perhaps. In the other countries, where the traditional agricultural sector and the exploitation of natural resources still predominate and where the private sector is limited to small traders and small-scale industry, the rebalancing process will require appropriate modalities. The uniform and premature application of liberalisation and privatisation programmes might have counter-productive effects by provoking the various groups threatened by the process to refuse to make the necessary structural adjustment. Applied more gradually, the rebalancing process will act as a form of apprenticeship. In this perspective, the foundations of appropriate rebalancing will be the decentralisation of economic and political responsibilities and the move towards individual initiative, the support of small and medium-sized enterprises, the implementation of a gradual and acceptable liberalisation, the institution of a body of law, training and education. Subject to this proviso, in the long run rebalancing will likely lead to the development of a private sector genuinely able to take over the reins from the state.

Whatever the country in question, rebalancing implies a reform of state institutions that is not merely quantitative but qualitative as well. The developing countries no longer have the means — did they ever? — to service a multitude of public and parapublic bodies serving as refuges for an urban élite and an educated middle class. The function of rebalancing is both to transform the way that the administration is run, by abandoning omnipotent and omniscient control in favour of promotion and encouragement, and to submit the public enterprises to the rules of economic reasoning. If it succeeds in these two tasks, rebalancing might, not without paradox, lead to the rehabilitation of the public function. Finally, it would strengthen both the private sector *and* the public sector. In this case, the rebalancing process will be not a temporary change in stance dictated by economic constraints but a sustainable advance, because it will be linked with the new equilibrium of the economic, social and political structures.

## PUBLIC BODIES IN CHARGE OF THE VARIOUS RESTRUCTURING/PRIVATISATION PROGRAMMES

GHANA

1. The State Enterprises Commission (SEC) is responsible for evaluating the performance of public enterprises and preparing planning contracts. It has been restructured with a view to these new objectives.

2. The Divestiture Implementation Committee (DIC), created in June 1988, prepares dossiers relating to "privatisable" enterprises (setting out financial information, valuation report, determination of enterprises' market value).

MOROCCO

A Commission for Transfers and an interministerial committee, chaired since the end of 1989 by a minister responsible for privatisation, supervises the completion of the programme. The Prime Minister decides by decree on the basis of the minister's proposals. The task of setting up economic and financial data banks, evaluating the performance of public enterprises and pinpointing target enterprises was entrusted to a firm of Canadian auditors, Lavalin International, in October 1987. Report issued in 1989.

TUNISIA

The National Commission for Reorganisation and Restructuring of Public Enterprises (CNAREP), directly under the aegis of the Prime Minister's office, was created in August 1987 by merging three bodies: the Interministerial Commission (selection of "privatisable" public enterprises), the Restructuring Commission (preparatory stages, valuation of assets, transfer price) and the Audit Commission (follow-up of the transaction on the securities market). Restructurings are decided by the Prime Minister on the proposal of the CNAREP.

| | |
|---|---|
| BOLIVIA | 1. The Systema Integrado de Administracion Financiera y Control (SAFCO), a project undertaken in 1987, groups Bolivian professionals, advised by an international firm of consultants, whose aim is to improve the administrative, financial control and planning systems in the public enterprises.

2. COMTRAIN (Commission for Industrial Transition), set up in 1987 with the financial support of USAID, is responsible for the preparatory stages of privatisation, in particular the valuation of the enterprises' assets. Its action is hampered by its lack of legal capacity (each meeting has to be voted by Congress). |
| CHILE | Ever since the start of the privatisation programme (1974-75), the administrative structure has been integrated in the public holding company Corporation de Fomento de la Produccion (CORFO). This became the appropriate institution for transferring all the public enterprises, including those under the aegis of the government ministries and agencies. It comprises the Council, which is responsible for the privatisation process; the Privatisation Committee, which supervises the implementation of the Council's decisions; and the Normalisation Commission, which completes the transfer in accordance with the procedure selected (transaction, restructuring if necessary, selection of national and foreign purchasers). |
| JAMAICA | In accordance with the case-by-case approach defined by the Prime Minister, the decision-making and supervisory structures are largely decentralised: at the level in particular of the Ministry of Agriculture, the Jamaican Industrial Development Bank, the National Investment Bank of Jamaica, the Divestment Committee (1981), the Joint National Investment Commission and the municipal assemblies. |
| MEXICO | No body has been specially constituted to supervise the privatisation and restructuring programme. The decision-making and operational structures are nonetheless grouped under the Ministry of Finance. The Economic Cabinet, made up of representatives of the ministries concerned (Finance, Budget) and the President, is the institution of final appeal. |

BANGLADESH The process of privatising the firms abandoned at the time of independence unites four bodies: the Tender Committee, supervising the tender procedure; the Scrutiny Committee, responsible for examining evidence of title; the Working Group on Divestment, in charge of valuing the assets and fixing the transfer price (National Reserve Price, minimum acceptable price); and the Disinvestment Board, which decides on final appeal. Since 1987, the Denationalization Amendment Ordinance has laid down rules on partial transfers (limited to 49 per cent of the capital). A variety of entities with the task of assessing performance and management control in public enterprises have been set up since 1984 (ABW, CPC).

MALAYSIA The Economic Planning Unit (EPU) of the Prime Minister's Cabinet initiated the general plan, completed in 1989, on the basis of an exhaustive study of public institutions and enterprises (using data collected about public enterprises since 1985 by the Central Information Collection Unit). The general plan should serve as a framework for future privatisations. Moreover, an interministerial committee responsible for the evaluation, co-ordination and control of the privatisation programme has been set up under the direction of the EPU.

PHILIPPINES 1. The Government Corporate Monitoring and Coordinating Committee (GCMCC) is in charge of evaluating performance and economic and financial control of public enterprises.

2. Two bodies created in 1987 were assigned the task of reducing the size of the public sector: the Committee on Privatization (COP), which defines the general framework and selects the enterprises to be privatised, and the Asset Privatization Trust (APT), which implements the transfer of assets.

## IDENTIFICATION OF PRIVATISED ENTERPRISES
## IN THE SAMPLE COUNTRIES

A total of 208 privatisation operations have been identified in the developing countries in our sample. This is not in any way an exhaustive list of privatisations undertaken up to the beginning of 1990, but the main operations are included. For each enterprise, in addition to the country of origin, the sector of activity and the date of the operation, three characteristics are considered: the technique or techniques used, the identity of the purchaser or contracting party, the amount of the transfer or contract.

### GHANA: 11 0perations

Agriculture:

1. GHANA SUGAR ESTATES LTD.
   Transfer of management and ownership of various sugar plantations. Public enterprise included on the list of 21 "privatisable" firms.
2. SUGAR PLANTATIONS
   Transfers of sugar plantations to private investors.

Industry:

3. STATE GOLD MINING CORPORATION OF GHANA, 1985
   Management contract concluded with Canada-Ghana Mining Group relating to a gold-mining enterprise listed as a "non-privatisable" public firm.
4. VOLTA ALUMINIUM
   Management contract signed with the American group Kaiser Aluminum.
5. D.L. STEEL (GHANA) LTD.
   Transfer of this steel enterprise, included on the list of 21 "privatisable" firms.
6. NEOPLAN
   Transfer of a coach manufacturing enterprise, included on the list of 21 "privatisable" firms.
7. WILLOWBROOK BUS CORP.
   Transfer of a coach assembly enterprise, included on the list of 21 "privatisable" firms.

8.    GHACHEM LTD.
      Management contract signed with NORCEM (Norway) relating to a cement works.
9.    FULGURIT ASBESTOS
10.   WESTERN CASTINGS

Services:

11.   GHANA NATIONAL TRADING CORPORATION (GNTC)
      Management contract.   Management of the enterprise provided by a former
      manager of Unilever.


                        MOROCCO:  14 Operations[1]


Agriculture:

1.    COMPAGNIE SUCRIERE DE DOUKKALA, 1973-84
      Transfer of this sugar producer to investors and sugar-beet growers.
2.    SONAMER, ASMAK and INTERPORT, 1984
      Transfer to private investors of three fisheries, former subsidiaries of the Office
      National des Pêcheries (National Fisheries Office).
5.    OFFICE NATIONAL DES PÊCHERIES (ONP), 1984
      2 leases of vessels owned by THONAPECHE to a Spanish firm and Moroccan
      fishermen, 1 transfer of a vessel belonging to PROMER.
6.    CONSUMAR, 1986
      Transfer of 33.7 per cent of the capital of the main sugar-refining company to a
      major Moroccan holding company, then private, Omnium Nord Africain (ONA)[2].


Tourism:

7.    HOTELS, 1984-89
      10 hotels transferred, most often by management contracts, including:  EL BADII
      & FES, to DIAFA (1978) then Liwa International (1989).
      SIDI HAZAREM (5) and MAROC HOTELS, to Dounia Hotels (1984).
      CHELLAH IMMOBILIERE, to Hilton then Hyatt.
      ATLAS AGADIR, to Liwa International (1989).

---

1.    We have included in this list only privatisations considered to be certain; 20 or so other operations are,
      according to official terminology, "probable".  Most often, partial transfers of holdings by the Office de
      Développement Industriel (ODI) or the Société Nationale d'Investissement (SNI) are involved.

2.    *Le Monde*, 5th August 1986.

13.     HOTELS owned by ONMT, 1984
        Management contracts relating to 17 hotels belonging to the Moroccan National
        Office of Tourism.

Services:

14.     SOCIETE NOUVELLE DES CONDUITES D'EAU (SNCE)
        Transfer of 17 per cent of the capital held by the state to a private purchaser,
        Omar Laraki.


TUNISIA: 24 Operations

Agriculture:

1.      OFFICE NATIONAL DES PECHES
        Transfer of 12 trawlers.
2.      SOCIETE DE CONDITIONNEMENT DE PRODUITS AGRO-ALIMENTAIRES

Industry:

3.      MARBRERIE DE THALA, 1986
        Transfer by private sale to a private group backed by a Tuniso-Saudi bank.
        Transfer price: 92 500 dinars.
4.      FLUOBAR (Fluorspar and Barytes Mining Company), 1985-88
        Increase of capital ending in the following division of capital: state, 45 per cent,
        AMRICO (Arab mining company), 39 per cent, IFC/World Bank, 11 per cent.
5.      SITEX, 1986-89
        Increase of capital unsubscribed by the state followed by transfer of its minority
        holding mainly to the Canadian group Dominion Textile (other partners: the IFC,
        a Tuniso-Saudi bank). Total government divestiture. Transfer price: 11.5 million
        dinars.
6.      SITER, 1987-88
        Transfer of a majority of the capital to various interests including the French
        textile group DMC, the IFC and Tunisian development banks. Offers to purchase
        the state's minority holding (29 per cent) under consideration. Transfer price:
        2.5 million dinars.
7.      TUNISIE-BOIS, 1988
        Transfer of 98 per cent of the capital via the stock market. Transfer price:
        4.5 million dinars.
8.      COMPTOIRS SFAXIENS, 1988
        Transfer of 92 per cent of the capital via the stock market. Transfer price: 1.8
        million dinars.

9. SOTUVER, 1988

    Staff buy-out of the enterprise, first recourse to this type of privatisation procedure in the Maghreb.

10. CHAFFOTTEAUX ET MAURY, 1988-89

    Transfer via the stock market. Transfer price: 350 000 dinars.

11. SOCIETE TUNISIENNE DES EMBALLAGES METALLIQUES (STUMETAL), 1989

    Partial transfer of the capital ending in a new division of capital between the Franco-British group CMB Packaging (whose holding increased from 36.6 per cent to 50 per cent) and a Tunisian businessmen, M. Mokdad. Transfer price: 5.3 million dinars.

12. CARRELAGES DE THALA, 1989

    Transfer of assets items (Gabès girders unit) to a private buyer. Transfer price: 275 000 dinars.

13. CARRELAGES TUNISIENS, 1989

    Transfer of assets to a private buyer. Transfer price: 1.2 million dinars.

14. SOCIETE TUNISIENNE DE MOTEURS, 1989

    Subscription on an increase of capital by a private foreign promoter (40 per cent). Subscription price: 200 000 dinars.

Transport:

15. SRT

    Restructuring of capital and split-up of the enterprise's activities. The freight operations were separated and sold to the private sector.

Tourism:

16. SOCIETE HOTELIERE ET TOURISTIQUE DE TUNISIE (SHTT)

    Splitting-up of the enterprise and transfer in April 1990 of 7 hotels either to private local groups or to investors from the Gulf states. Main purchaser: Société Tunisienne de Banque, at a price in the region of 10 million dinars.

    Including: HOTEL ULYSSE DE DJERBA

    Transfer to Tunisian and German purchasers. Transfer price: 3.2 million dinars.

    Including: HOTEL MIRAMAR

    Transfer to a Tuniso-Kuweiti bank, BTKD. Transfer price: 3.3 million dinars.

    Including: TANIT, 1989

    Transfer of 85 per cent of the capital to the French hotel group ACCOR. Transfer price: 17 million dinars.

23. HOTEL HANNIBAL

    Transfer following bids to a Tunisian investor, M'Henni. Former property of Société de Développement de Sousse-Nord. Transfer price: 12 million dinars.

24. HOTEL INTERNATIONAL, 1989

    Transfer to a private buyer. Transfer price: 12.4 million dinars.

BOLIVIA: 1 Operation

Transport:

1.    ENTA
      Enterprise put into liquidation and road transport vehicles transferred to local
      authorities. They are allowed to choose between creating autonomous transport
      companies or selling the assets to the private sector.


CHILE: 43 Operations[3]

Agriculture:

1.    INFORSA & SUDAMERICA, 1986
      Transfer of a forestry and paper-manufacturing enterprise to a local private buyer,
      Papelera. Transfer price: $27.4 million.
2.    INDUS, 1986
      Transfer of an enterprise specialising in the production and marketing of
      agricultural products to the Spanish group Banesto. Transfer price: $16 million
      in a debt-equity swap.
3.    CCU, 1986
      Transfer of 51 per cent of the capital of a beverage manufacturer to the private
      foreign group Lukic & Paulaner. Transfer price: $4.5 million.
4.    HUCKE & MACKAY
      Transfer of a food-products enterprise to private purchasers.
5.    INDUSTRIA AZUCARERA NACIONAL (IANSA), 1985-89
      Gradual divestiture by the state, which had formerly held 100 per cent of the
      capital in the government sugar-farming monopoly . In 1988, transfer of 18 per
      cent of the capital to Chicago Continental Bank for $9.5 million. Division of the
      capital: AFP (51 per cent), employees (29 per cent), others (20 per cent)[4].

---

3.    Only the privatisations since 1985 are included. Prior to then, it was mainly a question of transferring
      enterprises that had been nationalised (1970-73) back to their former owners (1974-75) or non-definitive
      transfers of ownership (renationalisation in 1982-83). During the first stage, 241 state-owned enterprises
      were returned to the private sector; 18 enterprises were privatised between 1976 and 1979 (figures taken
      from Nankani, *Techniques of Privatization*, World Bank, 1988).

4.    The divisions of capital of the privatised enterprises are taken from M. Marcel (1989). The percentages
      express the percentage holding of the various shareholders in the capital that was transferred to the private
      sector.

Industry:

6.      EMEC, 1985
        Transfer of all the capital in an electricity distribution company to local private
        purchasers following negotiations.
7.      EMEL, 1985
        Staff buy-out of the whole of the capital in this company, created from the
        reorganisation of the large public sector group Endesa.
8.      ACERO DEL COMPANIA PACIFICO (CAP), 1985-87
        Total state divestiture by public offering of this steel enterprise.  9 000 new
        shareholders including 4 000 of the 6 500 employees of the firm (holding
        approximately one-third of the capital).  Division of the capital:  stock market
        (58.5 per cent), employees (41.5 per cent).
9.      SOCIETAD QUIMICA Y MINERA DE CHILE (SOQUIMICH), 1985-88
        Transfer of the whole of the capital in three stages; in 1985, first public offering
        (partial failure owing to over pricing); in 1988, sale of 45 per cent of the capital
        still held in this nitrate manufacturer.  Division of the capital:  AFT (23 per cent),
        stock market (59 per cent), employees (18 per cent).
10.     COPEC, 1986
        Transfer of a gas and forestry enterprise to a New Zealand investor, Carter Hot
        Harvey (in association with the Chilean businessman A. Angelini).  Transfer price:
        $212 million in a debt-equity swap operation[5].
11.     POPAILCO, 1986
        Transfer of 40 per cent of the capital in the cement works to a private buyer,
        Gasco.  Transfer price:  $6.1 million.
12.     EMPRESA HIDROELECTRICA PILMAIQUEN, 1986
        Transfer of the whole of the capital in this hydro-electric complex to a consortium
        of Chilean investors (including Inversiones Imsa) led by the American group
        Bankers Trust.  Transfer price:  $20.8 million in a debt-equity swap operation[6].
13.     CHILECTRA METROPOLITANA, 1986-87
        Public offering subscribed for by local investors and the employees of this
        electricity distribution enterprise.  CORFO divested all its capital.  Division of the
        capital:  AFP (24 per cent), stock market (45 per cent), employees (31 per cent).
14.     CHILECTRA QUINTA REGION, 1986-87
        Public offering of the government holding in this electricity distribution enterprise,
        resulting in total divestiture.  Division of the capital:  AFP (17 per cent), stock
        market (74 per cent), employees (9 per cent).

---

5.      *South*, March 1989.

6.      *Center for Privatization*, July 1989.

15. **CHILECTRA GENERACION, 1986-88**

   Total government divestiture of the capital of this electricity-generating enterprise. Division of the capital: AFP (14 per cent), stock market (80 per cent), employees (6 per cent).

16. **ENAEX, 1987**

   Transfer of the whole of the capital of this explosives manufacturer by Chilean and foreign interests. Austin Powder (USA) acquired the whole of the capital. Price paid by Austin Powder: $8.5 million in a debt-equity swap operation[7].

17. **PULLINQUE, 1987**

   Sale of 100 per cent of the capital of this electricity producer to a private purchaser.

18. **EMELAT, 1987**

   Transfer of 100 per cent of the capital of this electricity producer to a private purchaser.

19. **LABORATORIO CHILE, 1987-89**

   Public offering of 49 per cent of the capital of this pharmaceuticals enterprise. Subsequently, total state divestiture. Division of the capital: AFP (14 per cent), stock market (61 per cent), employees (25 per cent).

20. **EMPRESA NACIONAL DE ELECTRICIDAD (ENDESA), 1987-89**

   Partial transfers bringing private sector's share in the capital of the largest electricity producer in the country up to 20 per cent, then 51 per cent and finally 90 per cent. Division of the capital: AFP (36 per cent), stock market (45 per cent), employees (11 per cent), others (8 per cent).

21. **SCHWAGER, 1987-89**

   Divestiture of 95 per cent of the capital in this carbon enterprise. Division of the capital: AFP (13 per cent), stock market (68 per cent), employees (7 per cent), others (12 per cent).

**Finance:**

22. **Administradoras de Fondos de Pensiones PROVIDA, 1985**

   Transfer of 50 per cent of the capital by public offering and, among the foreign investors, acquisition of 40 per cent of the equity by the American group Bankers Trust. Bankers Trust acquisition financed by a $60 million debt-equity swap operation.

23. **BANCO DE CHILE, 1986**

   Public offering of 350 million shares in one of the two largest commercial banks in the country. Example of encouragement "popular capitalism" (25 000 new shareholders holding 88 per cent of the capital). Transfer price: $9.1 million.

---

7. *Center for Privatization*, July 1989.

24. BANCO DE SANTIAGO, 1986

Public offering of Chile's other large commercial bank. Same objective as the previous transfer: reprivatisation following nationalisation in the light of the economic crisis in 1983, popular capitalism.

25. Administradoras de Fondos de Pensiones SANTA MARIA

Transfer of 50 per cent of the capital in this pension fund management institution by public offering and 50 per cent directly to foreign investors (the American group AETNA).

26. ISAPRE CRUZ BLANCA

Transfer of this health-insurance company to private purchasers.

27. ISAPRE LUIS PASTEUR

Transfer of this health-insurance company to private purchasers.

28. ISAPRE COLMENA

Transfer of this health-insurance company to private purchasers.

29. BANCO DE CONCEPCION

Transfer of a commercial bank to one single investor, the Association of Private Mining Producers.

30. BANCO INTERNACIONAL

Transfer of a commercial bank to private investors.

31. BANCO OSORNO Y LA UNION, 1986

Transfer of a commercial bank to private investors, Inversiones Chileno-Arabe. Transfer price: $11.7 million.

32. BHIF

Transfer of a banking institution to private investors.

33. AETNA INSURANCE COMPANY

Acquisition by the American AETNA of Banco de Chile's holding (50 per cent), giving it the whole of the capial.

34. CONSORCIO NACIONAL DE SEGUROS

Transfer of an insurance company to the American group Bankers Trust.

35. CONSORCIO NACIONAL DE SEGUROS DE VIDA

Acquisition by the American group Bankers Trust of 97 per cent of the capital of the largest life insurance company in the country.

36. LA PREVISION, 1989

Transfer of 25 per cent of Banco del Estado's holding purchased by Inversiones Mahuida. Transfer price: $500 000.

37. INSTITUT DES ASSURANCES DE L'ETAT, 1989

Acquisition of 88 per cent of the general insurance branch by the French groups Mutuelles du Mans and Crédit Lyonnais. Transfer price: $3 million.

Transport:

38. LADECO, 1986

Transfer of 55 per cent of the capital in this airline company to the local private consortium Frupac, Icarosan, Bancard. Transfer price: $5.1 million.

39. LANCHILE, 1989

Transfer of 51 per cent of the capital in the Chilean national airline company to the Icarosan group, 60 per cent of which is held by G. Carey and 40 per cent by the Banque Européenne pour l'Amérique Latine. In November 1988, a first operation involving Irish purchasers had failed. Transfer price: $42.3 million.

Telecommunications:

40. ECOM, 1985

Staff buy-out of the whole of the capital of the largest computer-equipment manufacturer in the country. Financial facilities granted by the public holding company CORFO to enable the operation to take place. Transfer price: $1.5 million.

41. TELEX CHILE, 1986

Total state divestiture (100 per cent) to a local purchaser, Chile-Pak, after a tender procedure. Transfer price: $7.3 million.

42. COMPANIA DE TELEFONOS DE CHILE (CTC), 1987

Transfer of the (very profitable) telephone monopoly to the employees (4 500 out of 6 800) and a 30 per cent (later 45 per cent) holding to the Australian Bond Group. Price of the Bond Group's acquisition: $115 million plus $135 million from a subscription on an increase of capital[8]. Division of the capital: AFP (10 per cent), stock market (19.5 per cent), employees (8 per cent), private groups (62.5 per cent).

43. ENTEL, 1986-89

Gradual reduction of the state holding, in the region of 51 per cent of the capital by means of a public offering followed by the acquisition of 20 per cent of the capital by the Spanish companies Telefonica and Banco de Santander.

JAMAICA: 44 Operations

Agriculture:

1. NATIONAL SUGAR COMPANY (NSC), 1984

Ten-year management contract signed with the British sugar group Tate and Lyle, for the operation and reorganisation of certain entities (Frome, Monymusk, B. Lodge) belonging to the public holding company NSC. Value of the contract: 7.2 million Jamaican dollars.

2. CORNWALL DAIRY DEVELOPMENT CO., 1987

Lease agreement involving a small dairy producer, a subsidiary of Jamaica Industrial Development Corporation (JIDC). Annual income: 600 000 Jamaican dollars.

---

8. Economist Intelligence Unit, *Country Report*, No. 2, 1988.

3.  HANOVER SPICES, 1987

    Transfer to private buyers of this small agriculture-based food production enterprise. Transfer price: 100 000 Jamaican dollars.

4.  HELLSHIRE FISHING FARM LTD., 1987

    Transfer and lease to private purchasers relating to the operation of this small fishery.

5.  SERGE ISLAND DAIRIES LTD., 1987

    Transfer of a small dairy producer to private interests. Transfer price: 1.8 million Jamaican dollars.

6.  JAMAICA FISHERIES COMPLEX LTD., 1988

    Lease agreement relating to the operation of a fishery. Annual rent: 300 000 Jamaican dollars.

7.  WEST INDIES PULP AND PAPER, 1988

    Transfer of this paper-manufacturing enterprise to private purchasers. No income from the transfer but cancellation of reimbursements of debts (33.1 million Jamaican dollars) and issue of convertible bonds (5 million Jamaican dollars). Transfer price: 38.1 million Jamaican dollars.

8.  NATIONAL CASSAVA PRODUCTS LTD., 1988

    Transfer of a food-processing firm, a subsidiary of the JIDC. Transfer price: 2 million Jamaican dollars.

9.  JAMAICA FROZEN FOOD LTD., 1988

    Transfer of a frozen-food products firm, a subsidiary of the JIDC. Transfer price: 9.5 million Jamaican dollars.

10. COCOA INDUSTRY BOARD

    Transfer to private managers of this marketing body.

11. BANANA COMPANY OF JAMAICA

    Transfer of all the maintenance, packing and marketing activities owned by Banana Company to a variety of private purchasers (in particular the Banana Growers Association in a joint venture with the Banana Export Co.)

12. FARMLAND

    Long-term leases relating to farming 57 000 acres of land out of the 200 000 acres owned by the state[9]. For example, lease involving the Black River Upper Morass Dev. Co. (500 acres to Italian and Jamaican investors for an annual rent of $175 000)[10].

---

9.  Dagnino-Pastore, 1991.

10. *Center for Privatization*, July 1989.

Industry:

13.  SEPROD LTD., 1985

Transfer of an enterprise involved in the production and distribution of everyday consumer goods by means of a private sale and a public offering. Transfer price: 30 million Jamaican dollars for the private sale and 8 million Jamaican dollars for the public offering.

14.  CARIBBEAN CEMENT COMPANY, 1987

Public offering of 100 per cent of the capital. 24 000 subscribers, including the Norwegian partner Scancem (acquisition of 10 per cent of the capital one month before the public offering), acquired only 72 per cent of the capital of the only cement works in the country. Transfer price: 178 million Jamaican dollars ($32 million).

15.  COTTON POLYESTER COMPANY

Transfer to private purchasers of an enterprise in the textile sector.

16.  ARIGUANABO COMPANY OF JAMAICA

Transfer to private purchasers of an enterprise in the textile sector (cotton).

17.  ZERO PROCESSING AND STORAGE LTD., 1987

Transfer to private purchasers of this refrigerated storage enteprise. Transfer price: 4 million Jamaican dollars.

18.  RURAL ICE AND COLD STORAGE LTD., 1987

Transfer to private purchasers of this small refrigerated storage enteprise. Transfer price: 500 000 Jamaican dollars.

19.  JAMAICA OXYGEN AND ACETYLENE LTD. and JAMAICA CARBONICS, 1987

Transfer to private purchasers of a small chemicals group. Transfer price: 2 million Jamaican dollars.

20.  NATIONAL GYPSUM AND QUARRIES LTD., 1988

Transfer of quarries to private investors, subsidiary of Jamaican National Investment Corp. Transfer price: 3 million Jamaican dollars.

21.  AGRICULTURAL MECHANICAL SERVICES, 1988

Transfer of a workshop specialising in agricultural machinery. Transfer price: 7 million Jamaican dollars.

Finance:

22.  NATIONAL COMMERCIAL BANK OF JAMAICA, 1986

Public offering of 51 per cent of the capital of one of the two largest banks in the country. 24 000 subscribers of which 2 000 employees benefiting from a special scheme. Transfer price: 90 million Jamaican dollars.

Transport:

23. JAMAICA OMNIBUS SERVICE (JOS), 1983
   Lease of assets, buses, operating licences for routes previously covered by JOS. The private sector now provides all bus transport services. JOS is only a regulatory body.
24. PORT AUTHORITY
   Management contract relating to the port authorities.
25. TRANS-JAMAICA AIRLINES LTD., 1988
   Transfer to local and foreign private purchasers of this domestic airline company. Transfer price: 4 million Jamaican dollars.

Telecommunications:

26. JAMAICA BROADCASTING CORPORATION (JBC)
   Lease and transfer of assets in respect of a number of JBC's activities (AM radio, television). Nonetheless, maintenance of most of the television activities (very profitable) to subsidise FM educational radio.
27. TELEPHONE COMPANY OF JAMAICA (TOJ), 1988
   Partial transfer of the new telephone company created by the merger of two companies: Jamaican Telephone Company, operating the domestic lines, and Jamaican International Telecommunication, operating the the international lines. Transfer of 39 per cent of the capital in TOJ to the British firm Cable & Wireless, then 13 per cent to the employees and Jamaican financial institutions (8 per cent being already held by private interests). The state holding was subsequently reduced to 40 per cent of the capital. Total transfer price: about 500 million Jamaican dollars.

Tourism:

28. NATIONAL HOTELS AND PROPERTIES, 1985-89
   Management contract for the 12 state-owned hotels. Transfer operations supervised by the British merchant bank S. Montagu. Effective transfer of nine hotels including the Royal Caribbean to a Jamaican hotel proprietor, G. Stewart, for a total of 49 million Jamaican dollars[11].
40. GRAY'S INN PROPERTIES, 1987
   Lease agreement. Annual rent: 400 000 Jamaican dollars.
41. PORT ANTONIO MARINA, 1987
   Lease agreement. Annual rent: 40 000 Jamaican dollars.
42. FORT CLARENCE & PALISADOES BEACH COMPLEX, 1987 and 1988
   Lease agreement. Annual rent: 120 000 Jamaican dollars.

---

11. Dagnino-Pastore, *op. cit.*

43.   MARTINS GROUP/TRAVEL SERVICES, 1988
      Transfer to private investors. Transfer price: 5.7 million Jamaican dollars.

Services:

44.   VERSAIR, 1981
      Transfer of this catering enterprise to a consortium of purchasers, some Jamaican
      (Grace, Kennedy and Co.) and some foreign (the American Marriot Company in
      particular).

MEXICO: 31 Operations[12]

Industry:

1.    RENAULT DE MEXICO, 1983
      Transfer of the government's majority holding in this automobile construction
      enterprise to the industrial and commercial partner, La Régie Renault (France).
2.    VEHICULOS AUTOMOTORES MEXICANOS, 1983
      Transfer of this automobile construction enterprise to La Régie Renault (France).
      Price of the two transfers: $30 million[13].
3.    DIESEL NACIONAL
      Transfer of part of the capital in the heavy-goods vehicle construction enterprise
      to Chrysler and Navistar.
4.    GARCI CRESPO
      Enterprise producing soft drinks.
5.    N.A.
      Bicycle factory.
6.    CEMENTOS ANAHUAC DEL GOLFO, 1985
      Transfer of 40 per cent of the capital to a group of Mexicans and Americans,
      already partners in the cement works.
7.    TEREFTALATOS MEXICANOS
      Transfer of 42.2 per cent of a petrochemicals plant to the consortium Petrocel,
      which became the leading shareholder. Transfer price: $95 million.

---

12.   It has been possible to identify only the significant privatisations. Therefore this list is not exhaustive.
      According to I. Pichardo Pagaza's report, *El Proceso de Desincorporacion de Entidades Parestatales*,
      published in July 1988, 116 public enterprises were transferred to the private sector between December 1982
      (beginning of President de la Madrid's term of office) and mid-June 1988.

13.   Economist Intelligence Unit, *Country Report*, No. 3, 1983.

8.  HULES MEXICANOS, 1988
    Transfer to Mexican purchasers[14].
9.  SOSA TEXCOCO, 1988
    Transfer to Mexican purchasers[14].
10. CLORO DE TEHUANTEPEC, 1988
    Transfer to Mexican purchasers[14].
11. TORRES MEXICANOS, 1988
    Transfer to Mexican purchasers[14].
12. GRUPO TEXTIL CADENA, 1988
    Transfer to the trades union confederation CTM[14].
13. MEXICANA DE ACIDO SULFURICO, 1988
    Transfer twinned with that of Mexicana del Cobre, of which the firm is a subsidiary.
14. MEXICANA DEL COBRE, 1988
    Transfer of 56 per cent of the capital in the largest copper producer in the country by a consortium led by an important mining group, Fomento Industrial del Norte de Mexico, and including the miners union. Belonged to the holding company Nacional Financiera (NAFINSA). Transfer price (total including the takeover of Mexicana de Acido Sulfurico) $680 million, financed by a $1.36 billion debt-equity swap[15].

Finance:

15. BANCO NACIONAL DE MEXICO (BANAMEX), 1987
    Public offering of 34 per cent of the capital in February 1987. Transfer of 12 per cent of the capital to employees of the bank. Transfer price: $36 million[16].
16. BANCO DE COMERCIO (BANCOMER), 1987
    Public offering of 34 per cent of the capital. Transfer price: $33 million[16].
17. BANCA SERFIN, 1987
    Transfer of 34 per cent of the capital mainly to employees and customers of the bank. Transfer price: $24 million.
18. 10 banking institutions
    (ATLANTI, BANCEN, BANORIE, BANORO, BANORTE, COMRMEX, CONFIA, CREMI, INTERNAL, PROMEX). Transfers of 34 per cent of the capital via the stock market.

---

14. Economist Intelligence Unit, *Country Report*, No. 1, 1989.

15. Economist Intelligence Unit, *Country Report*, No. 4, 1988.

16. The first amount is taken from *Privatization 1987*, by the Research Foundation, the second from the World Bank's *Techniques of Privatization*, Volume 3.

Transport:

28.    COMPANIA MEXICANA DE AVIACION, 1988
       Transfer of 58 per cent of the capital in the company, which had been private until
       1982, to a consortium of investors both national (led by Grupo Empresas Xabre)
       and foreign (in particular Sir J. Goldsmith and Chase Manhattan)[17].  Transfer
       price:  $140 million.
29.    AEROMEXICO, 1988
       Transfer of 65 per cent of the capital in October 1988, after the government had
       put the company into liquidation in April.  Transfer price:  $345 million.

Telecommunications:

30.    TELEPHONE COMPANY OF MEXICO, 1984

Tourism:

31.    NACIONAL HOTELERA, 1985
       Sale of a chain of 28 hotels to Mexican private purchasers with the backing of two
       public sector banks as minority partners.  Transfer price:  $84 million.


BANGLADESH:  539 Operations[18]


Agriculture:

1.     DHAKA VEGETABLE OIL INDUSTRIES LTD., 1987-88
       Transfer of 49 per cent of the capital in a vegetable-oil refining enterprise (34 per
       cent by public offering and 15 per cent earmarked for employees).  Price of the
       partial transfer:  40.7 million taka.
2.     ZEAL BANGLA SUGAR MILLS LTD., 1987-88
       Transfer of 49 per cent of the capital in a sugar group (34 per cent by public
       offering and 15 per cent earmarked for employees).  Price of the partial transfer:
       29.4 million taka.

---

17.   *Development Business*, 31st October 1989.

18.   The public enterprises derive from three origins: creation by the state prior to 1971, nationalisation in 1972
      of firms abandoned by their Pakistani owners, nationalisation in 1972-73 by the new state of Bangladesh
      of a large number of firms owned by Bengalis.  However, it is impossible to assess the exact number of
      privatisations carried out.  Chishty (1985) estimates that 117 enterprises were returned to their former
      proprietors following negotiations with the government.  The other privatised firms are generally very small
      manufacturing enterprises (textiles and derivatives, tanning, chemicals) and firms in the agricultural sector
      (rice, sugar, oil), which it is impossible to present in detail.  Accordingly, only privatisations carried out
      since the Denationalization Amendment Ordinance of June 1987 are identified.

Industry:

3. USMANIA GLASS SHEET FACTORY LTD., 1987-88
   Transfer of 49 per cent of the capital in a glass-manufacturing enterprise (34 per cent by public offering and 15 per cent earmarked for employees), a subsidiary of Bangladesh Chemical Industries Corp. Price of the partial transfer: 16.1 million taka.

4. EASTERN CABLES LTD., 1987-88
   Transfer of 49 per cent of the capital in a cable-manufacturing enterprise (34 per cent by public offering and 15 per cent earmarked for employees), a subsidiary of Bangladesh Steel and Engineering Corp. Price of the partial transfer: 98 million taka.

5. KOHINOOR CHEMICAL CO. LTD., 1987-88
   Transfer of 49 per cent of the capital in this chemicals group (34 per cent by public offering and 15 per cent earmarked for employees), a subsidiary of Bangladesh Chemical Industries Corp. Price of the partial transfer: 24.5 million taka.

6. EAGLE BOX AND CARTON MANUFACTURING LTD., 1988-89
   Transfer of 49 per cent of the capital in a packaging enterprise (34 per cent by public offering and 15 per cent earmarked for employees), a subsidiary of Bangladesh Chemical Industries Corp. Price of the partial transfer: 2.5 million taka.

7. RENURICK LTD., 1988-89
   Transfer of 49 per cent of the capital (34 per cent by public offering and 15 per cent earmarked for employees). Price of the partial transfer: 9.8 million taka.

8. METALEX CORPORATION LTD., 1988-89
   Transfer of 49 per cent of the capital in an iron and steel group (34 per cent by public offering and 15 per cent earmarked for employees), a subsidiary of Bangladesh Steel and Engineering Corp. Price of the partial transfer: 2.5 million taka.

9. ATLAS BANGLADESH LTD., 1987-88
   Transfer of 49 per cent of the capital of this subsidiary of Bangladesh Steel and Engineering Corp. (34 per cent by public offering and 15 per cent earmarked for employees). Price of the partial transfer: 4.9 million taka.

MALAYSIA: 15 Operations

Industry:

1.  LABUAN-BEAUFORT POWER INTERCONNECTION, 1988
    15-year contract granted to a private joint venture, LBI Pte Ltd. Financing, construction and management of two electric power stations and 85 kilometers of power lines[19]. Value of the contract: $35 million.

Transport:

2.  MALAYSIAN AIRLINE SYSTEM (MAS), 1985
    Public offering of 30 per cent of the capital. The state holding was reduced to 62 per cent of the new division of capital. The share offer was subscribed as follows: 50 per cent by the public, 17 per cent by employees and 33 per cent by institutional investors. Price of the transfer: $90 million.

3.  NORTH KELANG STRAITS BYPASS, 1985
    Construction and management of a toll motorway between Port Kelang and Kuala Lumpur (50 kilometers) by the contractors Shapadu Sdn Bhd.

4.  KEPONG-KUCHING ROAD INTERCHANGE, 1985
    Construction and management of a highway by a private Malaysian company, Seri Angkasa Sdn Bhd.

5.  MALAYSIAN INTERNATIONAL SHIPPING COMPANY (MISC), 1986
    Public offering of 17 per cent of the capital. State holding reduced from 60.8 per cent to 48.6 per cent.

6.  PORT KELANG CONTAINER TERMINAL, 1987
    Transfer of 51 per cent of the capital to Kontena Terminal Kelang, a joint venture between the Malaysian firm Kontena Nasional (80 per cent) and an Australian company, P & O. Transfer coupled with a long-term lease. Amount of the operation: management contract (annual payment: $500 000), lease (annual rent: $5.7 million), sale of 51 per cent of the capital ($58 million)[20].

7.  PORT PENANG

8.  NORTH-SOUTH HIGHWAY, 1988
    Construction and management of a toll motorway (504 kilometers) provided, for 25 years, by the contractors United Engineers Malaysia, held indirectly by the party in power, UMNO. Value of the contract: $1.3 billion.

---

19.  *Development Business*, 31st October 1988.

20.  "Case Studies: Malaysia", in *Management Dynamism in SOEs in Asia*, Asian Productivity Organization, 1989, pp. 161-99.

Telecommunications:

9.    TV 3, 1983
      Licence for a new television channel managed by a private group, Sistem
      Televisyen Malaysia. Introduction on the Kuala Lumpur Stock Exchange.

10.   JABATAN TELEKOM NEGARA, since 1986
      Creation of a public entity independent of the Ministry of Telecommunications,
      taking over the employees, assets and liabilities of JTN. Transfer of this entity to
      private investors after five years' operation. Creation in 1986 of Syarikat Telekom
      Malaysia (public company) to manage the telecommunications network under
      licence. Value of the contract: royalties between 3 and 7 per cent of the annual
      gross income of STM.

Tourism:

11.   NATIONAL PARK RECREATION FACILITIES, 1987
      Lease to a private enterprise, River Park Sdn Bhd.

Services:

12.   SPORT TOTO, 1985
      Transfer of 70 per cent of the shares to two private Malaysian groups, BMB and
      Makusawa Securities. Stock-market introduction on the KLSE. Transfer price:
      $28 million.

13.   GENERAL HOSPITAL, 1985
      Transfer to a private group of doctors.

14.   AIRCRAFT OVERHAULING DEPOT (AIROD), 1986
      Air-base maintenance activities transferred by both transfer and lease to a private
      company, held 51 per cent by Aerospace Industrial Malaysia (Malaysian semi-
      public company) and 49 per cent by Lockheed International Services.

15.   LABUAN WATER SUPPLY
      Management contract concluded with Antah-Biwater, a joint venture between a
      Malaysian semi-public company, Antah Holding Sdn Bhd and a British company,
      Biwater PLC, relating to 174 municipal projects. Value of the contract:
      $450 million.


PHILIPPINES: 16 Operations

Agriculture:

1.    PHILIPPINE COTTON CORPORATION
      Sale of assets by tender. Procedure completed in the third quarter of 1988, final
      decision of the government awaited. Value of assets: 209 million pesos.

2.     BUKIDNON SUGAR CENTRAL MINING, 1988
       Sale of assets of this sugar refinery to local entrepreneurs by a debt-equity swap.
       Transfer price: $34 million[21].

Industry:

3.     MINDANAO TEXTILE CORPORATION, 1987
       Transfer carried out by National Development Corporation (NDC)[22].
4.     ACOJE MINING CORPORATION, 1988
       Transfer carried out by National Development Corporation (NDC).
5.     ASIA NDUSTRIES, 1988
       Transfer carried out by National Development Corporation (NDC).
6.     BETA ELECTRIC CORPORATION, 1988
       Transfer carried out by National Development Corporation (NDC).

Finance:

7.     INTERBANK, 1986
       Acquisition of National Development Corporation holding (40 per cent) by
       American Express. Operation financed by a debt-equity swap[22].
8.     COMMERCIAL BANK OF MANILA, 1987
       Acquisition by Bank of Boston and a group of Philippine investors of the holding
       of Government Service Insurance System (GSIS). The Bank of Boston financed
       its operation by a debt-equity swap. Value of assets: $88 million[23].
9.     PHILIPPINAS BANK, 1987
       Transfer by Philippine National Bank. Value of assets: $82 million[23].
10.    CONSOLIDATED BANK AND TRUST, 1988
       Acquisition by Banque Nova Scotia of 40 per cent of the capital (maximum
       authorised for foreign investors). Financed by a $17 million debt-equity swap[24].
11.    PHILIPPINE NATIONAL BANK, 1989
       Public offering of 30 per cent of the capital in June 1989. Success of stock-market
       introduction (subscription, volume of transactions since the public offering). Price
       of the transfer: $90 million[25].

---

21.    *Center for Privatization*, Reason Foundation, 1989.

22.    Total amount of these four transfers (Mindanao, Interbank, Tacoma, National Stevedoring): 289 million
       pesos. *Center for Privatization*, July 1989.

23.    *Asiaweek*, 2nd October 1987.

24.    Economist Intelligence Unit, *Country Report*, No. 1, 1988.

25.    Economist Intelligence Unit, *Country Report*, No. 3, 1989.

Transport:

12.     TACOMA BAY SHIPPING COMPANY, 1988
        Transfer carried out by National Development Corporation (NDC)[22].

Tourism:

13.     TAAL VOLCANO
        Holiday village transferred to the Japanese group Prince Hotel. Transfer price: $1.8 million.
14.     CEBU PLAZA HOTEL
        Sale of a prestige hotel to a group belonging to a large Saudi bank. Transfer price: $16 million.
15.     PINES HOTEL
        Sale of a hotel to Chinese and Philippine buyers. Transfer price: $4.2 million.

Services:

16.     NATIONAL STEVEDORING AND LIGHTERAGE
        Transfer of a docks-handling enterprise carried out by National Development Corporation[22].

# BIBLIOGRAPHY

## General References

A.A.P.A.M. (Association for Public Administration and Management) (1987), *Public Enterprises Performance and Privatisation Debate: A Review of the Options for Africa*, Vikas Publishing House, New Delhi.

AHARONI, Y. (1986), *The Evolution and Managment of State Owned Enterprises*, Ballinger Publishing Company, Cambridge, MA.

AHMAD, M. (1982), "Political Economy of Public Enterprise", in Jones, pp. 49-63.

ALCHIAN, A. and H. DEMSETZ (1972), "Production, Information Costs and Economic Organization", *American Economic Review*, pp. 777-795, Vol. 62.

AMIN, S. (1970), *L'accumulation à l'échelle mondiale*, Anthropos, Paris.

AMIN, S. (1986), *La déconnexion : pour sortir du système mondial*, La Découverte, Paris.

ANGLADE, C. and C. FORTIN (1985), *The State and Capital Accumulation in Latin America*, Volume 1, MacMillan, New York.

AOKI, M. (1986), "Horizontal vs Vertical Information Structure of the Firm", *American Economic Review*, Vol. 76, December.

ASIAN DEVELOPMENT BANK (1985), *Privatization: Policies, Methods and Procedures*, Asian Development Bank, Manilla.

ASIAN PRODUCTIVITY ORGANIZATION (1989), *Managment Dynamism in State-Owned Enterprises in Asia*, Tokyo.

AVERCH, H. and L. JOHNSON (1962), "Behavior of the Firm under Regulatory Constraint", *American Economic Review*, pp. 1052-1069, Vol. 52.

AYUB, M. and S. HEGSTAD (1986), "Public Industrial Enterprises, Determinants of Performance", *Industry and Finance Series*, Volume 17, World Bank, Washington, D.C.

BALASSA, B. (1988), *Toward Renewed Economic Growth in Latin America*, Institute for International Economics, Washington, D.C.

BERG, E. and M. SHIRLEY (1987), *Divestiture in Developing Countries*, World Bank Discussion Papers, No. 11, World Bank, Washington, D.C.

de BERNIS, G. (1968), *Les industries industrialisantes et l'intégration économique régionale*, ISEA, Neuilly-sur-Seine.

259

BIENEN, H. and J. WATERBURY (1989), "The Political Economy of Privatization in Developing Countries", *World Development*, pp. 617-632, Vol. 17, No. 5.

BISHOP, M. and J. KAY (1989), "Privatization in the United Kingdom: Lessons from Experience", *World Development*, pp. 643-657, Vol. 17, No. 5.

BLEJER, M. and Chu. DE-YOUNG (1988), *Measurement of Fiscal Impact: Methodological Issues*, Occasional Paper No. 59, International Monetary Fund, Washington, D.C.

BLEJER, M. and S. SAGARI (1987), "The Structure of the Banking Sector and the Sequence of Financial Liberalization", in Connolly and Gonzalez-Vega, pp. 93-107.

BÖS, D. (1986), "A Theory of the Privatization of Public Enterprises", *Zeitschrift für Nationalökonomie, Journal of Economics*, pp. 17-40, suppl. 5.

BÖS, D. (1987a), "Privatization of Public Enterprises", *European Economic Review*, Vol. 31, pp. 352-360.

BÖS, D. (1987b), "Privatization of Public Firms: A Government/Trade-Union/Private Shareholder Cooperative Game", *Public Finance and Performance of Enterprises*, Proceedings of the 43rd Congress of the International Institute of Public Finance, pp. 343-363, Paris.

BORCHEDRING, T., W. POMMEREHNE and F. SCHNEIDER (1982), "Comparing the Efficiency of Private and Public Production: The Evidence for Five Countries", *Zeitschrift für Nationalökonomie: Journal of Economics*, suppl. 2.

BOYER, R. (1986), *La théorie de la régulation : une analyse critique*, La Découverte, Paris.

BUCHANAN, J., R. TOLLISON and G. TULLOCK (1980), *Towards a Theory of the Rent-Seeking Society*, Texas University Press, College Station, Texas.

BUCHANAN, J. and R. TOLLISON (eds.) (1984), *The Theory of Public Choice*, University of Michigan Press, Ann Arbor, Michigan.

CALVO, G. (1987), "On the Costs of Temporary Liberalization/Stabilization Experiments", in Connolly and Gonzalez-Vega, pp. 3-17.

CANDOY-SESKE, R. (1988), *Techniques of Privatization of State-Owned Enterprises, Volume III*, World Bank Technical Paper, No. 90, World Bank, Washington, D.C.

CAVES, D. and L. CHRISTENSEN (1978), "The Relative Efficiency of Public and Private Firms in a Competitive Environment: A Case of Canadian Railroads", Social Systems Research Institute, Workshop Series, October.

CENTER FOR PRIVATIZATION (1989), "Privatization Survey for Developing Countries", prepared for International Development Bureau for Private Enterprise, Washington, D.C., July.

CHOKSI, A. and D. PAPAGEORGIOU (1986), *Economic Liberalization in Developing Countries*, Basil Blackwell, Oxford.

COMMANDER, S. and T. KILLICK (1988), "Privatisation in Developing Countries: A Survey of the Issues", in Cook and Kirkpatrick, pp. 91-121.

CONNOLLY, M. and C. GONZALEZ-VEGA (1987), *Economic Reform and Stabilization in Latin America*, Praeger, New York.

COOK, P. and C. KIRKPATRICK (eds.) (1988), *Privatisation in Less Developed Countries*, Wheatsheaf, Sussex, and St Martin's Press, New York.

COOK, P. and C. KIRKPATRICK (1988), "Privatisation in Less Developed Countries: An Overview", pp. 3-43, in Cook and Kirkpatrick.

CORBO, V. and J. de MELO (1987), "Lessons from the Southern Cone Policy Reforms", *The World Bank Research Observer*, Vol. 2, No. 2, World Bank, Washington, D.C.

CORBO, V., M. GOLDSTEIN and M. KHAN (1987), "Growth-oriented Adjustment Programs", World Bank and International Monetary Fund, Washington, D.C.

CORDEN, M. (1987), *Protection and Liberalization: A Review of Analytical Issues*, Occasional Papers, No. 54, International Monetary Fund, Washington, D.C.

COWAN, G. (1989), "Political, Institutional and Employment Factors in Privatization", Draft prepared for the Office of Policy Development Program Review, Washington, D.C., February.

CROISSET, C., B. de PROT, M. ROSEN (eds.) (1986), "Dénationalisations : les leçons de l'étranger", *Economica*, Paris.

DATA RESOURCES INC. (1986), *Latin American Review*, 4th Quarter, DRI, Lexington, Mass.

DELAPIERRE, M. and C.A. MICHALET (1989), "Vers un changement des structures des multinationales : le principe d'internalisation en question", *Revue d'économie industrielle*, No. 47, 1st Quarter.

DEMSETZ, H. (1968), "Why Regulate Utilities?", *Journal of Law and Economics*, pp. 55-65, Vol. 11.

DOMBERGER, S. and J. PIGGOT (1986), "Privatization Policies and Public Enterprises: A Survey", *Economic Record*, pp. 145-162, Vol. 62, No. 177.

DORNBUSCH, R. and F. HELMERS (eds.) (1988), *The Open Economy*, Oxford University Press, Oxford.

ECKEL, C. and A. VINING (1982), "Towards a Positive Theory of Joint Enterprise", in Stanbury and Thompson (eds.), pp. 209-222.

ECKEL, C. and A. VINING (1985), "Elements of a Theory of Mixed Enterprise", *The Scottish Journal of Political Economy*, pp. 82-94, Vol. 32, No. 1.

EDWARDS, S. (1986), "Stabilization with Liberalization: An Evaluation of Ten Years of Chile's Experience with Free Market Policy: 1973-83", in Choksi and Papageorgiou, pp. 241-271.

EDWARDS, S. (1989), "On the Sequencing of Structural Reforms", *Economic and Statistic Department Working Papers*, No. 70, OECD, Paris.

EDWARDS, S. and S. Van WIJNGBERGEN (1986), "The Welfare Effects of Trade and Capital Market Liberalization", *International Economic Review*, pp. 141-148, Vol. 27, No. 1.

EMMANUEL, A. (1969), *L'échange inégal*, Maspéro, Paris.

FEIGENBAUM, H. (1985), *The Politics of Public Enterprise*, Princeton University Press, Princeton, N.J.

FIXLER, P., W. POOLE and L. SCARLETT (1987), *Privatization 1987: Second Annual Report on Privatization*, The Reason Foundation, Santa Monica, CA.

FIXLER, P., W. POOLE and L. SCARLETT (1989), *Privatization 1989: Third Annual Report on Privatization*, The Reason Foundation, Santa Monica, CA.

FLOYD, R., C. GRAY and R. SHORT (1984), *Public Enterprise in Mixed Economy: Some Macroeconomic Aspects*, International Monetary Fund, Washington, D.C.

FRISHTAK, C. (1989), "Competition Policies for Industrializing Countries", *Policy and Research Series*, World Bank, Washington, D.C.

GALAL, A. (1989), "*Ex-post* Performance of Divested State-Owned Enterprises", research outline, World Bank, Washington, D.C.

GALAL, A. (1990), "Public Enterprise Reform", *Policy, Research, and External Affairs, Working Papers*, World Bank, Washington, D.C.

GLADE, W. (ed) (1986), *State Shrinking: A Comparative Inquiry Into Privatization*, University of Texas at Austin, Institute of Latin American Studies, Office of Public Sectors Studies, Texas.

GLADE, W. (1989), "Privatization in Rent-seeking Societies", *World Development*, pp. 673-682, Vol. 17, No. 5.

GOLDSCHEID, R. (1917), "A Sociological Approach to Problems of Public Finance", in Musgrave and Peacock (eds.), (1964).

GRAY, C. (1984), "Toward a Conceptual Framework for Macroeconomic Evaluation of Public Enterprise Performance in Mixed Economies", in Floyd, Gray and Short, pp. 35-109.

GREFFE, X. (1972), "L'approche contemporaine de la valeur en finances publiques", *Economica*, Paris.

HAMILTON, C. (1989), "The Irrelevance of Economic Liberalization in the Third World", *World Development*, No. 10.

HEALD, D. (1985), "Privatization: Policies, Methods and Procedures", in Asian Development Bank, pp. 57-95.

HEALD, D. (1987), "Performance Measurement of Public Enterprises: Resolving Conceptual Issues", *International Institute of Public Finance*, 43th Congress, 24th-28th August 1987, Paris.

HEALD, D. (1988), "The Relevance of UK Privatisation for LDC's", in Cook and Kirkpatrick, pp. 68-90.

HELLER, P. and C. SCHILLER (1989), "The Fiscal Impact of Privatization, with Some Examples from Arab Countries", *World Development*, pp. 757-767, Vol. 17, No. 5.

HEMMING, R. and A. MANSOOR, *Privatization and Public Enterprises*, Occasional Paper No. 56, International Monetary Fund, Washington, D.C.

HENSHER, D. (1986), "Privatisation: An Interpretative Essay", *Australian Economic Papers*, pp. 147-174, Vol. 25, No. 47.

HIRSCHMAN, A. (1981), "The Rise and Decline of Development Economics", in *Essays in Trespassing: Economics to Politics and Beyond*, Cambridge University Press.

HUGON, P. (1989), *Économie du développement*, Dalloz, Paris.

INTERNATIONAL MONETARY FUND (1986), *A Manual on Government Finance Statistics*, Washington, D.C.

ISRAEL, A. (1990), "The Changing Role of the State", Working Papers, World Bank, Washington, D.C.

JENSEN, M. and W. MECKLING (1976), "Theory of the Firm: Managerial Behaviour, Agency Costs and Ownership Structure", *Journal of Financial Economics*, Vol. 3, pp. 305-360.

JONES, L. (1982), *Public Enterprise in Less Developed Countries*, Cambridge University Press, Cambridge, MA.

JONES, L. (1985), "Public Enterprise for Whom? Perverse Distributional Consequences or Public Operational Decisions", *Economic Development and Cultural Change*, pp. 333-347.

JONES, L., P. TANDON and I. VOGELSANG (1988), "The Economics of Divestiture: *Ex-ante* Valuation and *Ex-post* Evaluation", Provisional Papers in Public Economics, Boston University, MA, April.

KAHLER, M. (1990), "Orthodoxy and Its Alternatives: Explaining Approaches to Stabilization and Adjustment", in Nelson (1990a).

KAKWANI, N., E. MAKKONNEN and J. van der GAAG (1989), "Structural Adjustment and Living Conditions in Developing Countries", World Bank Population and Human Resources, World Bank, September.

KAY, J. (1987), "Public Ownership, Public Regulation or Public Subsidy?", *European Economic Review*, pp. 343-345, Vol. 31.

KAY, J., C. MAYER and D. THOMPSON (eds.) (1986), *Privatisation and Regulation: The UK Experience*, Clarendon Press, Oxford.

KAY, J. and D. THOMPSON (1986), "Privatisation: A Policy in Search of a Rationale", *The Economic Journal*, pp. 18-32, Vol. 96.

KIERZKOWSKI, H. (ed.) (1984), *Monopolistic Competition and International Trade*, Clarendon Press, Oxford.

KRUEGER, A. (1978), "Liberalisation Attemps and Consequences", *NBER*, New York.

KRUEGER, A. *et al.* (eds.) (1981), *Trade and Employment in Developing Countries*, University of Chicago, Chicago, Illinois.

KRUEGER, A. (1986), "Problems of Liberalization", in Choksi and Papageorgiou, pp. 15-31.

KRUGMAN, P. (1984), "Import Protection and Export Promotion: International Competition in the Presence of Oligopoly and Economies of Scale", in Kierzkowski (ed.).

KRUGMAN, P. (ed.) (1986), *Strategic Trade Policy and the New International Economics*, MIT Press, Cambridge, MA.

LAL, D. (1987), "The Political Economy of Economic Liberalization", *The World Bank Economic Review*, pp. 273-299, Vol. 1, No. 2.

LEIBENSTEIN, H. (1966), "Allocative Efficiency vs 'X-efficiency'", *American Economic Review*, pp. 392-415, June.

LITTLECHILD, S. (1983), *Regulation of British Telecommunications Profitability*, HMSO, London.

LORD ROLL OF IPSEN (ed.) (1982), *The Mixed Economy*, MacMillan, London.

MACKINNON, R. and D. MATHIESON (1981), "How to Manage a Repressed Economy", *Princeton Essays in International Finance*, No. 145, December.

MANSOOR, A. (1988), "The Budgetary Impact of Privatization", in Blejer and Ke-Young, pp. 48-56.

MARCHAND, M., P. PESTIAU and H. TULKENS (1984), *The Performance of Public Enterprises: Concepts and Measurements*, North-Holland, Amsterdam, New York, Oxford.

MEIER, G. and D. SEERS (eds.) (1985), *Pioneers in Development*, Oxford University Press, New York.

MICHALET, C.A. (1985), *Le capitalisme mondial*, Presses Universitaires de France, Paris.

MICHALET, C.A. (1989b), "Global Competition and Its Implications for Firms", OECD, International Seminar on Science, Technology and Economic Growth, June.

MICHAELY, M. (1986), "The Timing and Sequencing of a Trade Liberalization Policy", in Choksi and Papgeorgiou, pp. 41-67 (Comments).

MICHALOPOULOS, C. (1987), "World Bank Programs" in Corbo *et al.*

MILLWARD, R. (1982), "The Comparative Performance of Public and Private Ownership", in Lord Roll of Ipsen (ed.).

MILLWARD, R. (1988), "Measured Sources of Inefficiency in the Performance of Private and Public Enterprises in LDC's", in Cook and Kirkpatrick, pp. 143-161.

MUSGRAVE, R. (1959), *The Theory of Public Finance*, McGraw Hill, New York.

MUSGRAVE, R. and A. PEACOCK (eds.) (1964), *Classics in the Theory of Public Finance*, MacMillan, London.

MUSSA, M. (1987), "Macroeconomic Policy and Trade Liberalization: Some Guidelines", *The World Bank Research Observer*, Vol. 2, No. 1.

NAIR, G. and A. FILIPPIDES (1988), "How Much Do State-owned Enterprises Contribute to Public Sector Deficits in Developing Countries — and Why?", background paper to the 1988 World Development Report, WPS 45, World Bank, Washington, D.C.

NALEBUFF, B. and J. STIGLITZ (1983), "Information, Competition and Markets", *American Economic Review*, pp. 278-284, Vol. 73, May.

NANKANI, H. (1988), *Techniques of Privatization of State-Owned Enterprises*, Volume II, World Bank Technical Papers, No. 89, World Bank, Washington, D.C.

NELLIS, J. (1989), "Contract Plans and Public Enterprise Performance", World Bank Discussion Paper, No. 48, Washington, D.C.

NELLIS, J. and S. KIKERI (1989), "Public Enterprise Reform: Privatization and the World Bank", *World Development*, pp. 659-672, Vol. 17, No. 5.

NELSON, J. (ed.) (1990a), *Economic Crisis and Policy Choice*, Princeton University Press, Princeton, N.J.

NELSON, J. (1990b), "Poverty, Equity and the Politics of Adjustment", Symposium on the Politics of Stabilization and Structural Change in Developing Countries, Overseas Development Council, 11-12th June.

OHMAE, K. (1985), *Triad Power: The Coming Shape of Global Competition*, Free Press, New York.

OLSON, M. (1982), *The Rise and Decline of Nations*, Yale University Press, New Haven.

OMAN, C. (1989), *New Forms of Investment in Developing Countries' Industries: Mining, Petrochemicals, Automobiles, Textiles, Food*, with the collaboration of F. Chesnais, J. Pelzman and R. Rama, OECD Development Centre, Paris.

OMAN, C. and G. WIGNARAJA (1991), *The Postwar Evolution of Development Thinking*, Macmillan, London, for the OECD Development Centre, Paris.

PAPAGEORGIOU, D., A. CHOKSI and M. MICHAELY (1990), *Liberalizing Foreign Trade*, 7 volumes, Basil Blackwell, Oxford.

PERA, A. (1989), "La déréglementation et la privatisation dans une perspective macro-économique", pp. 183-236, No. 11, Spring.

PESTIAU, P. (1987), "Entreprise et propriété publiques", *Revue économique*, pp. 1191-1202, No. 6.

PIRIE, M. (1988), *Privatization*, Wildwood House, Aldershot, United Kingdom.

PORTER, M. (ed.) (1986), *Competition in Global Industries*, Harvard Business School, Boston, MA.

PORTER, M. (1990), *The Competitive Advantage of Nations*, Free Press, New York.

PRATT and ZECKHAUSER (eds.) (1985), *Principals and Agents: The Structure of Business*, Harvard Business School Press, Boston, MA.

RAMANADHAM, V. (ed.) (1988), *Privatization in Developing Countries*, Routledge, London.

REASON FOUNDATION (1987 and 1989), see Fixley, P. *et al.*

REES, R. (1988), "Inefficiency, Public Enterprise and Privatisation", *European Economic Review*, pp. 422-431, Vol. 32.

ROSA, J. (1985), "Théorie économique de la nationalisation et de la privatisation", *Politique économique*, July-August-September.

ROSA, J. (1988), "Théorie économique de la nationalisation et de la privatisation", *Finance*, pp. 91-114, Vol. 9, No. 2.

ROSS, J. (1973), "The Economic Theory of Agency: The Principal's Problem", *American Economic Review*, pp. 134-139, Vol. 63.

SAMUELSON, P. (1954), "The Pure Theory of Public Expenditures", *Review of Economics and Statistics*, Vol. 36, no. 4.

SANTINI, J. (ed.) (1986), "Les privatisations à l'étranger", *Notes et études documentaires*, No. 4821.

SAULNIERS, A. (1988), "Nationalisation/privatisation : bases d'une discussion", prepared for the Symposium "Secteur public-Secteur privé : vers un meilleur équilibre", 31st March-2nd April, Casablanca, Morocco.

SAUNDERS, P. and F. KLAU (1985), "The Role of the Public Sector: Cases and Consequences of the Growth of Government", *OECD Economic Studies*, special issue, No. 4, Spring.

SAVAS, E. (1977), *Alternatives for Delivering Public Service: Towards Improved Performance*, Westview Press, Boulder, Colorado.

SCHMALENSEE, R. (1979), *The Control of Natural Monopolies*, Lexington Books, Lexington, MA.

SHARPE, T. (1982), "The Control of Natural Monopoly by Franchising", mimeograph, Wolfson College, Oxford.

SHIRLEY, M. (1983), "Managing State-Owned Enterprises", *World Bank Staff Working Papers*, No. 577, World Bank, Washington, D.C.

SHIRLEY, M. (1989), "The Reform of State-Owned Enterprises: Lessons from World Bank Lending", *Policy and Research Series*, No. 4, World Bank, Washington, D.C.

SHORT, R. (1984), "The Role of Public Enterprises: An International Statistical Comparison", in Floyd, Gray and Short, pp. 110-194.

STANBURY and THOMPSON (1982), *Managing Public Enterprises*, Praeger, New York.

STEWART, F. (1984), "Recent Theories of International Trade: Some Implications for the South", in Kierzkowski.

Van de WALLE, N. (1989), "Privatization in Developing Countries: A Review of the Issues", *World Development*, pp. 601-615, Vol. 17, No. 5.

VERNON, R. (1966), "International Investment and International Trade", *Quarterly Journal of Economics*, May.

VERNON, R. (1985), *Eclipse of the State-Owned Enterprise: Causes and Consequences*, Kennedy School of Government, Cambridge, MA, July.

VERNON, R. (ed.) (1988), *The Promise of Privatization*, Council of Foreign Relations, New York.

VERNON, R. (1989), "Conceptual Aspects of Privatization", *CEPAL Review*, pp. 143-149, Vol. 37.

VICKERS, J. and G. YARROW (1985), *Privatization and the Natural Monopolies*, Public Policy Centre, London.

VICKERS, J. and G. YARROW (1988), *Privatisation: An Economic Analysis*, The MIT Press, Cambridge, MA.

VUYLSTEKE, C. (1988), *Techniques of Privatization of State-Owned Enterprises*, Vol. 1, World Bank Technical Paper, No. 88, World Bank, Washington, D.C.

WILLIAMSON, J. (1990), *Latin American Adjustment: How Much Has Happened?*, Institute for International Economics, Washington, D.C.

WILLIAMSON, O. (1981), "The Modern Corporation: Origins, Evolution, Attributes", *Journal of Economic Literature*, December.

WORLD BANK, *Annual Reports*, Washington, D.C, various issues.

WORLD BANK, *World Development Report*, Oxford University Press, Oxford, various issues.

WORLD BANK (1988), *Techniques of Privatization of State-Owned Enterprises*, World Bank Technical Paper, 3 volumes (Vuylsteke, Nankani and Candoy-Seske), No. 90, Washington, D.C.

WORLD BANK (1989), *Developing the Private Sector: A Challenge for the World Bank Group*, Washington, D.C.

WORLD DEVELOPMENT (1985), "Liberalization with Stabilization in the Southern Cone of Latin America", Special Issue, Vol. 13, August.

YARROW, G. (1985), "Privatisation in Theory and Practice", *Economic Policy*, pp. 324-377, Vol. 2.

# References by country

## For all countries:

THE ECONOMIST INTELLIGENCE UNIT, *Country Reports* (Quarterly), *The Economist*, London, United Kingdom.

## BANGLADESH

CHISHTY, S. (1985), "The Experience of Bangladesh", in Asian Development Bank, pp. 261-292.

GHAFUR, A. and O. CHOWDHURY (1988), *Financing Public Sector Development Expenditure in Selected Countries: Bangladesh*, Economics Office, Asian Development Bank, Manila.

HUMPHREY, C. (1990), *Privatization in Bangladesh: Economic Transition in a Poor Country*, Boulder, Westview Press.

LORCH, K. (1988), "The Privatization Transaction and Its Longer-term effects: A Case Study of the Textile Industry in Bangladesh", Harvard University, MA, April.

## BOLIVIA

ARGUEDAS, A. (1986), *Pueblo Enfermo*, Libreria Editorial Popular.

BANCO CENTRAL DE BOLIVIA (1984), *Participation del sector publico en el producto interno bruto de Bolivia, 1978-1983*, Banco Central de Bolivia, Division de Estudios Economicos, Departemento de Cuentas Nacionales, La Paz.

DAGNINO-PASTORE, J.M. (1991), *Rebalancing the Public and Private Sectors in Developing Countries: The Cases of Bolivia and Jamaica*, OECD Development Centre Technical Paper.

MOORE CASANOVAS, W. (1985), "Capital Accumulation and Revolutionary Nationalism in Bolivia (1952-1985)", in Anglade and Fortin.

## CHILE

BANCO CENTRAL DE CHILE (1988), "Economia chilena en los anos 80: ajuste y recuparacion", *Serie de Estudios Economicos*, No. 34.

*Bulletin de l'Ambassade de France au Chili*, various issues.

DAGNINO-PASTORE, J.M. (1989), "Privatisation in Chile, 1985-1989", mimeo, OECD Development Centre, Paris.

*Financial Times*, "Practical Privatisation in Chile", 16 June 1987.

*Financial Times*, "Pinochet Pushes Ahead with Privatisations", 10 October 1987.

*Financial Times*, "Chile Privatisation Steams Ahead", 13 May 1988.

*Financial Times*, "Debt Equity is Investment Key", 28 September 1988.

*Financial Times*, "Moving Further and Faster", 28 September 1988.

*Financial Times*, "Chile is Benchmark for Latin America", 11 April 1990.

LARRAIN, M. (1989), "How the 1981-83 Chilean Banking Crisis Was Handled", Working Paper, World Bank, Washington, D.C., December.

MAMALAKIS, M. (1989), *Historical Statistics of Chile*, Vol. 6, Greenwood Press, London.

MARCEL, M. (1989), "Privatizacion y Finanzas Publicas: El caso de Chile (1985-88)", *Estudios Cieplan*, pp. 5-61, Vol. 26, June.

MARSHALL, J. (1986), "Economic Privatisation: Lessons from the Chilean Experience", in Glade (ed.).

MARSHALL, J. and F. MONTT (1988), "Privatisation in Chile", in Cook and Kirkpatrick, pp. 281-307.

NANKANI, N. (1988), "Chile: Techniques of Privatization", in Nankani, pp. 17-45.

STALLINGS, B. (1990), "Politics and Economic Crisis: A Comparative Study of Chile, Peru and Colombia", in Nelson.

YOTOPOULOS, P. (1989), "The (rip)Tide of Privatization: Lessons from Chile", *World Development*, Vol. 17, No. 5.

## GHANA

ADDA, W. (1988), "Privatisation in Ghana", in Ramanadham, pp. 303-322.

AKUOKO-FRIMPONG, H. (1990), *Rebalancing the Public and Private Sectors in Developing Countries: The Case of Ghana*, OECD Development Centre Technical Paper, No. 19.

ASANTE, K. (1987), "Privatization of Public Enterprises: The Case of Ghana", in A.A.P.A.M.

KILLICK, T. (1978), *Development Economics in Action: A Study of Economic Policies in Ghana*, Heinemann, London.

PAUL, S. (1990), "Assessment of the Private Sector", World Bank Discussion Paper, No. 93, World Bank, Washington, D.C.

## JAMAICA

DAGNINO-PASTORE, J.M. (1991), *Rebalancing the Public and Private Sectors in Developing Countries: The Cases of Bolivia and Jamaica*, OECD Development Centre Technical Paper.

KENNEDY, P. (1986), "State Shrinkage: The Jamaican Experience", in Glade (ed.).

LEEDS, R. (1987), "Privatization of the National Commercial Bank of Jamaica: A Case Study", Center for Business & Government, Harvard University, October.

MILLS, G. (1988), "Privatisation in Jamaica, Trinidad and Tobago", in Ramanadham, pp. 378-399.

# MALAYSIA

ASLI, M. (1989), "Case Study: Malysia", in Asian Productivity Organization.

*Financial Times*, "Malaysia's Master Plan Sets the Pace for Privatisation", 21st September 1989.

KEAN, T. (1988), "Privatization in Malaysia", *Development Business*, pp. 1-2, 31st October.

LEEDS, R. (1989), *Rebalancing the Public and Private Sectors: The Case of Malaysia*, OECD Development Centre Technical Paper, No. 5.

MINISTÈRE DES ENTREPRISES PUBLIQUES (1988), in Ramanadham.

NANKANI, H. (1988), "Malaysia: Techniques of Privatization", in Nankani, pp. 62-95.

WOON, T. (1989), "Privatization in Malaysia: Restructuring or Efficency", in "Privatization and Deregulation in ASEAN", *ASEAN Economic Bulletin*, pp. 242-257, Vol. 5, No. 3.

# MOROCCO

DAMIS, J. (1987), "The Privatization of the Transport Sector in Morocco: A Case Study", Harvard University, Kennedy School of Government Center for Business and Government, Cambridge, MA, December.

KHOUZAM, M. (1989), "Le rééquilibrage entre le secteur public et le secteur privé : le cas du Maroc", OECD Development Centre, ronéo, Paris.

*Le Monde*, "Maroc : les limites d'une expérience", 5th August 1986.

OUDGHIRI, T, (1989), "Restructurations, privatisations : le patrimoine étatique à l'épreuve du temps", *Revue française de finances publiques*, pp. 15-28, No. 28.

SAULNIERS, A. (1990), "Privatization: Morocco", mimeo, Rabat.

# MEXICO

CASAR, A. and W. PERES (1988), "El estado impresario en Mexico: Agotamiento o renovacion ?", *Siglo XXI*.

CAULEY DE LA SIERRa, M. (1989), "Mexico Intensifies Efforts to Attract Investment", *Development Business*, pp. 1 and 16, 30th October.

*Financial Times*, "Mexico Modifies Its Privatisation Strategy", 25th April 1990.

*Mexico Service*, "The Privatization Program: De La Madrid's Legacy", pp. 14-29, 29th September 1988.

MICHALET, C.A. (1989a), *Le rééquilibrage entre secteur public et secteur privé : le cas du Mexique*, OECD Development Centre Technical Paper, No. 4.

SECRETARIA DE HACIENDA Y CREDITO PUBLICO (1990), Unidad de Desincorporacion, Mexico.

VILLAREAL, R. (1988), *Mitos et Realidades de la Empresa Publica*, DIANA, Mexico.

# PHILIPPINES

*Asian Wall Street Journal*, "Successful PNB Offering Stirs Manila Row", 28th-29th July 1989.

*Asiaweek*, "Going, going... kept", pp. 47-48, 2nd October 1987.

BRIONES, L. (1986), "The Role of the Government-Owned or Controlled Corporation in Development", *The Philippine Economic Journal*, No. 61.

CLAD, J., "Manila's Hardy Privateers", *Far Eastern Economic Review*, pp. 88-91, 7th July 1988.

GODINEZ, Z. (1989), "Privatization and Deregulation in the Philippines: An Option Package Worth Pursuing?", in "Privatization and Deregulation in ASEAN", *ASEAN Economic Bulletin*, pp. 259-289, Vol. 5, No. 3.

HAGGARD, S. (1988), "The Philippines: Picking Up After Marcos", in Vernon (ed.), pp. 91-121.

HAGGARD, S. (1990), "The Political Economy of the Philippines Debt Crisis", in J. Nelson, 1990a.

LEVISTE, J. (1985), "The Management of Public Enterprise and the Monitoring of Government Corporations", Philippine Budget Management IX, Manila.

MANASAN, R. (1988), *Financing Public Sector Expenditure Development in Selected Countries: Philippines*, Economics Office, Asian Development Bank, Manila.

MANASAN, R. and C. BUENAVENTURA (1986), "A Macroeconomic Overview of Public Enterprise in the Philippines, 1975-84", *Philippine Economic Journal*, pp. 24-50, Vol. 25, No. 1 and 2.

# TUNISIA

BEN REJEB, M. (1983), "Importance, évolution et orientation des entreprises publiques en Tunisie", *Conjoncture*, No. 81, July-August.

GUEN, M. (1988), *Les défis de la Tunisie*, L'Harmattan, Paris.

*Maghreb Développement*, "Le textile en Tunisie", No. 407 of 28th October 1989 and No. 413 of 22nd January 1990.

MINISTÈRE DU PLAN ET DES FINANCES (1981), "Liste des entreprises à participation publique", Institut National de la Statistique, Tunis.

PELLETREAU, P. (1988), "Perspectives on Privatization in Tunisia", prepared for 1988 Annual Meeting of the Middle East Studies Association, Los Angeles, 2nd-5th November 1988.

PERKINS, K. (1986), *Tunisia*, Westview Press, Boulder, Colorado.

RAVENEL, B. (1987), "Tunisie, le maillon faible", *Politique étrangère*, No. 4.

# WHERE TO OBTAIN OECD PUBLICATIONS – OÙ OBTENIR LES PUBLICATIONS DE L'OCDE

**Argentina – Argentine**
CARLOS HIRSCH S.R.L.
Galeria Güemes, Florida 165, 4° Piso
1333 Buenos Aires    Tel. 30.7122, 331.1787 y 331.2391
Telegram: Hirsch-Baires
Telex: 21112 UAPE-AR. Ref. s/2901
Telefax:(1)331-1787

**Australia – Australie**
D.A. Book (Aust.) Pty. Ltd.
648 Whitehorse Road, P.O.B 163
Mitcham, Victoria 3132    Tel. (03)873.4411
Telex: AA37911 DA BOOK
Telefax: (03)873.5679

**Austria – Autriche**
OECD Publications and Information Centre
Schedestrasse 7
DW–5300 Bonn 1 (Germany)    Tel. (49.228)21.60.45
Telefax: (49.228)26.11.04
Gerold & Co.
Graben 31
Wien I    Tel. (0222)533.50.14

**Belgium – Belgique**
Jean De Lannoy
Avenue du Roi 202
B-1060 Bruxelles    Tel. (02)538.51.69/538.08.41
Telex: 63220    Telefax: (02) 538.08.41

**Canada**
Renouf Publishing Company Ltd.
1294 Algoma Road
Ottawa, ON K1B 3W8    Tel. (613)741.4333
Telex: 053-4783    Telefax: (613)741.5439
Stores:
61 Sparks Street
Ottawa, ON K1P 5R1    Tel. (613)238.8985
211 Yonge Street
Toronto, ON M5B 1M4    Tel. (416)363.3171
Federal Publications
165 University Avenue
Toronto, ON M5H 3B8    Tel. (416)581.1552
Telefax: (416)581.1743
Les Publications Fédérales
1185 rue de l'Université
Montréal, PQ H3B 3A7    Tel.(514)954-1633
Les Éditions La Liberté Inc.
3020 Chemin Sainte-Foy
Sainte-Foy, PQ G1X 3V6    Tel. (418)658.3763
Telefax: (418)658.3763

**Denmark – Danemark**
Munksgaard Export and Subscription Service
35, Nørre Søgade, P.O. Box 2148
DK-1016 København K    Tel. (45 33)12.85.70
Telex: 19431 MUNKS DK    Telefax: (45 33)12.93.87

**Finland – Finlande**
Akateeminen Kirjakauppa
Keskuskatu 1, P.O. Box 128
00100 Helsinki    Tel. (358 0)12141
Telex: 125080    Telefax: (358 0)121.4441

**France**
OECD/OCDE
Mail Orders/Commandes par correspondance:
2, rue André-Pascal
75775 Paris Cédex 16    Tel. (33-1)45.24.82.00
Bookshop/Librairie:
33, rue Octave-Feuillet
75016 Paris    Tel. (33-1)45.24.81.67
(33-1)45.24.81.81
Telex: 620 160 OCDE
Telefax: (33-1)45.24.85.00 (33-1)45.24.81.76
Librairie de l'Université
12a, rue Nazareth
13100 Aix-en-Provence    Tel. 42.26.18.08
Telefax : 42.26.63.26

**Germany – Allemagne**
OECD Publications and Information Centre
Schedestrasse 7
DW–5300 Bonn 1    Tel. (0228)21.60.45
Telefax: (0228)26.11.04

**Greece – Grèce**
Librairie Kauffmann
28 rue du Stade
105 64 Athens    Tel. 322.21.60
Telex: 218187 LIKA Gr

**Hong Kong**
Swindon Book Co. Ltd.
13 - 15 Lock Road
Kowloon, Hong Kong    Tel. 366.80.31
Telex: 50 441 SWIN HX    Telefax: 739.49.75

**Iceland – Islande**
Mál Mog Menning
Laugavegi 18, Pósthólf 392
121 Reykjavik    Tel. 15199/24240

**India – Inde**
Oxford Book and Stationery Co.
Scindia House
New Delhi 110001    Tel. 331.5896/5308
Telex: 31 61990 AM IN
Telefax: (11)332.5993
17 Park Street
Calcutta 700016    Tel. 240832

**Indonesia – Indonésie**
Pdii-Lipi
P.O. Box 269/JKSMG/88
Jakarta 12790    Tel. 583467
Telex: 62 875

**Ireland – Irlande**
TDC Publishers – Library Suppliers
12 North Frederick Street
Dublin 1    Tel. 744835/749677
Telex: 33530 TDCP EI    Telefax: 748416

**Italy – Italie**
Libreria Commissionaria Sansoni
Via Benedetto Fortini, 120/10
Casella Post. 552
50125 Firenze    Tel. (055)64.54.15
Telex: 570466    Telefax: (055)64.12.57
Via Bartolini 29
20155 Milano    Tel. 36.50.83
La diffusione delle pubblicazioni OCSE viene assicurata
dalle principali librerie ed anche da:
Editrice e Libreria Herder
Piazza Montecitorio 120
00186 Roma    Tel. 679.46.28
Telex: NATEL I 621427
Libreria Hoepli
Via Hoepli 5
20121 Milano    Tel. 86.54.46
Telex: 31.33.95    Telefax: (02)805.28.86
Libreria Scientifica
Dott. Lucio de Biasio 'Aeiou'
Via Meravigli 16
20123 Milano    Tel. 805.68.98
Telefax: 800175

**Japan – Japon**
OECD Publications and Information Centre
Landic Akasaka Building
2-3-4 Akasaka, Minato-ku
Tokyo 107    Tel. (81.3)3586.2016
Telefax: (81.3)3584.7929

**Korea – Corée**
Kyobo Book Centre Co. Ltd.
P.O. Box 1658, Kwang Hwa Moon
Seoul    Tel. (REP)730.78.91
Telefax: 735.0030

**Malaysia/Singapore – Malaisie/Singapour**
Co-operative Bookshop Ltd.
University of Malaya
P.O. Box 1127, Jalan Pantai Baru
59700 Kuala Lumpur
Malaysia    Tel. 756.5000/756.5425
Telefax: 757.3661
Information Publications Pte. Ltd.
Pei-Fu Industrial Building
24 New Industrial Road No. 02-06
Singapore 1953    Tel. 283.1786/283.1798
Telefax: 284.8875

**Netherlands – Pays-Bas**
SDU Uitgeverij
Christoffel Plantijnstraat 2
Postbus 20014
2500 EA's-Gravenhage    Tel. (070 3)78.99.11
Voor bestellingen:    Tel. (070 3)78.98.80
Telex: 32486 stdru    Telefax: (070 3)47.63.51

**New Zealand – Nouvelle-Zélande**
GP Publications Ltd.
Customer Services
33 The Esplanade - P.O. Box 38-900
Petone, Wellington
Tel. (04)685-555    Telefax: (04)685-333

**Norway – Norvège**
Narvesen Info Center - NIC
Bertrand Narvesens vei 2
P.O. Box 6125 Etterstad
0602 Oslo 6    Tel. (02)57.33.00
Telex: 79668 NIC N    Telefax: (02)68.19.01

**Pakistan**
Mirza Book Agency
65 Shahrah Quaid-E-Azam
Lahore 3    Tel. 66839
Telex: 44886 UBL PK. Attn: MIRZA BK

**Portugal**
Livraria Portugal
Rua do Carmo 70-74
Apart. 2681
1117 Lisboa Codex    Tel.: 347.49.82/3/4/5
Telex: (01) 347.02.64

**Singapore/Malaysia – Singapour/Malaisie**
See "Malaysia/Singapore" – Voir «Malaisie/Singapour»

**Spain – Espagne**
Mundi-Prensa Libros S.A.
Castelló 37, Apartado 1223
Madrid 28001    Tel. (91) 431.33.99
Telex: 49370 MPLI    Telefax: 575.39.98
Libreria Internacional AEDOS
Consejo de Ciento 391
08009-Barcelona    Tel. (93) 301.86.15
Telefax: (93) 317.01.41

**Sri Lanka**
Centre for Policy Research
c/o Mercantile Credit Ltd.
55, Janadhipathi Mawatha
Colombo 1    Tel. 438471-9, 440346
Telex: 21138 VAVALEX CE    Telefax: 94.1.448900

**Sweden – Suède**
Fritzes Fackboksföretaget
Box 16356, S 103 27 STH
Regeringsgatan 12
DS Stockholm    Tel. (08)23.89.00
Telex: 12387    Telefax: (08)20.50.21
Subscription Agency/Abonnements:
Wennergren-Williams AB
Nordenflychtsvagen 74
Box 30004
104 25 Stockholm    Tel. (08)13.67.00
Telex: 19937    Telefax: (08)618.62.36

**Switzerland – Suisse**
OECD Publications and Information Centre
Schedestrasse 7
DW–5300 Bonn 1 (Germany)    Tel. (49.228)21.60.45
Telefax: (49.228)26.11.04
Librairie Payot
6 rue Grenus
1211 Genève 11    Tel. (022)731.89.50
Telex: 28356
Subscription Agency – Service des Abonnements
Naville S.A.
7, rue Lévrier
1201 Genève    Tél.: (022) 732.24.00
Telefax: (022) 738.48.03
Maditec S.A.
Chemin des Palettes 4
1020 Renens/Lausanne    Tel. (021)635.08.65
Telefax: (021)635.07.80
United Nations Bookshop/Librairie des Nations-Unies
Palais des Nations
1211 Genève 10    Tel. (022)734.60.11 (ext. 48.72)
Telex: 289696 (Attn: Sales)    Telefax: (022)733.98.79

**Taiwan – Formose**
Good Faith Worldwide Int'l. Co. Ltd.
9th Floor, No. 118, Sec. 2
Chung Hsiao E. Road
Taipei    Tel. 391.7396/391.7397
Telefax: (02) 394.9176

**Thailand – Thaïlande**
Suksit Siam Co. Ltd.
1715 Rama IV Road, Samyan
Bangkok 5    Tel. 251.1630

**Turkey – Turquie**
Kültur Yayinlari Is-Türk Ltd. Sti.
Atatürk Bulvari No. 191/Kat. 21
Kavaklidere/Ankara    Tel. 25.07.60
Dolmabahce Cad. No. 29
Besiktas/Istanbul    Tel. 160.71.88
Telex: 43482B

**United Kingdom – Royaume-Uni**
HMSO
Gen. enquiries    Tel. (071) 873 0011
Postal orders only:
P.O. Box 276, London SW8 5DT
Personal Callers HMSO Bookshop
49 High Holborn, London WC1V 6HB
Telex: 297138    Telefax: 071 873 8463
Branches at: Belfast, Birmingham, Bristol, Edinburgh, Manchester

**United States – États-Unis**
OECD Publications and Information Centre
2001 L Street N.W., Suite 700
Washington, D.C. 20036-4095    Tel. (202)785.6323
Telefax: (202)785.0350

**Venezuela**
Libreria del Este
Avda F. Miranda 52, Aptdo. 60337
Edificio Galipán
Caracas 106    Tel. 951.1705/951.2307/951.1297
Telegram: Libreste Caracas

**Yugoslavia – Yougoslavie**
Jugoslovenska Knjiga
Knez Mihajlova 2, P.O. Box 36
Beograd    Tel.: (011)621.992
Telex: 12466 jk bgd    Telefax: (011)625.970

Orders and inquiries from countries where Distributors
have not yet been appointed should be sent to: OECD
Publications Service, 2 rue André-Pascal, 75775 Paris
Cedex 16, France.

Les commandes provenant de pays où l'OCDE n'a pas
encore désigné de distributeur devraient être adressées à :
OCDE, Service des Publications, 2, rue André-Pascal,
75775 Paris Cédex 16, France.

75490-1/91

OECD PUBLICATIONS, 2, rue André-Pascal, 75775 PARIS CEDEX 16
PRINTED IN FRANCE
(4191041) ISBN 92-64-13440-9 No. 45489 1991